MISSION
UNACCOMPLISHED

ALSO BY TOM ENGELHARDT

The End of Victory Culture

The Last Days of Publishing (a novel)

MISSION
UNACCOMPLISHED

Tomdispatch Interviews with
American Iconoclasts and Dissenters

Tom Engelhardt

Nation Books
New York

MISSION UNACCOMPLISHED:
Tomdispatch Interviews with American Iconoclasts and Dissenters

Published by Nation Books
An Imprint of Avalon Publishing Group, Inc.
245 West 17th Street, 11th Floor
New York, NY 10011

www.nationbooks.org

AVALON

Nation Books is a co-publishing venture of The Nation Institute
and Avalon Publishing Group Incorporated.

Library of Congress Cataloging-in-Publication Data

ISBN-10: 1-56025-938-8
ISBN-13: 978-1-56025-938-1

9 8 7 6 5 4 3 2 1

Book design by Meryl Sussman Levavi

Printed in the United States of America
Distributed by Publishers Group West

For Maggie and Will.

Without you, Tomdispatch would never have happened.

You should have a world to come home to.

Contents

Introduction:
Mission Unaccomplished

On April 28, 2003, George W. Bush's advance men were preparing to stop an aircraft carrier returning from Iraq just short of its home base in San Diego, so he could dramatically land on its deck rather than clamber aboard. That same day, halfway across the planet, soldiers from the 82nd Airborne Division, occupying an elementary school in Fallujah, fired on a crowd of angry demonstrators. Perhaps fifteen Iraqis died and more were wounded. Two days later, in a second clash of demonstrators and troops, two more Iraqis died.

On May 1, the President performed his *Top Gun* victory stunt, landing in an S-3B Viking sub reconnaissance Naval jet on the USS *Abraham Lincoln*. At the perfect photogenic moment, under a banner reading "Mission Accomplished," he announced that "major combat operations have ended" in Iraq. On CNN's Web site the following day, the main headline read: "Bush calls end to 'major combat.'" But there would be a smaller secondary headline that read: "U.S. Central Command: Seven hurt in Fallujah grenade attack." Two grenades had been tossed into a U.S.

military compound, leaving seven American soldiers "slightly injured."

In the years to follow, those two headlines would jostle for dominance, a struggle now over. In retrospect, it was startling how quickly that "Mission Accomplished" banner started to shred. Within months, the President's men had pinned the idea for creating it on the sailors and airmen of the *Abraham Lincoln,* only to be forced to admit that the White House itself had produced the banner, and then to cease to mention the matter altogether.

By that time, those two grenades in Fallujah had multiplied into a fierce Sunni insurrection. Within six months, *Time Magazine* would be writing of the President's landing, "The perfect photo-op has flopped," and speaking in Vietnam-ish tones of "Bush's suddenly growing credibility problem." Long before May 1, 2004, rolled around, "mission accomplished" would be a scarlet phrase of shame—taken up only by administration critics.

By that May, Fallujah had morphed into a resistant enemy city that had withstood an assault by the Marines. And in November 2004, it would be largely destroyed by American firepower without ever being fully subdued. In those same months, the Bush administration's grandiose plans for Iraq, for the greater Middle East, and for much of the rest of the world would begin to shred like that banner.

"Imperial overreach" is perhaps too fancy a term for what the Bush administration has actually "accomplished" since September 12, 2001. But then, what would you expect of grand strategists who never made it out of the world of Washington think tanks, punditry, and politics, and who were desperately ready to be dazzled by the tales of a brilliant Iraqi schemer, Ahmed Chalabi, and other exiled Iraqi Scheherazades. While American officials talked a great game when it came to achieving "total victory" in Iraq and exporting democracy to the Middle East, the administration's main exports turned out to be mayhem, chaos, and ruins.

It's been a long five years, but for an imperial project launched by the Earth's lone "hyperpower," or "global sheriff," or "new Rome" (as right-wing pundits were proudly proclaiming back then), it's actually been a remarkably brief span of time. It was no more than a historical blink of an eye from the moment Bush administration officials proclaimed their global project to the moment they first stood in its ruins. Perhaps in our less than consoling world, there is something consoling in knowing that history remains filled with surprises and that the rubble-filled, disastrous career of the Bush administration looks likely to be one of them.

Give its top officials and their various neocon backers credit, though. They thought big; they were ready to connect the dots at a planetary level (and even beyond, if you include their plans for the militarization of space). They wanted to control nothing less than a vast swath of territory they labeled "the arc of instability." (Think: energy heartlands of the planet.) And they were ready to roll the dice big time. They were—except perhaps for Jefferson Davis and his compatriots—the biggest gamblers in our history. In their eyes, the invasion of Iraq, which they targeted as the soft underbelly of the Middle East, and the felling of Saddam Hussein's regime were to be but the first shock-and-awe pit stops on a far more ambitious tour of the region.

In May 2003, when the President made his "tailhook" landing on that aircraft-carrier deck, it looked to a lot of people like they were going to succeed. I had then been running Tomdispatch, a Web site and project of The Nation Institute, for just a few months, though I had been sending my thoughts to an unnamed e-list with a growing set of readers since November 2001. (For more on my history and that of the Web site, see the final interview in this book.) Like most people, my predictive powers are not normally striking. I've been wrong enough times in my life to prove that point. But in the case of the invasion of Iraq, what I knew of the long history of struggles to gain, regain, or preserve national sovereignty, of the perils of imperial hubris, and of our own history in Vietnam and elsewhere, left me convinced—and I wrote as much both before and after the invasion—about just what sort of disaster would indeed ensue.

In the meantime, I saw my mission, modestly accomplished, as connecting some of the "dots" not being connected by our largely demobilized media, while recording as best I could the "mission unaccomplished" moments I felt certain would come.

In the late summer of 2005, I started a new feature at Tomdispatch. On little more than a whim I sat down for an interview with historian and activist Howard Zinn and, soon after, *Boston Globe* columnist James Carroll. As a professional book editor much of my adult life, I had worked on a fair number of oral histories, but I had never done an interview myself for publication. I had few thoughts then about an interview series, and none about a book of interviews. I was, however, curious about a form I hadn't tried before. I also had the urge to explore our imperial world with critical thinkers (and activists) I admired, a sense that our media seldom allows us to hear voices speaking clearly at any length or to see minds at work, and the simple desire to have a little good company (and offer it to others) in bleak times.

The eleven interviewees in this book (as well as the protesters I interviewed at an antiwar march in Washington, DC) provided that good company. Their thoughts now constitute a rather striking record of almost a year of imperial failure and planetary destruction that, unfortunately, is not likely to end soon. Perhaps the saddest thing to say here is that there will undoubtedly be space in our world for more such Tomdispatch interview books in the years to come.

TOM ENGELHARDT
July 4, 2006

1. The Outer Limits of Empire

Howard Zinn

September 8, 2005

He's tall and thin, with a shock of white hair. A bombardier in the great war against fascism and an antiwar veteran of America's wars ever since, he's best known as the author of the pathbreaking *A People's History of the United States*, and as an expert on the unexpected voices of resistance that have so regularly made themselves heard throughout our history. At eighty-three (though he looks a decade younger), he is also a veteran of a rugged century and yet there's nothing backward looking about him. His voice is quiet and he clearly takes himself with a grain of salt, chuckling wryly on occasion at his own comments. From time to time, when a thought pleases him and his well-used face lights up or breaks out in a bona fide grin, he looks positively boyish.

We sit down on the back porch of the small coffee shop, alone, on a vacation morning. He has a croissant and coffee in front of him. I suggest that perhaps we start after breakfast, but he assures me that there's no particular contradiction between eating and talking and so, as a novice interviewer, I awkwardly turn on my two tape recorders—one of which, on pause, will still miss several minutes of our conversation (our equivalent, we joke, of Nixon's infamous eighteen-minute gap). In preparation, he pushes aside his half-eaten breakfast, never to touch it again, and we begin.

Tomdispatch: You and Anthony Arnove just came out with a new book, *Voices of a People's History of the United States*, featuring American voices of resistance from our earliest moments to late last night. Now, we have a striking new voice of resistance, Cindy Sheehan. I was wondering what you made of her?

Howard Zinn: Often a protest movement that's already underway— and the present antiwar movement was underway even before the Iraq War began—gets a special impetus, a special spark, from one person's act of defiance. I think of Rosa Parks and that one act of hers and what it meant.

TD: Can you think of other Cindy Sheehan-like figures in the past who made movements coalesce?

Zinn: In the antiwar movement of the Vietnam years, there wasn't one person, but when I think back to the abolitionist movement, Frederick Douglass was a special figure in that way. When he came north, out of slavery, and spoke for the first time to a group of antislavery people, the beginnings of a movement existed. [William Lloyd] Garrison had already started [his antislavery newspaper] the *Liberator*, but Frederick Douglass was able to represent slavery itself in a way that Garrison and the other abolitionists could not. His dramatic appearance, his eloquence, provided a special spark for the abolitionist movement.

TD: I guess Cindy Sheehan also represents something that can't be represented by anyone else, almost, in fact, can't be represented—the American dead in the war and, of course, her own dead son.

Zinn: It's interesting. There have been mothers other than Cindy Sheehan who have spoken out, but she decided on an act that had a special resonance, which was simply to find where Bush was going [he chuckles to himself at the thought] and have a confrontation between the two poles of this war, between its maker and the opposition. She just parked herself near Bush and became the center of national attention, of gravity, around which people gathered, hundreds and hundreds of people.

TD: The Bush administration has had such a long-term strategy of never venturing anywhere that the President might be challenged, but now, unless he's literally on a military base, I suspect he's no longer safe from that, and even then...

Zinn: Did you read about the Mayor of Salt Lake City speaking out before 2,000 people to protest a presidential speech there? This is just what began to happen in the Vietnam War. After a while, [President Lyndon] Johnson and [Vice President Hubert] Humphrey couldn't go anywhere except military bases. And the thing about Cindy Sheehan is that she's not a moderate voice either. I mean, she's saying we must withdraw from Iraq so boldly and clearly that even an antiwar person like [*New York Times* columnist] Frank Rich refers to her position as "apocalyptic" and kind of outside the pale. And that's terrible, because on the issue of withdrawal she represents, I think, the unspoken desires of a huge number of people and is willing to say what the politicians and the journalists have not yet dared to say. There are very few newspapers in the country—maybe the *Seattle Post-Intelligencer* and one other—that have simply called for withdrawal without talking about timetables and conditions.

TD: As the person who, in 1967, wrote *Vietnam: The Logic of Withdrawal*, how do you compare the logic of withdrawal discussions in this moment with that one?

Zinn: There was a point early in the Vietnam War when no major figure and no critic of the war was simply calling for immediate withdrawal. Everybody was hedging in some way. We must negotiate. We must compromise. We must stop the bombing north of this or that parallel. I think we're at a comparable point now, two years after the beginning of the Iraq War. When my book came out in the spring of '67, it was just two years after the escalation in early '65 when Johnson sent in the first major infusions of American troops. What's comparable, I think, are the arguments then and now. Even the language is similar. We mustn't cut and run. We mustn't give them a victory. We mustn't lose prestige in the world.

TD: …credibility was the word then.

Zinn: Yes, exactly, credibility. There will be chaos and civil war if we leave…

TD: …and a bloodbath.

Zinn: Yes, and a bloodbath—because the one way you can justify an ongoing catastrophe is to posit a greater catastrophe if you don't continue with the present one. We've seen that psychology operating again and again. We saw it, for instance, with

Hiroshima. I mean, we have to kill hundreds of thousands of people to avert a greater catastrophe, the death of a million people in the invasion of Japan.

It's interesting that when we finally did leave Vietnam, none of those dire warnings really came true. It's not that things were good after we left. The Chinese were expelled, and there were the boat people and the reeducation camps, but none of that compared to the ongoing slaughter taking place when the American troops were there. So while no one can predict what will happen—I think this is important to say—when the United States withdraws its troops from Iraq, the point is that we're choosing between the certainty of an ongoing disaster, the chaos and violence that are taking place in Iraq today, and an eventuality we can't predict which *may* be bad. But what *may* be bad is uncertain; what's bad with our occupation right now is certain. It seems to me that, choosing between the two, you have to take a chance on what might happen if you end the occupation. At the same time, of course, you do whatever you can to mitigate the worst possibilities of your leaving.

TD: I want to return for a moment to Cindy Sheehan. By the last years of the Vietnam War, the American military was almost incapable of fighting and, though there were military families against the war, the main resistance to the war was by then coming from draft-age soldiers themselves. Now we have an all-volunteer army; we know that morale is sinking and that there are specific cases of resistance—refusals to return to Iraq, for instance—within the military, but most of the resistance this time seems to be coming from the families of the soldiers. I wonder whether there's any historical precedent for that?

Zinn: I don't know of any previous war where something like this happened...in the United States anyway. The closest you might get would be in the Confederacy in the Civil War, when the wives of soldiers rioted because their husbands were dying and the plantation owners were profiting from the sale of cotton, refusing to grow grains for civilians to eat. David Williams in Valdosta, Georgia, is coming out this fall with *A People's History of the Civil War* in which he describes that phenomenon.

In the case of the Soviet Union, though, there may be a closer parallel. Russian mothers protested the continuing war in Afghanistan, their Vietnam. I don't know how strong a part that played in the Soviet decision to withdraw, but certainly there was something dramatic about that.

We had gold star mothers against the war in the Vietnam era, but nothing like this and I think you've pointed to the reason. The GIs in Iraq are not in the same position the draftees were in—although I have to temper that by noting that a lot of the resistance in the Vietnam War came from people who had enlisted in the Army. And, in a certain sense, there are also draftees in this war, people who didn't sign up to fight, or National Guards and Reserves who didn't expect to go to war. You might say that they had been drafted.

Still, because it's a largely all-volunteer army, the protesting has been left to the parents in an unprecedented way. Their children just aren't in a position to protest as easily and yet I think there's going to be more and more GI protest as the war goes on. That's inevitable. I imagine—there's no way of proving this—that there's already a lot more subterranean protest and disaffection in the military than has been reported, maybe much more than can be reported because it's probably not visible.

When I try to think what would really compel the Bush administration to get out of Iraq, the one thing is a rebellion in the military. David Cortright [author of *Soldiers in Revolt: GI Resistance During the Vietnam War*] believes that what happened to the military in Vietnam was the crucial factor in finally bringing the United States out of Vietnam.

TD: And what about military resistance at the top rather than the bottom? As far back as Korea, there was a feeling among officers of being in the wrong war in the wrong place at the wrong time and that was replicated in Vietnam. It's clear that the top people in the field in Iraq have known for a long time that they're involved in a catastrophe. They were the ones recently who began talking about draw-downs and withdrawals without permission from the Bush administration.

Zinn: It's a very important development, because when cracks occur in what had previously seemed to be the solidity of the top, it becomes that much more difficult to carry on. One example I think of—it's not a war situation—is McCarthyism. When [red-baiting Senator Joseph] McCarthy began to go after important figures in the Eisenhower administration, when he went after General [George] Marshall and his forays came closer and closer to the top, more and more people moved away from him, and that was critical to his demise. Disaffection in the top ranks of the military has been evident for some time now. [Retired Centcom commander] General [Anthony] Zinni, for instance, has been speaking out from the beginning. For a while I was worried about the similarity between our names [he laughs], but I feel better about it now that he's come out speaking the way he has.

TD: And retired generals like him are always speaking for others inside the military.

Zinn: That's right. They're in a position to say what others can't say. I mean there's been military resistance in many of our wars, but until Vietnam it never reached the point where it actually changed policy. There were mutinies against Washington in the revolutionary army. In the Mexican War, even huge numbers of desertions didn't stop the war. I can't think of any military resistance in World War I. Of course, the United States was only in for a brief time, a year and a half really. Certainly, World War II was a different situation. That's what makes Vietnam such a historical phenomenon. It was the first time you had a movement in the military that was an important factor in changing government policy. And it's interesting that we've had short wars ever since, except for this one, and those wars were deliberately designed to be short so that there wouldn't be time for an antiwar movement to develop. In this case, they miscalculated. Now, I don't think it's a question of if, just when. When and how. I don't think there's any question that the United States is going to have to get out of Iraq. The only questions are: How long will it take? How many more people will die? And how will it be done?

TD: Let me turn to another issue you certainly wrote about in the sixties, war crimes, which was the last charge to arrive in the mainstream in those years and the first to depart. We've certainly experienced many crimes in the last few years, from Abu Ghraib and Guantánamo to Afghanistan. I wonder why, as a concept, it sticks so poorly with Americans?

Zinn: It does seem like a hard concept—war crimes, war criminals —to catch on here. There's a willingness to say the leadership is wrong, but it's a great jump from there to saying that the leadership is vicious. Unfortunately, in American culture, there's still a kind of monarchical idea that the President, the people up there, are very special people and while they may make mistakes, they couldn't be criminals. Even after the public had turned against the Vietnam War, there was no widespread talk about Johnson, [Secretary of Defense Robert] McNamara, and the rest of them being war criminals. And I think it has to do with an American culture of deference to the President and his men—beyond which people refuse to think.

TD: How does an American culture of exceptionalism play into this?

Zinn: I would guess that a very large number of Americans against the war in Vietnam still believed in the essential goodness of this country. They thought of Vietnam as an aberration. Only a minority in the antiwar movement saw it as part of a continuous policy of imperialism and expansion. I think that's true today as well. It's very hard for Americans to let go of the idea that we're an especially good nation. It's comforting to know that, even though we do wrong things from time to time, these are just individual aberrations. I think it takes a great deal of political consciousness to extend the criticism of a particular policy or a particular war to a general negative appraisal of the country and its history. It strikes too close to something Americans seem to need to hold on to.

Of course, there's an element that's right in this as well—in that there are principles for which the United States presumably stands that are good. It's just that people confuse the principles with the policies—and so long as they can keep those principles in their heads (justice for all, equality, and so on), they are very reluctant to accept the fact that they have been crassly, consistently violated. This is the only way I can account for the stopping short when it comes to looking at the President and the people around him as war criminals.

TD: Stepping back from the catastrophe in Iraq, what do you make of the Bush administration's version of the American imperial project?

Zinn: I like to think that the American empire has reached its outer limits with the Middle East. I don't believe it has a future in Latin America. I think it's worn out whatever power it had there and we're seeing the rise of governments that will not play ball with the United States. This may be one of the reasons why the war in Iraq is so important to this administration. Beyond Iraq there's no place to go. So, let's put it this way: I see withdrawal from Iraq whenever it takes place—and think of this as partly wish and partly belief [he chuckles at himself]—as the first step in the retrenchment of the American empire. After all we aren't the first country in history to be forced to do this.

I'd like to say that this will be because of American domestic opposition, but I suspect mostly it will be because the rest of the world won't accept further American forays into places where we don't belong. In the future, I believe 9/11 may be seen as representing the beginning of the dissolution of the American empire; that is, the very event that immediately crystallized popular support for war, in the long run—and I don't know how long that will be—may be seen as the beginning of the weakening and crumbling of the American empire.

TD: There would be an irony in that.

Zinn: Yes, certainly.

TD: I wanted to turn to the issue of war. You've written about the possible end of war not being a purely utopian project. Do you really believe war could end or is it in our genes?

Zinn: Although lots of things are unclear to me, one thing is very clear. It's not in our genes. Whenever I read accounts, even by people who have been in war, that suggest there's something in the masculine psyche that requires this kind of violence and militarism

I don't believe it. I say this on the basis of historical experience; that is, if you compare the instances in which people, mostly men, have committed violent acts and gone to war to those in which people have not gone to war, have rejected war, it seems people don't *naturally* want war.

They may want a lot of things associated with war—the comradeship, the thrill that comes from holding a weapon. I think this is what confuses people. Thrills, comradeship, all of that can come in many different ways; it comes from war, though, only when people are manipulated into it. To me the strongest argument against an inherent drive to war is the extent to which governments have to resort to get people to go to war, the huge amounts of propaganda and deception of which we had an example very recently. And don't forget coercion. So I discard that idea of a natural inclination to war.

TD: You went to war yourself...

Zinn: I was twenty years old. I was a bombardier in the 8th Air Force on a B-17 crew that flew some of the last missions of the war out of England. I went in as a young, radical antifascist, believing in this war and believing in the idea of a just war against fascism. At war's end I was beginning to have doubts about whether the mayhem we had engaged in was justified: the bombing of cities, Hiroshima and Nagasaki, the bombings I had engaged in. And then I was beginning to suspect the motives of the Allied leaders. Did they really care that much about fascism? Did they care about the Jews? Was it a war for empire? In the Air Force I encountered a young Trotskyite on another air crew who said to me, "You know, this is an imperialist war." I was sort of shocked. I said, "Well, you're flying missions! Why are you here?" He replied, "I'm here to talk to people like you." [He laughs.] I mean, he didn't convert me, but he shook me up a little.

After the war, as the years went by, I couldn't help contemplating the promises that had been made about what the war would accomplish. You know, General Marshall sent me—and 16 million others—a letter congratulating us for winning the war and telling us how the world would now be a different place. Fifty million people were dead and the world was not really that different. I mean, Hitler and Mussolini were gone, as was the Japanese military machine, but fascism and militarism, and racism were still all over the world, and wars were still continuing. So I came to the conclusion that war, whatever quick fix it might give you—Oh, we've defeated this phenomenon, fascism; we've gotten rid of Hitler (like we've gotten rid of Saddam Hussein, you see)—whatever spurt of enthusiasm, the after-effects were like those of a drug; first a high and then you settle back into something horrible. So I began to think that any wars, even wars against evil, simply don't accomplish much of anything. In the long run, they simply don't solve the problem. In the interim, an enormous number of people die.

I also came to the conclusion that, given the technology of modern warfare, war is inevitably a war against children, against civilians. When you look at the ratio of civilian to military dead, it changes from 50-50 in World War II to 80-20 in Vietnam, maybe as high as 90-10 today. Do you know this Italian war surgeon, Gino Strada? He wrote *Green Parrots: A War Surgeon's Diary*. He was doing war surgery in Afghanistan, Iraq, and other places. Ninety percent of the people he operated on were civilians. When you face that fact, war is now always a war against civilians, and so against children. No political goal can justify it, and so the great challenge before the human race in our time is to solve the problems of tyranny and aggression, and do it without war. [He laughs quietly.] A very complex and difficult job, but something that has to be faced—and that's what accounts for my becoming involved in antiwar movements ever since the end of World War II.

2. The Mosquito and the Hammer

James Carroll

September 11, 2005

We pull into the parking lot at the same moment in separate cars, both of us slightly vacation-disheveled. He wears a baseball-style cap and a half-length purple raincoat in anticipation of the downpour which begins soon after we huddle safely in a local coffee shop. As I fumble with my two tape recorders, he immediately demurs about the interview. He may have nothing new to say, he assures me, and then absolves me, now and forever, of the need to make any use whatsoever of anything we produce through our conversation.

The son of a lieutenant-general who was the founding director of the Pentagon's Defense Intelligence Agency, a former Catholic priest and antiwar activist in the Vietnam era (the subject of his book, *An American Requiem: God, My Father, and the War That Came Between Us*), Carroll has long pursued his interest in the ways in which faith and force can coalesce into historically fatal brews. From this came, for instance, his best-selling book *Constantine's Sword: The Church and the Jews.*

Within days of the attacks of September 11, 2001, he became perhaps our most passionate—and prophetic—columnist in the mainstream media. His weekly columns continue to appear in the *Boston Globe.* The Bush administration, with its fundamentalist religious base, its Manichaean worldview, its urge toward a civilizational conflict against Islam, and its deeply held fascination with and belief in the all-encompassing powers of military force, was, in a sense, made for him. And he grasped the consequences of its actions with uncanny accuracy from the first moments after our President announced his "war on terror," just days after 9/11. A remarkable collection of his *Globe* columns that begins with the fall of the World Trade Center towers and the damaging of the Pentagon and ends on the first anniversary of the invasion of Iraq, *Crusade: Chronicles of an Unjust War*, will certainly prove one of the best running records of that crucial period we have.

He speaks quietly and straightforwardly. You can almost see him thinking as he talks. As he reenters the world we've passed through these last years, his speech speeds up and gains a certain emphatic cadence. You can feel in his voice the same impressive combination of passion and intelligence, engagement and thoughtfulness that is a hallmark of his weekly column. I turn on the tape recorders and we begin to consider the world since September 11, 2001.

Tomdispatch: In September 2003, only five months after the invasion of Iraq, you wrote in a column, "The war in Iraq is lost. What will it take to face that truth this time?" Here we are two years later. What has it taken, what will it take, to face that truth?

James Carroll: It's interesting to me that the tribunes of the truth right now are the people who have felt the loss of the war most intensely, the parents of the dead American soldiers. I find it astounding that facing the truth in the month of August has been the business almost solely of these parents, pro and con. Cindy Sheehan on the one side, clearly saying that, whatever its imagined values, this war's not worth what it's costing us and it's got to end immediately; on the other side, parents, desperately trying to make some sense of the loss of their child, who want the war to continue so that he or she will not have died in vain. Both are facing a basic truth of parental grief and, I'd also say, responding to the same larger phenomenon: the war being lost. I'm not certain we'd hear from any parents if the war were being won. Given the great tragedy of losing your child to a war that's being lost, nobody gets to the question of whether it's just or not.

It's heartbreaking to me that, in American political discourse, what discussion there is of the larger human and political questions has fallen to these heartbroken parents. Where are the Democrats? Where, for that matter, are the Republicans? On the floor of Congress, has there been a discussion of this war? I mean in the Vietnam years you did have the astounding Fulbright hearings. [Democratic Senator William] Fulbright was in defiance of [Democratic President] Lyndon Johnson when those hearings were initiated, that's for sure. Where are the hearings today? We have a political system that is supposed to engage the great questions and they obviously aren't being engaged. How long will it take us to face the truth? It's just terrible that the truth has to be faced by these heartbroken parents, because even if they're opposed to the war—as I am—they're not the ones to whom we should look for political wisdom on how to resolve the terrible dilemma we're in.

TD: In March 2004, on the first anniversary of the invasion—and this was the piece with which you ended your book, *Crusade*—you wrote again, "Whatever happens from this week forward in

Iraq, the main outcome of the war for the United States is clear, we have defeated ourselves."

Carroll: I was already instructed by the history of the twentieth century, summarized so well by Jonathan Schell in his book *The Unconquerable World*. He cites numerous instances in which broad-based, national resistance movements couldn't be defeated even by massively superior military power. It was his insight that the last century was rife with examples—the most obvious for Americans being Vietnam—where a huge superiority in fire-power was irrelevant against even a minority resistance move-ment based in an indigenous population; and it's clear that this so-called insurgency in Iraq is a minority resistance movement, largely Sunni, and that it doesn't matter if it's a minority. There's an indigenous population within which it resides and which fuels it. And all of that was quickly evident. In fact, I think it was evi-dent to George H.W. Bush in 1991. It wasn't Vietnam we needed to learn from first in this case; it really was the first Gulf War and Bush's realpolitik decision to stop it based on the sure knowledge that there was no way of defeating an indigenous popular reli-gious movement prepared to fight to the death.

TD: So where are we now as you see it?

Carroll: It's already become clear to people that we can't win this. Who knows what being defeated means? I said we had lost because there's no imposing our will on the people of Iraq. That's what this constitutional imbroglio demonstrates. A month ago, Donald Rumsfeld was insisting that there had to be a three-party agreement. In August, it became clear that there would be none. So now there's a two-party agreement and the Sunnis are out of it. Basically, this political development has endorsed the Sunni resistance movement, because they've been cut out of the future of Iraq. They have no share of the oil. They have no access to real political power in Baghdad. They have nothing to lose and that's a formula for endless fighting.

TD: I was struck by recent statements by top American generals in Iraq about draw-downs and withdrawals, all of them clearly unauthorized by Washington. At the bottom, you have angry military families, lowering morale, and the difficulties of signing people on to the all-volunteer army; at the top, generals who didn't want to be in Iraq in the first place and don't want to be there now.

Carroll: Well, they've been forced to preside over the destruction of the United States Army, including the civilian system of support for the Army—the National Guard and the active Reserves. This is the most important outcome of the war and, as with Vietnam, we'll be paying the price for it for a generation.

TD: Knowing the Pentagon as you do, what kind of a price do you think that will be?

Carroll: I would say, alas, that one of the things we're going to resume is an overweening dependence on air power and strikes from afar. It's clear, for instance, that the United States under the present administration is not going to allow Iran to get anywhere near a nuclear weapon. The only way they could try to impede that is with air power. They have no army left to exert influence. If the destruction of the United States Army is frightening, so is the immunity from the present disaster of the Navy and the Air Force, which are both far-distance striking forces. That's what they exist for and they're intact. Their Tomahawk and Cruise missiles have basically been sidelined. We have this massive high-firepower force that's sitting offshore and we're surely going to resume our use of such power from afar.

One of the things the United States of America claims to have learned from the nineties is that we're not going to let genocidal movements like the one in Rwanda unfold. Well, we've basically destroyed the only military tool we have to respond to genocidal movements, which is a ground force. You can't use air power against a machete-wielding movement. And if you think that kind of conflict won't happen in places where poverty is overwhelming and ecological disaster is looming ever more terrifyingly, think again. What kind of response to such catastrophe will a United States without a functional army be capable of?

You know, in this way, we're now like the Soviet Union once it collapsed into Russia. When it could no longer pay the salaries of its soldiers, Russia fell back on its nuclear arsenal as its only source of power. In a way the Soviet Union never was, Russia is now a radically nuclear-dependent military power. The Red Army doesn't really count for much anymore. And we've done that to ourselves in Iraq. This is what it means to have lost the war already. We didn't need an enemy to do it for us. We've done it to ourselves.

TD: "We" being the Bush administration?

Carroll: Yes, the Bush administration, but "we" also being John Kerry and the Democrats who refused to make the war an issue in the presidential election campaign last year. I fault them every bit as much as I fault the Republicans. At least Bush is being consistent and driven ideologically by his unbelievably callow worldview. The Democrats were radical cynics about it. They didn't buy the preventive war doctrine. They didn't buy the weapons of mass destruction justification for this war. They didn't buy any of it and yet they didn't oppose it! The cynicism of the Democrats is one of the most stunning outcomes of this war. And even now, as the political conversation for next year's congressional election begins, where's the discussion from the Democrats about this, the second self-inflicted military catastrophe since World War II. At least the first time, the Democrats were there. In the election of 1972, when they lost badly, George McGovern and company really did engage this question.

We're desperately in need of a Eugene McCarthy, someone who will speak the truth in a really clear and powerful way and in a political context so that we can respond to it as a people. Eugene McCarthy is putting it positively. I'd say negatively what we could use is a Newt Gingrich, someone who could marshal political resistance going into this next election period in a way that would make the war a lively issue in every senatorial and congressional election. We really need someone. In America, our system requires someone of the political culture to invoke this discussion.

TD: In the first column you wrote after September 11, 2001, you said, "How we respond to this catastrophe will define our patriotism, shape the century, and memorialize our beloved dead." Four years later, how do you assess our response to each?

Carroll: Patriotism has become a hollow, partisan notion in our country. It's been in the name of patriotism that we've turned our young soldiers into scapegoats and fodder. The betrayal of the young in the name of patriotism is a staggering fact of our post-9/11 response. The old men have carried the young men up the mountain and put them on the altar. It's Abraham and Isaac all over again. It's the oldest story, a kind of human sacrifice, and that's what's made those cries of parents so poignant this August. But those cries also have to include an element of self-accusation, because parents have done it to their children. We've done it to our children. That's what it means to destroy the United States Army. Night after night, we see that the actual casualties of that destruction are young men, and occasionally women, between the ages of eighteen and thirty. And this in the name of patriotism.

On the second point, the shape of the world for the century to come, look what the United States of America has given us— civilizational war against Islam! Osama bin Laden hoped to ignite a war between radically fundamentalist Islam and the secular West. And he succeeded. We played right into his hands. Now, we see that war being played out not just in Iraq and the Arab world generally, but quite dramatically in Europe.

TD: You picked up on this in the first few days after 9/11 when you caught Bush in a little slip of the tongue. He spoke of us entering a "crusade"...

Carroll: "This war on terrorism, this crusade."

TD: Yes, which, you said, "came to him as naturally as a baseball reference." Are we now, with the protesting military families, seeing a retreat from this kind of sacralizing of violence?

Carroll: No! I think the warnings signs are all around us for what has happened—the politicization of fundamentalist Christianity. I mean, we've had that since the early days of the Cold War when Billy Graham became a tribune of anticommunism. But what's new is the way in which this marginal fundamentalist Christianity has entered the political mainstream and taken hold on Capitol Hill. Dozens and dozens of congressmen and senators are now overt Christian fundamentalists who apply their theology—including religious categories like Armageddon and end-of-the-world justifications for violence—to their political decisions. The kind of apocalyptic political thinking that Robert Jay Lifton has written about has now become so mainstream that we even see it in the United States military. For the first time, at least in my lifetime, overt religiosity has emerged as a military virtue and I'm not just talking about General [William] Boykin, the wacko who deliberately and explicitly insulted the Islamic religion...

TD: ...and who was promoted.

Carroll: And is still in power. Not just him but this most alarming and insufficiently noted phenomenon of the rise of fundamentalist Christianity at the Air Force Academy, conveniently located in the neighborhood of the two most politicized fundamentalist religious congregations in the country, Focus on the Family and the New Life Ministries. A significant proportion of the cadet population is reliably understood to be overt, born-again Christians and the commandant has been explicit in his support of religious conformity in the cadet corps. These are the people we are empowering with custodianship over our most powerful weapons in a war increasingly defined in religious terms by the President of the United States. All of this is our side of a religious war against an increasingly mobilized jihadist Islam.

Meanwhile in Europe, Great Britain had, until recently, been a far more tolerant culture than the United States (as indicated by the British welcome to large populations of Muslim immigrants over the last generation). All of that is now being firmly and explicitly repudiated by British lawmakers. You see it in the great cities of Europe everywhere. When people in the Netherlands and France vote against the European Constitution in some measure because it represents to them an opening to Turkey and the world of Islam, something quite large is happening.

TD: Doesn't this take us back to a period you've studied deeply—
the Middle Ages?

Carroll: It's true. We don't sufficiently appreciate how the paradigm of the crusades never ended for Europe. Europe came into
being in response to the threat of Islam. The European structure
of government, the royal families of Europe, they're all
descended from Charlemagne, grandson of the man who
defeated the Islamic armies at Tours. More than a thousand years
ago, a system of identity first took hold in Europe that defined
itself against Islam. This is the ultimate political Manichaeism in
the European mind.

We're the children of this. Of course, Islam had been forgotten in our time. Never mind that there were more than a billion Muslims in the world. All through the Cold War, we thought
that the other, the stranger, the enemy was the Communist. But
the Muslim world never forgot about us. The crusades are yesterday to them. They've understood better than we have that the
West has somehow defined itself against them.

It's in this context that we have to understand the Israeli-
Palestinian conflict. A thousand years ago, as now, the political
fate of Jerusalem was the military spark for the marshaling of a
holy war. The crusaders, after all, were going to Jerusalem to
rescue the Holy Land from the infidel, and the infidel was defined
as a twin-set, Muslims and Jews. The attack on Muslims happened
simultaneously with the first real attacks against Jews inside
Europe. The ease with which, in the Middle East, the conflict in
Israel has come to be subsumed as the defining conflict with the
West is part of this phenomenon.

In Cologne [Germany] last week, I met with the head of the
Jewish congregation and also the imam who heads the Muslim
community, and they both reported the same experience. They
both feel they're on the table—the table of sacrifice—in Europe.

They're both feeling vulnerable to attack and they're right to feel that way. It's a very curious turn.

Anyway, the United States of America didn't understand the tinder it was playing with and George Bush, in his naïve reference to the crusades, demonstrated his profound ignorance of how deep in the history of our culture these conflicts go. Osama bin Laden understood this much better than Bush. It's no accident that the two epithets of choice the jihadists use for the American enemy are "crusaders" and "Jews," and they're mobilizing epithets for vast numbers of Muslim Arabs.

TD: Do you think that, in dancing with Osama bin Laden, Bush has somehow turned him into something like a superpower? You know, a word you used early on caught my eye. You said, "Mr. Bush's hubristic foreign policy has been officially exposed as based on nothing more than hallucination." However clever bin Laden has been, isn't there also something hallucinatory about all this?

Carroll: It's true that if you begin to treat an imagined enemy as transcendent, at a certain point he becomes transcendent.

TD: You said we "forgot" Islam. A theme of your writings and maybe your life—if you'll excuse my saying so—is an American-style willed forgetfulness. Two key concerns of yours that seem "forgotten" in American life are the militarization of our society and nuclear weapons. Your father was a general. Your next book is about the Pentagon. What's the place of the Pentagon in our life that we don't see?

Carroll: When George W. Bush responded to the crisis of 9/11, two things came into play: his own temperament—his ideological impulses which were naïve, callow, dangerous, Manichaean, triumphalist—and the structure of the American government, which was sixty years in the making. What's not sufficiently appreciated is that Bush had few options in the way he might have responded to 9/11.

What was called for was vigorous diplomatic activity centered around cooperative international law enforcement, but our government had invested little of its resources in such diplomatic internationalism in the previous two generations. What we had invested in since World War II was massive military power, so it was natural for Bush to turn first to a massive military response. The meshing of Bush's temperament and a long-prepared American institutional response was unfortunate, but there it was. As somebody said, when he turned to his tool bag to respond to the mosquito of Osama bin Laden, the only tool he had in it was a hammer, so he brought it down on Afghanistan and destroyed it; then he brought it down on Iraq and destroyed it, missing the mosquito, of course.

Something has happened in our country since the time of Franklin Roosevelt that we haven't directly reckoned with. The book I've just written has as its subtitle, "The Pentagon and the Disastrous Rise of American Power." That polemical phrase "disastrous rise" comes from Eisenhower's famous military-industrial-complex speech where he explicitly warned against "the disastrous rise of misplaced power" in America—exactly the kind that has since come into being.

TD: And yet one of the hallucinatory aspects of this, don't you think, is that when we responded after 9/11…

Carroll: …the power was empty. That's the irony, of course. We've created for ourselves the disaster an enemy might have liked to create for us. That was the essence of the Eisenhower warning. We've sacrificed democratic values. What accounts for Abu

Ghraib and Guantánamo? What accounts for the abandonment of basic American principles of how you treat accused people? We've abandoned this fundamental tenet of American democracy ourselves! We didn't need an invading force to take away this one chief pillar of the Constitution. We took it down ourselves.

And we've barely begun to reckon with the war machine that we created to fight the Soviet Union and that continued intact when the Soviet Union disappeared. Of course, that was the revelation at the end of the Cold War when the threat went away and our response didn't change. This isn't a partisan argument, because the person who presided over the so-called peace dividend which never came was Bill Clinton; the person who presided over the time when we could have dismantled our nuclear arsenal, or at least shrunk it to reasonable levels (as even conservative military theorists wish we had done) was Bill Clinton. Bill Clinton was the person who first undercut the ideas of the International Criminal Court, the Nuclear Non-Proliferation Treaty, and the Anti-Ballistic Missile Treaty. When George Bush became president, he stepped into space created for him by Bill Clinton. This isn't to demonize Clinton. It's just to show that our political system had already been corrupted by something we weren't reckoning with—and the shorthand for that something was "the Pentagon."

TD: The bomb also arrived at that moment sixty years ago and you often write about it as the most forgotten of things.

Carroll: Marc Trachtenberg, the political scientist, has this phrase "atomic amnesia." Everything having to do with atomic weapons we seem to forget which is why the United States of America has had such trouble reckoning with the authentic facts of what happened in 1945, the negotiations around the Japanese surrender impulse, the invasion of Japan, and all of that. The first week of

August every year we see this flurry of American insistence on the
necessity of the bomb (almost all of which has been thoroughly
debunked by professional historians across the ideological spectrum). At the other end of the spectrum, we have not begun to
reckon at all with the nonsense of American policies toward
nuclear weapons today—the fact that we're resuming their production even now, that we continue to threaten their use even
now. How can these questions be so unreckoned with? Well, the
answer is that they're part of this larger phenomenon, the ele-
phant in the center of the American living room that we just walk
around and nobody speaks about.

TD: I was thinking of that relatively brief moment just after 9/11
and before Iraq when pundits were talking about us as the new
Roman Empire; when there was this feeling, very much connected
to the Pentagon, that we had the power to dominate the world,
from land, from space, from wherever. Do you have anything to
say about that now?

Carroll: We're not sufficiently attuned to the fact that we of the
West are descended from the Roman Empire. It still exists in us.
The good things of the Roman Empire are what we remember
about it—the roads, the language, the laws, the buildings, the
classics. We're children of the classical world. But we pay very
little attention to what the Roman Empire was to the people at its
bottom—the slaves who built those roads; the many, many slaves
for each citizen; the oppressed and occupied peoples who were
brought into the empire if they submitted, but radically and completely smashed if they resisted at all.

We Christians barely remember the Roman war against the
Jewish people in which historians now suggest that hundreds of
thousands of Jews were killed by the Romans between 70 and
135 CE. Why were the Jews killed? Not because the Romans

were anti-Semites. They were killed because they resisted what for them was the blasphemous occupation of the Holy Land of Israel by a godless army. It would remain one of the most brutal exercises of military power in history until the twentieth century. That's the Roman story.

We Americans are full of our sense of ourselves as having benign imperial impulses. That's why the idea of the American Empire was celebrated as a benign phenomenon. We were going to bring order to the world. Well, yes... as long as you didn't resist us. And that's where we really have something terrible in common with the Roman Empire. If you resist us, we will do our best to destroy you, and that's what's happening in Iraq right now, but not only in Iraq. That's the saddest thing, because the way we destroy people is not only by overt military power, but by writing you out of the world economic and political system that we control. And if you're one of those benighted people of Bangladesh, or Ghana, or Sudan, or possibly Detroit, then that's the way we respond to you. We'd do better in other words if we had a more complicated notion of what the Roman Empire was. We must reckon with imperial power as it is felt by people at the bottom. Rome's power. America's.

3. Katrina Will Be Bush's Monica

Cindy Sheehan

SEPTEMBER 29, 2005

My brief immersion in the almost unimaginable life of Cindy Sheehan begins on the Friday before a massive antiwar march past the White House. I take a cab to an address somewhere at the edge of Washington DC—a city I don't know well—where I'm to have a quiet hour with her. Finding myself on a porch filled with peace signs and vases of roses (assumedly sent for Sheehan), I ring the doorbell, only to be greeted by two barking dogs but no human beings. Checking my cell phone, I discover a message back in New York from someone helping Sheehan out. *Good Morning America* has just called; plans have changed. Can I make it to Constitution and 15th by five? I rush to the nearest major street and, from a bus stop, fruitlessly attempt to hail a cab. The only empty one passes me by and a young black man next to me offers an apologetic commentary: "I hate to say this, but they probably think you're hailing it for me and they don't want to pick me up."

On his recommendation, I board a bus, leaping off (twenty blocks of crawl later) at the sight of a hotel with a cab stand.

A few minutes before five, I'm finally standing under the Washington monument, beneath a cloud-dotted sky, in front of "Camp Casey," a white tent with a blazing red "Bring them home tour" banner. Behind the tent is a display of banged-up, empty soldiers' boots; and then, stretching almost as far as the eye can see or the heart can feel, a lawn of small white crosses, nearly two thousand of them, some with tiny American flags planted in the nearby ground. In front of the serried ranks of crosses is a battered looking metal map of the United States rising off a rusty base. Cut out of it are the letters, "America in Iraq, killed ▬, wounded ▬." (It's wrenching to note that, on this strange sculpture with eternal letters of air, only the figures of 1,910 dead and 14,700 wounded seem ephemeral, written as they are in white chalk over a smeared chalk background, evidence of numerous erasures.)

This is, at the moment, Ground Zero for the singular movement of Cindy Sheehan, mother of Casey, who was killed in Sadr City, Baghdad on April 4, 2004, only a few days after arriving in Iraq. Her movement began in the shadows and on the Internet, but burst out of a roadside ditch in Crawford, Texas, and, right now, actually seems capable of changing the political map of America. When I arrive, Sheehan is a distant figure, walking with a crew from *Good Morning America* amid the white crosses. I'm told by Jodie, a stalwart of Code Pink, the women's antiwar group, in a flamboyant pink-feathered hat, just to hang in there along with Joan Baez, assorted parents of soldiers, vets, admirers, tourists, press people, and who knows who else.

As Sheehan approaches, she's mobbed. She hugs some of her greeters, poses for photos with others, listens briefly while people tell her they came all the way from California or Colorado just to

see her, and accepts the literal T-shirt off the back of a man, possibly a vet, with a bandana around his forehead, who wants to
give her "the shirt off my back." She is brief and utterly patient.
She offers a word to everyone and anyone. At one point, a man
shoves a camera in my hand so that he and his family can have
proof of this moment—as if Cindy Sheehan were already some
kind of national monument, which in a way she is.

But, of course, she's also one human being, even if she's on
what the psychiatrist Robert Jay Lifton would call a "survivor
mission" for her son. Exhaustion visibly inhabits her face. (Later,
she'll say to me, "Most people, if they came with me for a day,
would be in a coma by eleven A.M.") She wears a tie-dyed, purple
T-shirt with "Veterans for Peace" on the front and "waging
peace" on the back. Her size surprises me. She's imposing, far
taller than I expected, taller certainly than my modest five-feet,
six inches. Perhaps I'm startled only because I'd filed her away—
despite every strong commentary I'd read by her—as a grieving
mother and so, somehow, a diminished creature.

And then, suddenly, a few minutes after five, Jodie is hustling
me into the backseat of a car with Cindy Sheehan beside me, and
Joan Baez beside her. Cindy's sister Dede, who wears an "Anything war can do, peace can do better" T-shirt and says to me
later, "I'm the behind-the-scenes one, I'm the quiet one," climbs
into the front seat. As soon as the car leaves the curb, Cindy turns
to me: "We better get started."

"Now?" I ask, flustered at the thought of interviewing her
under such chaotic conditions. She offers a tired nod—I'm surely
the 900th person of this day—and says, "It's the only way it'll
happen." And so, with my notebook (tiny printed questions scattered across several pages) on my knees, clutching my two cheap
tape recorders for dear life and shoving them towards her, we
begin:

Tomdispatch: You've said that the failed bookends of George Bush's presidency are Iraq and Katrina. And here we are with parts of New Orleans flooded again. Where exactly do you see us today?

Cindy Sheehan: Well, the invasion of Iraq was a serious mistake, and the invasion and occupation have been seriously mismanaged. The troops don't have what they need. The money's being dropped into the pockets of war profiteers and not getting to our soldiers. It's a political war. Not only should we not be there, it's making our country very vulnerable. It's creating enemies for our children's children. Killing innocent Arabic Muslims, who had no animosity toward the United States and meant us no harm, is only creating more problems for us.

Katrina was a natural disaster that nobody could help, but the man-made disaster afterwards was just horrible. I mean, number one, all our resources are in Iraq. Number two, what little resources we did have were deployed far too late. George Bush was golfing and eating birthday cake with John McCain while people were hanging off their houses praying to be rescued. He's so disconnected from this country—and from reality. I heard a line yesterday that I thought was perfect. This man said he thinks Katrina will be Bush's Monica. Only worse.

TD: It seems logical that the families of dead soldiers should lead an antiwar movement, but historically it's almost unique. I wondered if you had given some thought to why it happened here and now.

Sheehan: That's like people asking me, "Why didn't anybody ever think of going to George Bush's ranch to protest anything?"

TD: I was going to ask you that too…

Sheehan: [Laughs.] I don't know. I just thought of it and went down to do it. It was so serendipitous. I was supposed to go to England for a week in August to do Downing Street [Memo] events with [Congressman] John Conyers. That got cancelled. I was supposed to go to Arkansas for a four-day convention. That got cancelled. So I had my whole month free. I was going to be in Dallas for the Veteran's for Peace convention. The last straw was on Wednesday, August 3—the fourteen Marines who were killed and George Bush saying that all of our soldiers had died for a noble cause and we had to honor the sacrifices of the fallen by continuing the mission. I had just had it. That was enough and I had this idea to go to Crawford.

The first day we were there—this is how unplanned it was—we were sitting in lawn chairs, about six of us, underneath the stars with one flashlight between us, and we were going to the bathroom in a ten-gallon bucket.

DeDe: Five-gallon . . .

Sheehan: A five-gallon bucket, sorry. So that's how well planned this action was. We just planned it as we were going along and, for something so spontaneous, it turned out to be incredibly powerful and successful. It's hard for some people to believe how spontaneous it was.

TD: You've written that George Bush refusing to meet with you was the spark that lit the prairie fire—and that his not doing so reflected his cowardice. You also said that if he had met you that fatal . . . fateful day . . .

Sheehan: Fatal day . . .

TD: Fatal—it was fatal for him—things might have turned out quite differently.

Sheehan: If he had met with me, I know he would have lied to me. I would have called him on his lies and it wouldn't have been a good meeting, but I would have left Crawford. I would have written about it, probably done a few interviews, but it wouldn't have sparked this exciting, organic, huge peace movement. So he really did the peace movement a favor by not meeting with me.

TD: I thought his fatal blunder was to send out [National Security Advisor Stephen] Hadley and [Deputy White House Chief of Staff Joe] Hagin as if you were the prime minister of Poland. [She laughs.] And it suddenly made you in terms of the media . . .

Sheehan: . . . credible.

TD: So what did Hadley and Hagen say to you?

Sheehan:: They said, "What do you want to tell the President?" I said, "I want to ask the President, what is the noble cause my son died for?" And they kept telling me: Keep America safe from terrorism for freedom and democracy. Blah-blah-blah . . . all the excuses I wasn't going to take, except from the President. Then we talked about weapons of mass destruction and the lack thereof, about how they had really believed it. I was: Well, really, Mr. Stephen (Yellowcake Uranium) Hadley... I finally said, "This is a waste of time. I might be a grieving mother, but I'm not stupid. I'm very well informed and I want to meet with the President." And so they said, "Okay, we'll pass on your concerns to the President."

They said at one point, "We didn't come out here thinking

we'd change your mind on policy." And I said, "Yes you did." They thought they were going to intimidate me, that they were going to impress me with the high level of administration official they had sent out, and after they explained everything to me, I was going to go [her voice becomes liltingly mocking], "Ohhhh, I really never saw it that way. Okay, let's go guys." You know, that's exactly what they thought they were going to do to me. And I believe it was a move that did backfire because, as you said, it gave me credibility and then, all of a sudden, the White House press corps thought this might be a story worth covering.

TD: What was that like? I had been reading your stuff on the Internet for over a year, but . . .

Sheehan: I think in progressive circles I was very well known. But all of a sudden I was known all over the world. My daughters were in Europe when my mother had her stroke. My husband and I decided not to tell the girls. We didn't want to ruin their vacation, but they saw it on TV. So it really just spread like wildfire. And not only did it bring wanted attention, it brought unwanted attention from the right-wing media. But that didn't affect me, that didn't harm me at all.

I'd been doing this a long time. I'd been on Wolf Blitzer, Chris Mathews, all those shows. I'd done press conferences. It was just the intensity that spiked up. But my message has always remained the same. I didn't just fall off some pumpkin truck on August 6th and start doing this. The media couldn't believe someone like me could be so articulate and intelligent and have my own message. Number one, I'm a woman; number two, I'm a grieving mother; so they had the urge to marginalize me, to pretend like somebody's pulling my strings. Our President's not even articulate and intelligent. Someone must be pulling his strings, so someone must be pulling Cindy Sheehan's too. That offended me. Oh my gosh, you think someone has to put words into my mouth! [She laughs.] Do some research!

TD: Did you feel they were presenting you without some of your bluntness?

Sheehan: God forbid anybody speak bluntly or tell the truth. Teresa Heinz Kerry, they marginalized her too because she always spoke her mind.

TD: Would you like to speak about your bluntness a little because words you use like "war crimes" aren't ones Americans hear often.

Sheehan: All you have to do is look at the Nuremberg Tribunal or the Geneva Conventions. Clearly they've committed war crimes. *Clearly*. It's black and white. It's not me coming up with this abstract idea. It's like, well, did you put a bullet in that person's head or didn't you? "Yes I did." Well, that's a crime. It's not shades of grey. They broke every treaty. They broke our own Constitution. They broke Nuremberg. They broke the Geneva Conventions. Everything. And if somebody doesn't say it, does it mean it didn't happen? Somebody has to say it, and I'll say it. I've called George Bush a terrorist. He says a terrorist is somebody who kills innocent people. That's his own definition. So, by George Bush's own definition, he is a terrorist, because there are almost 100,000 innocent Iraqis that have been killed. And innocent Afghanis that have been killed.

And I think a lot of the mainstream opposition is glad I'm saying it, because they don't have to say it. They're not strong enough or brave enough or they think they have something politically at stake. We've had Congress members talk about impeachment and war crimes. I've heard them. But they're the usual suspects. They're marginalized too. They've always been against the war, so we can't listen to them.

You know, I had always admired people like the woman who started Mothers Against Drunk Driving or John Walsh for starting the Adam Walsh Foundation after his son was killed. I thought I could never do anything like that to elevate my suffering or my tragedy, and then, when it happened to me, I found out I did have the strength.

[It's about 5:30 when we pull up at a Hyatt Hotel. Cindy, Dede, and I proceed to the deserted recesses of the hotel's restaurant where Cindy has her first modest meal of the day. The rest of the interview takes place between spoonfuls of soup.]

TD: I've read a lot of articles about you in which your son Casey is identified as an altar boy or an Eagle Scout, but would you be willing to tell me a little more about him?

Sheehan: He was very calm. He never got mad. He never got too wild. One way or the other, he didn't waver much. I have another son and two daughters. He was the oldest one and they just idolized him. He never gave anybody trouble, but he was a procrastinator, the kind of person who, if he had a big project at school, would wait until the day before to do it. But when he had a job—he worked full time before he went into the Army and he was never late for work or missed a day in two years. I think that's pretty amazing. The reason we talk about him being an altar boy was that church was his number one priority, even when he was away from us in the Army. He helped at the chapel. He never missed Mass. He was an usher. He was a Eucharistic minister. When he was at home, he was heavily involved in my youth ministry.

For eight years I was a youth minister at our parish and for three of those years in high school he was in my youth group; then for three of those years in college he helped me.

TD: Tell me about his decision to join the Army.

Sheehan: A recruiter got hold of him, probably at a vulnerable point in his life, promised him a lot of things, and didn't fulfill one of the promises. It was May of 2000. There was no 9/11. George Bush hadn't even happened. When George Bush became his commander-and-chief, my son's doom was sealed. George Bush wanted to invade Iraq before he was even elected president. While he was still governor of Texas he was talking about: "If I was commander-and-chief, this is what I would do."

Back then, my son was promised a twenty thousand dollar signing bonus. He only got four thousand dollars of that when he finished his advanced training. He was promised a laptop, so he could take classes from wherever he was deployed in the world. He never got that. They promised him he could finish college because he only had one year left when he went in the Army. They would never let him take a class. They promised him he could be a chaplain's assistant which was what he really wanted to do; but, when he got to boot camp, they said that was full and he could be a Humvee mechanic or a cook. So he chose Humvee mechanic. The most awful thing the recruiter promised him was: Even if there was a war, he wouldn't see combat because he scored so high on the ASVAB [Career Exploration] tests. He would only be in war in a support role. He was in Iraq for five days before he was killed in combat.

TD: Did you discuss Iraq with him at all?

Sheehan: Yes we did. He didn't agree with it. Nobody in our family agreed with it. He said, "I wish I didn't have to go, Mom, but I have to. It's my duty and my buddies are going." I believe we as Americans have every right to, and should be willing to, defend our country if we're in danger. But Iraq had nothing to do with keeping America safe. So that's why we disagreed with it. He reenlisted after the invasion of Iraq, because he was told if he didn't, he'd have to go to Iraq anyway—he'd be stop-lossed—but if he did, he'd get to choose a new MOS [military specialty] when he got home.

TD: Can you tell me something about your own political background?

Sheehan: I've always been a pretty liberal democrat, but I don't think this issue is partisan. I think it's life and death. Nobody asked Casey what political party he belonged to before they sent him to die in an unjust and immoral war.

TD: You met with Hillary Clinton yesterday, didn't you? What do you think generally of the Democratic... well, whatever it is?

Sheehan: They've been very weak. I think Kerry lost because he didn't come out strong against the war. He came out to be even more of a nightmare than George Bush. You know, we'll put more troops in; I'll hunt down terrorists; I'll kill them! That wasn't the right thing to say. The right thing to say was: This war was wrong; George Bush lied to us; people are dead because of it; they shouldn't be dead; and if I'm elected, I'll do everything to get our troops home as soon as possible. Then, instead of seeing the failure Kerry was with his middle-of-the-road, wishy-washy, cowardly policies, the rest of the Democrats have just kept saying the same things.

Howard Dean came out and said he hopes that the President

is *successful* in Iraq. What's that mean? How can somebody be successful when we have no goals or defined mission or objectives to achieve there? They've been very cowardly and spineless. What we did at Camp Casey was give them some spine. The doors are open to them, Democrats and Republicans alike. As [former Congressman and Win Without War Director] Tom Andrews said, if they won't see the light, they'll feel the heat. And I think they're feeling the heat.

I can see it happening. I can see some Republicans like Chuck Hagel and Walter Jones breaking ranks with the party line. We met with a Republican yesterday—I don't want to say his name because I don't want to scare him off—but he seems to be somebody we can work with. Of course, as it gets closer to the congressional elections, we'll be letting his constituents know that he can be worked with.

TD: So you're planning to go into the elections as a force?

Sheehan: It's totally about the war, about their position on the war. If people care about that issue, then that's what they should make it about too. We're starting a "Meet with the Moms" campaign. We're going to target every single congressman and senator to show their constituents exactly where they stand on the war. People in the state of New York, for instance, should look at their senators and say, if you don't come out for bringing our troops home as soon as possible, we're not going to reelect you.

TD: Did Hillary give you any satisfaction at all?

Sheehan: Her position is still to send in more troops and honor the sacrifices of the fallen, which sounds like a Bush position, but the dialogue was open.

TD: Don't you think it's strange, these politicians like [Senator] Joe Biden, for example, who talk about sending in more troops, even though we all know there are no more troops?

Sheehan: Yes... Where you gettin' 'em? Where you gettin' 'em? It's crazy. I mean we're going to send more troops in there and leave our country even more vulnerable? Leave us open for attack somewhere else, or to be attacked by natural and man-made disasters again?

TD: You want the troops out now. Bush isn't about to do that, but have you thought about how you would proceed if you could?

Sheehan: When we say *now*, we don't mean that they can all come home tomorrow. I hope everybody knows that. We have to start by withdrawing our troops from the cities, bringing them to the borders and getting them out. We have to replace our military with something that looks Arabic, something that looks Iraqi, to rebuild their country. You know, they have the technology, they have the skills, but they don't have any jobs right now. How desperate for a job does one have to be to stand in line to apply to the Iraqi National Guard? I mean, they're killed just standing in line! Give the Iraqis as much help and support as they need to rebuild their country which is in chaos. When our military presence leaves, a lot of the violence and insurgency will die. There will be some regional struggles with the different communities in Iraq, but that's happening right now. The British put together a country that should never have been put together. Maybe it should be split into three different countries—who knows? But that's up to them, not us.

TD: And what do you actually expect? We have three and a half more years of this administration...

Sheehan: No we don't! [She chuckles.] I think Katrina's going to be his Monica. It's not a matter of "if" anymore, it's a matter of "when," because clearly... *clearly*, they're criminals. I mean, look at the people who got the first no-bid contracts to clean-up and rebuild New Orleans. It's Halliburton again. It's crazy. One negative effect of Camp Casey was it took a lot of heat off Karl Rove for his hand in the [Valerie] Plame case. But I hear indictments are coming down soon. So that's one way it's going to come about. George Bush is getting ready to implode. I mean have you seen him lately? He's a man who's out of control.

4. "No Iraqis Left Me on a Roof to Die"

Voices from the
Frontlines of Protest

SEPTEMBER 25, 2005

George was out of town, of course, in the "battle cab" at the U.S. Northern Command's headquarters in Colorado Springs, checking out the latest in homeland-security technology and picking up photo ops; while White House aides, as the *Washington Post* wrote that morning, were attempting "to reestablish Bush's swagger." The Democrats had largely fled town as well, leaving hardly a trace behind. Another hurricane was blasting into Texas and the media was preoccupied, but nothing, it seemed, mattered. Americans turned out in poll-like numbers for the Saturday antiwar demonstration in Washington and I was among them. So many of us were there, in fact, that my wife (with friends at the back of the march) spent over two hours as it officially "began," moving next to nowhere at all.

This was, you might say, the "connection demonstration." In the previous month, two hurricanes, one of them human, had blown through American life; and between them, they had, for many people, linked the previously unconnected—Bush administration policies and the war in Iraq—to their own lives. So, in a sense, this might be thought of as the demonstration created by Hurricanes Cindy Sheehan and Katrina. It was, finally, a protest that, not just in its staggering turnout but in its make-up, reflected the changing opinion-polling figures in this country. This was a majority demonstration and the commonest statement I heard in the six hours I spent talking to as many protesters as I could was: "This is my first demonstration."

In addition, there were sizeable contingents of military veterans and of the families of soldiers in Iraq, or of those who were killed in Iraq. No less important, scattered through the crowd were many, as I would discover, whose lives had been affected deeply by George Bush's wars.

This was an America on very determined parade. Even though the march, while loud and energetic, had an air of relaxed calmness to it, the words that seemed to come most quickly to people's lips were: infuriated, enraged, outraged, had it, had enough, fed up. In every sense, in fact, this was a demonstration *of* words. I have never seen such a sea of words—of signs, almost invariably handmade, along with individually printed posters, T-shirts, labels, stickers. It often seemed that, other than myself, there wasn't an individual in the crowd without a sign and that no two of them were quite the same.

The White House, which the massed protesters marched past, was in every sense the traffic accident of this event. The crowds gridlocked there; the noise rose to a roar; the signs waved, a veritable sea of them, and they all, essentially said, "No more, not me!"

Here's just a modest sample of those that caught my eye, reflecting as they did humor, determination, and more than anything else, outrage: "Yeeha is not a foreign policy"; "Making a killing"; "Ex-Republican. Ask me why"; "Blind Faith in Bad

Leadership is not Patriotism"; "Bush is a disaster!" (with the President's face in the eye of a hurricane); "He's a *sick nut* my Grandma says" (a photo of an old woman in blue with halo-like rays emanating from her); "Osama bin Forgotten"; "Cindy speaks for me"; "Make levees not war"; "W's the Devil, One Degree of Separation"; "Dick Cheney Eats Kittens (with a photo of five kittens)"; "Bush busy creating business for morticians worldwide"; "Liar, born liar, born-again liar"; "Dude—There's a War Criminal in *My* White House!!!"; "Motivated moderates against Bush"; "Bored with Empire"; "Pro Whose Life?"; "War is Terrorism with a Bigger Budget."

Because just about everybody had the urge to express him or herself, I largely followed the signs to my interviewees. People were unfailingly willing to talk (and no less unfailingly polite as I desperately tried to scribble down their words). The meetings were brief and, for me, remarkably moving, not least because Americans regularly turn out to be so articulate, even eloquent, and because so many people are thinking so hard about the complex political fix we find ourselves in today. I've done my level best to catch (sometimes in slightly telescoped form and hopefully without too many errors) just what people had to say and how open they were—the first-timers and the veterans of former demonstrations alike.

A day of walking and intensive talking still gave me only the smallest sampling of such a demonstration. To my amazement, on my way to the Metro heading back to New York at about 5:30 (almost seven hours after I first set out for the Mall), I was still passing people marching. So I can't claim that what follows are *the* voices of the Washington demonstration, just that they're the voices of my demonstration, some of the thirty-odd people to whom I managed to talk in the course of those hours. They are but a drop in the ocean of people who turned out in Washington, while the President was in absentia and the Democrats nowhere to be seen, to express in the most personal and yet collective way possible their upset over the path America has taken in the world. As far as I'm concerned, we seldom hear the voices of Americans in our media society very clearly. So I turn the rest of this dispatch over to those voices. Dip in wherever you want—as if you were at the march too.

Angry Graphic Designer: On the corner by the Metro, we meet Bill Cutter and a friend. Cutter is carrying a sign with a Bush image and enough words to drown a city. We stop to copy it down. It has a headline that asks, "What did you do on your summer vacation?" Inside a bubble is the President's reply: "Well, I rode my bike, killed some troops, killed even more Iraqis, raised lots of money for my friends, ignored a grieving mom and, for extra credit, I destroyed an American city!" Cutter, a forty-five-year-old Washingtonian with a tiny goatee, says simply enough, "I'm just an angry graphic designer with a printer." The previous day he made his sign and his friend's (an image of Bush over the question, "Intelligent design?"—and, on the back, Dick Cheney with quiz-like, check-off boxes that say, "Evil, Crazy, or Just Plain Mean, Pick any three!"). We're all looking for the demonstration's initial gathering place, and so we fall in step and begin to chat. This sign-maker will prove an omen for the day—the march will be a Katrina, a cacophony, of handmade signs, waves and waves of them, expressing every bit of upset and pent-up frustration that the polls tell us a majority of Americans feel.

Cutter explains his presence this way: "I figure that if we live here and don't do something, it's ridiculous. Cindy Sheehan's sacrifice is so much huger than anything anyone has done, so how could we not?"

On what is to be done in Iraq itself, he first says, "It's a tough one"—a comment I will hear again and again, even from those intent on seeing American troops withdraw immediately. On this

day, you would be hard pressed not to come away with a sense of
Americans in protest over Bush's war and the mess he's brought
to our very doorstep, and yet deeply puzzled by what is now to
be done and how exactly to do it. "We've gotten ourselves down
a rat hole," he continues. "I don't know what to do. Ultimately, I
think it's going to end up as a civil war there and we'll have
caused it. I only wish the Democratic Party had the balls and
would seize the moment. It's like they're practicing the politics of
safety. Do what's safe, not what's right." He pauses. "It's the politics of expediency," he adds with disgust just as we arrive at a
plaza filled with a sea of pink balloons—a sign that the antiwar
women's group Code Pink is gathering here. We part at this point
with him saying brightly, "I'm not sure 'enjoy yourself' is quite
the right thing to say…but enjoy yourself!"

Disabled (Peacetime) Vet: On the plaza we run into forty-eight-year-
old Steve Hausheer ("Howser," he says, "but if you look at the
spelling, you'll never pronounce it right.")—or rather he rolls
past us at quite a clip in his wheelchair. He's dressed severely in
black, but has a kindly, open face. When I stop him, he swivels
around, removes his black-leather wheeling gloves ("my hands
are a mess…") and shakes firmly. "I'm disabled," he says, "but I
was in the peacetime military. I'm a peacetime vet. Seventy-six,
seventy-seven. I just missed the Vietnam War." He's unsure about
giving an interview. "I get really excited. I'm impassioned about
this cause, but then everything just flies out of my head!" He's
from New York, he tells me, and adds, excitement in his voice,
"I've looked forward to doing something more than just talk to
my friends and donate. I'm just so tired of seeing this country
head in the wrong direction. It's time to get proactive!

"We need to support the troops," he insists with feeling and
then, after a pause, "by bringing them home. We're stuck now.
We've torn Iraq apart and there are going to be no easy answers.

George Bush has taken us so far down the wrong road that it's going to be very difficult to find our way back. My wish is that the people speak up until Congress and the other 40 percent of America that still thinks he's doing a good job change their mind.

"The men we're trying to bring home are true heroes and we need to treat them as such. It isn't bad enough that he put them in harm's way through a lie, now he's working to treat them as anything but heroes. Can you believe it? He wants to cut their disability payments!"

I thank him, we shake hands, he begins to don his gloves and then, at the last second, he calls me back. "One more thing," he says and begins to give me this final comment in a slow, measured way as you might dictate to a stenographer: "I want to put this country back into the hands of men and women who are dedicated to serving the American people instead of themselves and their cronies." He stops, satisfied, and then adds, "This would be my quote, if you have to pick one."

Ms. Statue of Liberty: Just down the plaza near a "Montana Women For Peace" sign, a group of women of all ages are scurrying to get their Styrofoam green Statue-of-Liberty crowns and green robes in place. A welcoming, white-haired Norma Buchanan is among them. "I am fifty-six years old. I have never been in a peace march in my life. I just snapped and I had to be here. Enough is enough. This war, the leadership, is against the law. What I hope is that, at a grassroots level, we're going to wake up the 40 percent of Americans who are still asleep at the wheel. I hope we're going to stop worrying about what kind of dog Paris Hilton is carrying around or who's divorcing whom, and pay some attention to what matters!"

Suddenly a cry goes up, "The march is starting!" It's true. Hundreds of pink balloons, all attached to Code Pink women, are slowing beginning to bob out of the plaza heading for the gathering area near the Washington Monument where Cindy Sheehan is to speak and the official march is to begin. So Norma Buchanan excuses herself, picks up her placard, and a bevy of Montana-style Lady Liberties, hoisting aloft a cumulative painting of a Western mountain scene, head off to join what will soon be an ocean of protesting humanity, much of it, like Buchanan, at such an event for the first time.

Vietnam Nurse: In a jaunty pink beret and a white "Stop the War" T-shirt ("My daughter made this for me!"), Peggy Akers is carrying a colorful hand-lettered sign that says, "Another Veteran for Peace." She's fifty-eight, cheery, has flown in from Portland, Maine, and is marching in the Code Pink contingent with her daughter and sister. She's active in Veterans for Peace and promptly tells me, "I was a nurse in Vietnam." If I want to get a sense of her sentiments about her Vietnam experience, she suggests, I should check out the Commondreams Web site which has posted a poem of hers on the subject, "Dear America." ("I hear a helicopter coming in—I smell the burning of human flesh. It's Thomas, America, the young Black kid from Atlanta, my patient, burned by an exploding gas tank... And Pham. He was only eight, America, and you sprayed him with napalm and his skin fell off in my hands and he screamed as I tried to comfort him... America, we have sent another generation of children to see life through an M-16 and death through the darkness of a body bag.")

"I just feel it's so important for people like myself to speak out about what I saw and did in Vietnam. I'm part of the conscience of this country. If people like myself don't speak about what war does, it'll never end. The images of war are not being shown to Americans. Not really. No one here knows what it's like to see a young soldier, eighteen or nineteen years old, in a body bag, or an Iraqi mother who has lost her son. If Americans really saw that, this couldn't go on.

"If it wasn't for people marching like today, if they hadn't done that during Vietnam, that Wall [the Vietnam Wall honoring America's war dead] would be wrapped around this city ten times over.

"You know," she says with excitement, "we met so many people coming in who had never marched before. From Utah, from the Midwest, from everywhere. I think we should bring our troops home and instead send in a Peace Corps—plumbers, electricians, carpenters—to help rebuilt that country; whatever the Iraqi people want from *us*, not what *we* want from them."

Republican for Impeachment: Approaching the rally, we notice Cathy Hickling, a financial consultant from Maryland, standing on the curb in a bright red T-shirt holding a "Republicans for impeachment" sign on a pole and can't resist a stop. "My odyssey," she says, "simply is: I've been a registered Republican for in excess of thirty years and I think the Party's been hijacked by the policies of George Bush! I think a president should be smarter than I am.

"This is my first demonstration. I felt strongly enough to come. What I hope will happen is that the Democrats and Republicans with a mind-set similar to mine get people to change their minds about the direction this country is taking. Remember, Clinton was impeached for a lot less. I saw a sign that said, 'Clinton lied, no one died,' and that just about sums it up.

"This is an antiwar protest, but I'm not here to support the idea that we should be leaving Iraq immediately. Now that we're there, we need to finish the job, but it's folly to think that the people who got us there can get us out."

"Right on!" says a woman who happens to be standing next to her.

And after just a moment's hesitation, she says it too: "Right on."

Sign of the Times: As we head into the rally, I run into Susan, a social worker from the New York area, and ask her to stop so I can copy down her sign. Its front says: "What if they gave a war and nobody came?" The back reads: "What if they had a hurricane and nobody came because... They were all at *War!!*" She insists I get front and back in the right order. "See, the front is that old sixties slogan and on the back it's been adapted to the present. A teacher I work with made it. She's more artistic than I am. I was absolutely infuriated after the hurricane. All our resources were at war. There was nothing to help our people here. I was infuriated and, after thinking about it, wanted to be here with this."

The Man from Alabama: He's white-haired, wears a striped oxford shirt, and carries an "Alabama has lost too many young people to this war" sign. He's with a small group of fellow Alabamans. When I introduce myself and mention the Tomdispatch Web site, he responds, "Do I know it! I send it to my lists, maybe one hundred people. I can't believe I'm actually meeting you here." He introduces himself as Wythe ("Get Wythe it!") Holt. I ask— as I do of many people— "What do you do in real life?"

"Protest," he says definitively. And then he chuckles. "But in the business world, I'm a retired professor of law at the University of Alabama. What I really do now is work for democracy, which means protesting, which is, of course, what democracy's all about. Even those nitwits who are protesting on the other side are exercising their democratic rights.

"Alabama has lost a lot of children to this war. It's making its mark on the state. The *Tuscaloosa News* is beginning to come out and question what's going on. So the truth is filtering through to Alabama. There are, at this moment, big demonstrations in Birmingham and in a little while we're going to be in communication with our colleagues there. We belong to Tuscaloosa People for Peace. We meet two or three times a month for discussions. We read books together. We go to protests.

"I was against Vietnam in 1971. Then, we had two busloads of people driving up here. Now we have one SUV.

"I agree with Jefferson that unless you're vigilant, you're not going to have liberty. And this country is slowly losing its liberties. But we're making liberty here today. Unfortunately, we don't make enough of it in Alabama, but we try.

"As for Iraq, I say get out now. Leave Iraq to the Iraqis. Bring our young people home this minute. All that equipment that could have been used in New Orleans and Galveston and Houston. If we want democracy in Iraq, we should encourage it, not impose it. I saw a sign earlier that said, 'Read between the pipelines,' but it's deeper than oil. Oil just happens to be the greedy object of the moment. The real struggle is between those of us who want to speak up for ourselves and want to have a government we have a part in, and those who have other goals, which are mostly selfish and greedy, and are interested in imposing their wills on others."

Mother Lion: She's holding up a hand-scribbled sign which reads, "Not with my sons." She's Robbie from New York. "I'm a writer and a mom. I have three sons. One is almost nineteen, one's almost eighteen. I wrote this sign. I mean it. You know, the mother lion. I feel so outraged. It's the outrage of mothers—and fathers too—to see children sacrificed for these lies. We have to start getting angry and that's why I'm here.

"I thought of this sign when I was home and identifying with those mothers who had lost their sons. Seeing all of these banners here representing each child who has been killed, that is just so graphic. You stop thinking of the war as being fought by another group of people. I feel this outrage, this energy. Like Cindy Sheehan said, we have to get back to our humanity, and so we mothers have to begin to be teachers. We've lost our way."

College Students: Samantha Combs and Andrea Solazzo are weaving happily through the crowd, wearing matching tie-dyed T-shirts, pink and blue. Samantha's says, "Peace Takes Time, Not Lives!" They're startled to be stopped, embarrassed at the thought of being interviewed. Extremely charming, a little giggly, they're both eighteen, from Eckerd College in St. Petersburg, Florida and they've spent nineteen hours on the Alliance for Concerned Individuals' bus to get here. ("It's a campus group that focuses on everything that deals with human rights," Samantha tells me.)

Why are they at the demonstration? The responses are brief and to the point. Samantha: "So much money's being spent in Iraq, when it should be spent here."

Andrea: "My cousin went to Afghanistan and then Iraq. He's been trying to go to college for years and he keeps getting called up! I don't think Iraq's worth his life."

And then they exclaim in unison, "Our group's leaving," and with another round of embarrassed giggles they bound off.

School Teacher: Sadida Athaullah is a social studies teacher in metropolitan Baltimore. She's wearing a blue "March on Washington/End the Iraq War" T-shirt and a light blue headscarf. She's quiet-spoken and thoughtful. "This is my first time at such a demonstration. I'm a naturalized American of twenty-five years, originally from India. I gave up my heritage to be an American because I admired American values, and I don't like what this country is turning into. When the war first began, I didn't really take an active part against it. I thought it would be a quick action, over in weeks, not months, and not turning into this big, long disaster, which makes no sense to me. I don't think the Iraqis are going to drink the oil in their country. They're going to have to sell it on the open market and we could buy it like anyone else."

Father and Daughter: As we leave the rally grounds, in a milling mass of humanity and pour out onto 15th Street, the sound level beginning to rise, I notice Frank Medina in a reddish baseball cap, and on his shoulders, his young daughter in a pink shirt and bright yellow dress. As I ask for his name, she leans over and shouts out with delight: "Claire Elizabeth Medina!" He's a lawyer with the Securities and Exchange Commission. "I was at the demonstration before the war," he tells me. "And now, this is just an appalling circumstance. That's why I'm back. It's an appalling war and it needs to end immediately. There needs to be a coherent plan to turn the country back over to the Iraqis, with definite dates for the return of American troops. What can't be done is to continue to justify the war there by the sacrifices that have already been made. It's like saying that, when you've lost everything at the casino, you're going to double-down. At some point, you need to cut your losses.

"However, it's an administration that can't admit its mistakes, that can't admit the truth, and consequently that can't change. So there is no hope."

Why bother to come then, I ask.

"It's important," he says firmly, "to express your views, to protest."

Grandfather and Daughter: Only moments later, another man with a little girl on his shoulders catches my eye. I approach him, introduce myself, and mention that he's the second father I've seen this way in so many minutes. Joe Stone promptly corrects me: "I'm her grandfather. Her father's in Iraq." He lifts MacKenzie down from his shoulders, tired and ready for her nap, and puts her in a stroller pushed by his actual daughter Cindy. Then he turns back to me. "I haven't done this in thirty years. I was here in 1970. I was tear-gassed at the University of Maryland. Same kind of war, different time."

From Virginia, he's the assistant controller at a dairy ("an accountant basically"). Like a lot of people at this demonstration, he speaks calmly, even quietly, but with a deep-seated disgust. "I'm just sick of it. I think Bush is immoral. You have to say something. We're proud to be here. I'd slam the door in George Bush's face if he came knocking."

His daughter, like most of the demonstrators, is dressed casually—sweat shirt, blue jeans, sneakers. She tells me her husband, a combat engineer who joined the military in 2002, is back for his second tour of duty in Iraq. He was gone for his daughter's birth, home for nine months, returned in the winter and now is stop-lossed. They're not certain when he'll be back.

I ask whether he knows she's at the demonstration—her first, it turns out, other than a small "free Tibet" one.

"He wouldn't say not to," she replies in almost a whisper. "But I haven't had a chance to tell him yet. I just feel the same as my dad, though. I'd had it. I can't believe there are so many people in this country who still think the President's so great, especially after his first term. I couldn't get a single one of my friends to come. I work at a government contracting company and my co-workers thought it was strange to do this because I might not have a job if the war ended. One of them even said, 'You know, there's video cameras down there.' So what!"

Her father chimes in: "Defense contractors don't need a war to keep going."

She adds, "I don't really know what to do about Iraq now. They can't just leave, but I don't see a plan of action for how we're going to get out. I wish George Bush could get out of office. I just don't see how, though."

The Farmer: His sign reads, "U.S. Farmers Say No to War" and we bump into him just as we turn the corner and head for the White House, the march slowing into gridlock, the roaring of the crowd ahead rising to a din. But Michael O'Gorman's voice carries well. "I'm a real farmer," he says in response to my query. "I farm a thousand acres of organic vegetables for sale to the U.S. market in Baja, California [Mexico]. I've been farming for thirty-five years. I've earned all these wrinkles." And indeed his face is deeply creased.

"When I began in 1970, U.S. farmers were feeding the world. This is the first year, possibly in our history, when we're importing more than we're exporting, when we're not feeding ourselves. China will feed itself. India will feed itself. We won't. When I began farming, there were two million farmers in the U.S. Three hundred thousand of us remain; average age, sixty-two. I'm almost there." He laughs.

He tells me that he sits on the steering committee of United for Peace and Justice, which helped organize this demonstration. He flew in from Baja. "I was supposed to be in the lead contingent." He shows me a badge that indicates exactly that. "But we were swamped by the crowd and so I'm here. I remember joining protests back on July 4, 1987, in my community. We were supposed to speak about local issues, but I was protesting that the U.S. was arming Saddam Hussein's Iraq and [Ronald Reagan aide] Oliver North was arming Iran in a war between those two countries where two million young men would die. I warned that it would come back to haunt us.

"On 9/11, my oldest daughter was at Ground Zero, right across the street, and she survived. My son volunteered after that because his sister had been there. Now, he's at Guantánamo, so that war is haunting not just our society, but my own family.

"My son joined the Coast Guard Reserves. He thought it was a peaceable way to serve. Then they shipped him off to Cuba. I support him. We don't argue about it too much. I'm waiting for him to make his peace with it. He had a week off recently and—can you believe it—they didn't even fly him to Florida. We had to pay $750 to get him home.

"It's a horrible situation. People say it'll be a total mess if we pull out, but it's a mess and we're there. I don't see any argument for the United States staying. If, in pulling out, we could create an alternative to the U.S. military that would, of course, be best."

He shakes hands and invites us to visit his farm in Baja. "I believe," he says in parting, "that this is a very American movement. We're reclaiming our country."

Protester with Cane: I approach Camille Hazeur, who works for George Mason University's Office of Equity and Diversity, because of her cane ("arthritic hip"). I say that I think, in a march like this, the cane indicates real commitment. "Darn right!" she replies. "I'm against this war. It's indescribable that we're even there. It's my small way of saying, no, get out! And it's for our kids over there. To bring them back. And for the Iraqis. You never even hear what's happening to them. And I feel we're just sitting here while atrocities are going on, and I'm afraid our kids will have to suffer the impact of what we're doing there now. Those of us who are reading and thinking people . . . I'm not naïve about the Middle East or Saddam Hussein, but none of it justifies *this*.

"I was here in the seventies. I went to college in this town. I remember the demonstrations. I remember them all. They had a distinctive smell, of tear gas and grass, and we haven't smelled either of those today."

Protester with Cane (2): We're past the White House now and Ann Galloway is walking with determination, cane well deployed ("I need a knee replacement"). The gridlock of the march has ended and open space has appeared. She has a blue backpack strapped on. A little sign sticks out: "Support our troops, Bring them home alive."

"I hosted a Cindy Sheehan vigil in Stanford, Connecticut, and have been a leader of one of the MoveOn teams there. This is the first big march I have been in since Doctor Martin Luther King, Doctor Benjamin Spock, and the Reverend William Sloan Coffin demonstrated in maybe 1967 against the Vietnam War. I actually became energized again because everything this administration does is so antithetical to what America is about and I intend to be part of a movement that takes back the Congress in 2006.

"I'm a grandmother and, if anything, I am marching for my grandchild's future. She'll be two in December. I wrote to a friend that I'm going to show up with a cane and a floppy hat [which indeed she's wearing] and become one of those little old ladies we used to joke about. But this—the abuses, there are just so many—*has* to stop. They won't take the tax cuts off the table, but they're willing to squander our precious dollars on the war in Iraq that could be used for a myriad of other things in this country, including"—she says it emphatically—"homeland security. These guys don't care about any of it, just those tax cuts for their people who are not sending their children to fight this war."

Flight Attendant: She's standing at the curb in a green shirt with a sticker on the back that reads, "Sex is back in the White House. Bush is screwing us all!" She introduces herself as Liane. "I'm a flight attendant," she says. "I got this sticker from a woman I met at a union rally by the Labor Department. I liked it and she was so interesting. She had a history of coming to protests. She told me, if I gave her my address, she would send one my way. It was at least six months ago. I just haven't had a chance to use it until now."

This is her first antiwar protest. "I don't know what to do," she says. "I just think that the war in Iraq is a big mistake. Especially when I saw New Orleans and thought about the money for the levee system diverted to Iraq. *That* was upsetting. Even before that, though, I got the impression that the ones pushing the war were really planning for the best-case scenario, that they hadn't planned for anything but the best outcome. I think what they're doing is creating more terrorism."

Toy Soldiers: As we turn the corner, heading up 17th away from the White House, I'm approached by a young man dressed all in black and wearing headgear that looks like a cross between a fedora and a top hat. It's fronted by a yellow piece of cardboard with images of toy soldiers stamped on it. He hands me a little bag of green plastic soldiers of the sort I played with as a child and, strangely enough, in the midst of this antiwar demonstration, my heart takes a leap. I genuinely want them.

Each soldier, whether shooting or throwing a grenade, turns out to have a little piece of paper attached that says, "Bring me home" and includes the Mouths Wide Open Web site address. There's even a small explanation in the bag that begins, "We're spreading plastic Army Men around the country and around the globe as small, everyday reminders of the ongoing horrors of the war in Iraq—using them as tools to foster dialogue, action and resistance to the war."

I ask if he'd mind being interviewed, which flusters him. He finally indicates Merry Conway, who is older. "She's better to talk to," he says. And it's true. She's happy to talk. In fact, she's an enthusiast as well as an artist who "creates performance and installation shows with a very large community element."

So I ask about Mouths Wide Open. "We're a little group of friends in New York. Many are artists. We came together after 9/11 to see what we could do. We created the Four Horsemen of the Apocalypse Crusade. Maybe you've seen it at other demonstrations. It's huge. But we were still thinking about how to create a dialogue, because so many people were acting as if the war wasn't happening if they didn't have a relative involved. It was business as usual. What, we thought, if we left a trace, started that dialogue with a poignant emotional effect. And these little toy soldiers that so many boys have played with are it.

"The other night in New York at a Cindy Sheehan event, we were handing these out and I gave a packet to one of the mothers there. She recoiled. She said, 'My son's in Iraq. I can't take those. I used to hide them from him.' But you know what she said then? She said, 'Keep going. *But keep going!*'

"People get very excited about putting them in places and then other people find them. The other day we got an e-mail from a cop who had found one in the Federal Courthouse in New York and he was so moved he wrote us.

New Orleans Evacuee: She's holding up a bright red sign that says, "New Orleans Evacuees for Peace." Erica Smith is twenty-five, a law student at Loyola in New Orleans. ("We've been relocated to the University of Houston law school.") "I've probably met about ten people from New Orleans today and I've had lots of people come up to give me a hug.

"I was planning to come to this anyway. But with what happened in New Orleans, well… I was lucky, I live uptown and my place is on the third floor and a friend had a key and checked. It's okay. But all of our National Guard troops were off in Iraq instead of rescuing people here. Instead of being here to help out, they were off making problems in the rest of the world."

Mother and Son: As we circle back toward the Mall, we pass a mother and son standing on the sidewalk. She's holding what, for me, is the most striking sign of the day: "No Iraqis left me on a roof to die." Her twelve-year-old son, Muata Hunter, holds a sign too. It's simple and eloquent. "No war." Just as I approach them, a young black woman comes up to ask (as I was about to do), "Is your home in New Orleans?"

"No," the woman answers, "but my heart is. It's my people."

She's Aziza Gibson-Hunter, a local artist. "I've been thinking and thinking," she says, "trying to figure out how to make my people understand the direct correlation of this war and our well-being and I just thought this put it succinctly."

Her son shyly tells me that he made his sign that morning. "I just think war shouldn't be done. War isn't necessary. My uncle's been in war and my cousin Jimmy was in Iraq."

His mother adds, "*He* made it back."

5. "A Felon for Peace"

Ann Wright

November 11, 2005

She's just off the plane from Tulsa, Oklahoma, the cheapest route back from a reunion in the little Arkansas town where she grew up in the 1950s. For thirty years, she and her childhood friends have climbed to the top of Penitentiary Mountain, where the local persimmon trees grow, for a persimmon-spitting contest. ("All in the great spirit of just having fun and being crazy.") She holds out her hands and says, "I probably still have persimmon goop on me!"

We seat ourselves at a table in my dining room, two small tape recorders between us. She's dressed all in black with a bright green over-shirt, a middle-aged blond woman wearing gold earrings and a thin gold necklace. As she settles in, her sleeves pull back, revealing the jewelry she'd rather talk about. On her right wrist is a pink, plastic band. "This one was to be a volunteer in the Astrodome for Hurricane Katrina. I did two days work there, then three days in Covington, Louisiana, the first week after." On her left wrist, next to a watch from another age, are two blue plastic bands: "And this one," she says with growing animation, fingering the nearest of them, "was my very first arrest of my whole life on September 26th in front of the White House with four hundred of my closest friends. This is the bus number I was on and this is the arrest number they gave me and then, later on, I had to date it because now I have two." She fingers the second band. "Last week twenty-six of us were arrested after a die-in right in front of the White House in commemoration of the two thousandth American and maybe one hundred thousandth Iraqi who died in this war. So now," she announces, chuckling heartily, "I'm a felon for peace."

When she speaks—and in the final g's she drops from words ("It's freezin' in Mongolia!")—you can catch just a hint of the drawl of that long-gone child from Bentonville, Arkansas. In her blunt, straightforward manner, you can catch something of her twenty-nine years in the Army; and in her ease perhaps, the sixteen years she spent as a State Department diplomat. Animated, amused by her foibles (and those of her interviewer), articulate and thoughtful, she's just the sort of person you would want to defend—and then represent—your country, a task she continues to perform, after her own fashion, as one of the more out-of-the-ordinary antiwar activists of our moment.

Last August, she had a large hand in running Camp Casey for Cindy Sheehan at the President's doorstep in Crawford, Texas; then again, that wasn't such a feat, given that in 1997 she had overseen the evacuation of 2,500 foreigners from the war zone that was then Sierra Leone, a harrowing experience for which she was given the State Department's Award for Heroism. "That's why I joined the foreign service," she comments, her voice still filled with some residual excitement from those years. "I wanted to go to places you wouldn't visit on vacation." In fact, the retired colonel opened and closed embassies from Africa to Uzbekistan and took some of the roughest diplomatic assignments on Earth, including the reopening of the American embassy in Kabul in December 2001.

On March 19, 2003, the day before the first Cruise missiles were launched against Baghdad, she resigned from the Foreign Service in an open letter sent from the U.S. embassy in Mongolia (where she was then Deputy Chief of Mission) to Secretary of State Colin Powell. In it she wrote, in part:

"This is the only time in my many years serving America that I have felt I cannot represent the policies of an administration of the United States. I disagree with the administration's policies on Iraq, the Israeli-Palestinian conflict, North Korea, and curtailment of civil liberties in the U.S. itself. I believe the Administration's policies are making the world a more dangerous, not a safer, place. I feel obligated morally and professionally to set out my very deep and firm concerns on these policies and to resign from government service as I cannot defend or implement them."

Once used to delivering official U.S. statements to other governments, she now says things like: "Everyone should have to be handcuffed with the flexi-cuffs they use now and feel just how unflexible they are, just how they cut, and then imagine Iraqis, Afghans, and other people we pick up in them twenty-four hours a day." She relaxes, sits back, awaits the first question, and responds with gusto.

Tomdispatch: I thought we'd start by talking about two important but quite different moments in your life. The first was not so long ago. Let me quote from a *New York Times* article on a recent Condoleezza Rice appearance before the Senate Foreign Relations Committee. "It was a day that echoed the anguish, anger and skepticism that opinion polls show have begun to dominate the thinking of Americans. The hearing was punctuated by a heckler who called for an end to the war, only to be hustled out." Now, I believe this was you.

Ann Wright: [She chuckles.] Yes! Not a heckler, I was a protester.

TD: Tell me about it.

Wright: It was as much a protest against the Senators as against Condoleezza Rice, because they were not holding our Secretary of State responsible. I picked up the *Washington Post* that morning and noticed that Condoleezza was going to testify on Iraq, and I thought, well, I'm free until noon. When I walked in, I was not planning on doing anything.

But I sat there for two hours and Senators were saying: We've heard the administration is discussing a military option in Syria and perhaps Iran. The committee needs to be brought in on this, because we've only given you authorization for military action in Iraq. In an almost rude, dismissive tone, the Secretary of State essentially replied: We'll talk to you when we want to; all options are on the table; and thank you very much. Then the senators just kind of sat there. It was like: Come on, guys talk! Pin that woman down! We, the people, want to know. I want to know. And then they just started off on something else. It was like: No! Come back to this question. We don't want to go to war in Syria or Iran . . .

TD: And did you stand up?

Wright: So I stood up. I was back in the peanut gallery. I've never done anything like it before in my whole life. I took a deep breath and went, "Stop the killing! Stop the war! Hold this woman accountable! You, the Senate, were bamboozled by the administration on Iraq and you cannot be bamboozled again! Stop this woman from killing!"

At that point, I ran out of things to say because I hadn't really planned it. [She laughs.] I was looking around. There was only one police officer and he was just ambling toward me. It was like he enjoyed what I was saying. I thought, until he gets here I've got to say something more, so I went: "You failed us in Iraq, you can't fail us on Syria!" The police office finally said, "Uh, ma'am, you've got to come with me." This is the first time—somebody told me later—anyone's ever seen a protester put her arm around a police officer. [She laughs.]

TD: So you weren't "hustled" out?

Wright: Noooooo. It was a slow walk and there was silence in the room, so I thought: Well, I can't let this go by and I started another little rant on the way out. That part wasn't mentioned in the news reports.

TD: At least some papers like the *Washington Post* mentioned you by name. The *Times* merely called you a heckler.

Wright: Well, how rude! I wasn't heckling anyway. I was speaking on behalf of the people of America.

TD: This obviously takes you a long way from your professional life, because you were in the Foreign Service for . . .

Wright: Sixteen years . . .

TD: . . .and in all those years this would have been rather inconceivable.

Wright: Having testified at congressional hearings as a Foreign Service officer, particularly on Somalia issues back in '93 and '94, I was always humbled to go into those rooms as a government employee. I always found it interesting when people in the audience stood up to say something. You know, I learned later that most protestors do it in the first ten minutes because that's when the cameras and all the reporters are sure to be there.

As it happened, the chairman of the committee declined to have me arrested. The police officer said, "Well, if you're disappointed, I can arrest you." I replied, "If you don't mind, I'll just run on over to my lunch appointment." I was actually on my way to a presentation by Larry Wilkerson, Colin Powell's former chief of staff, where he would describe the secrecy of the administration and the way the State Department had been isolated by the White House and the National Security Council.

TD: Another moment of protest, one I'm sure you thought about very carefully, took place the day before the shock-and-awe campaign against Iraq began. That day you sent a letter of public resignation to Colin Powell which began—and not many people could have written such a sentence—"When I last saw you in Kabul in 2002 . . ."

Wright: Indeed I had volunteered to go to Kabul, Afghanistan, in December 2001 to be part of a small team that reopened the U.S. embassy. It had been closed for twelve years. I have a background in opening and closing embassies. I helped open an embassy in Uzbekistan, closed and reopened an embassy in Sierra Leone. I've been evacuated from Somalia and Sierra Leone. And with my military background, I've worked in a lot in combat environments.

I volunteered because I felt the United States needed to respond to the events of 9/11, and the logical place to go after al-Qaeda was where they trained, knowing full well that you probably weren't going to get a lot of people. The al-Qaeda group is very smart and few of them, in my estimation, would have been hanging out where we were most likely to go after them in Afghanistan. Actually, I was amazed the administration went in physically. I thought, like the Clinton administration, they would send in cruise missiles. Considering the severity of September 11, I guess the military finally said: Well, it looks like we're going into that hell-hole where the Russians got their butts whipped. Everybody knew it was going to be tough.

TD: You've commented elsewhere that a crucial moment for you was watching the President's axis-of-evil State of the Union Address from a bunker in Kabul.

Wright: A bunker outside the chancellery building meant to protect against the rockets the mujahedeen were sending against each other after they defeated the Soviets. We had taken [then interim leader] Hamid Karzai, who had been invited to the State of the Union, to Bagram Air Base and sent him off three days before. We told him, "You've got to start getting together some detailed plans for economic development funds because the attention of the United States doesn't stay on any country for long; so, get your little fledgling cabinet moving fast." Well, the President started talking about other interests that the United States had after 9/11 and these interests were Iran, Iraq, and North Korea. Just as he said that, the cameras focused on Karzai and you could almost see him going: Hmmmm [she mugs a wince], now I know what they were telling me at the embassy. And we were sitting there thinking, Oh my God . . .

TD: You had a functioning TV?

Wright: Barely. We had a satellite dish made of pounded-out coke cans—these were being sold down in Kabul—and a computer chip sent in from Islamabad, because we wanted to hear from Washington what was going to happen with Afghanistan. When, instead of talking much about Afghanistan, the President started in on this axis-of-evil stuff we were stunned. We were thinking: Hell's bells, we're here in a very dangerous place without enough military. So for the President to start talking about this axis of evil . . . everyone in the bunker just went: Oh Christ, here we go! No wonder we're not getting the economic development specialists in here yet. If the American government was going after al-Qaeda in Afghanistan, and clearing out the Taliban and preparing to help the people of Afghanistan, why the hell was it taking so long? Well, that statement said it all.

TD: Did you at that moment suspect a future invasion of Iraq?

Wright: I'm a little naïve sometimes. I really never, ever suspected we would go to war in Iraq. There was no attempt at that moment to tie 9/11 to Iraq, so it didn't even dawn on me.

Anyway, that was the preface to my letter of resignation. I wanted to emphasize that I had seen Colin Powell on his first trip to Kabul. I wanted to show that this was a person who had lots of experience.

TD: In the whole Vietnam era, few, if any, government officials offered public resignations of protest, but before the invasion of Iraq even began, three diplomats—Brady Kiesling, John Brown, and yourself—resigned in a most public fashion. It must have been a wrenching decision.

Wright: I had been concerned since September 2002 when I read in the papers that we had something like 100,000 troops already in the Middle East, many left behind after the Bright Star [military] exercise we have every two years in Egypt. I thought: Uh-oh, the administration is doing some sneaky-Pete stuff on us. They were claiming they wanted UN inspectors to go back into

Iraq, when a military build-up was already underway. It's one thing to put troops in the region for pressure, but if you're leaving that many behind, you're going to be using them. Then, as the mushroom-cloud rhetoric started getting stronger, it was like: Good God! These guys mean to go to war, no matter what the evidence is.

By November, I was having trouble sleeping. I would wake up at three, four in the morning—this was in Mongolia where it was freezing cold—wrap up in blankets, go to the kitchen table, and just start pouring my soul out. By the time I finally sent that resignation letter in, I had a stack of drafts like this. [She lifts her hand a couple of feet off the table.] I did know two others had resigned, but quite honestly I hadn't read their letters and I didn't know them.

TD: You were ending your life in a way, life as you had known it . . .

Wright: Thirty-five years in the government between my military service and the State Department, under seven administrations. It was hard. I liked representing America.

TD: Was there a moment when you knew you couldn't represent this government anymore?

Wright: I kept hoping the administration would go back to the Security Council for its authorization to go to war. That's why I held off until virtually the bombs were being dropped. I was hoping against hope that our government would not go into what really is an illegal war of aggression that meets no criteria of international law. When it was finally evident we were going to do so, I said to myself: It ain't going to be on my watch.

TD: Was it like crossing a border into a different world?

Wright: It was a great relief. During the lead-up to war, I had begun showing symptoms of an impending heart attack. The State Department put me on a medivac flight to Singapore for heart tests. The doctors said, "Lady, you're as strong as a horse. Are you just under some kind of stress?" "Yes, I am!" The moment I sent in that letter, it was like a great burden had been lifted from my shoulders. At least I had made my stand and joined the other two who had resigned.

TD: And what of those you left behind?

Wright: In the first couple of days, while I was still in Mongolia, I received over four hundred e-mails from colleagues in the State Department saying: We're so sad you're not going to be with us, but we're so proud of the three of you who resigned because we think this going-to-war is just so horrible; then each one would describe how anti-American feeling was growing in the country where they were serving. It was so poignant, all those e-mails.

TD: Why don't you think more people in the government—and in the military where there's clearly been opposition to Iraq at a very high level—quit and speak out?

Wright: There were a few. [General] Eric Shinseki talked about the shortchanging of the [Iraq] operations plan by a couple of hundred thousand people. He was forced out. But see, in the military, in the Foreign Service, you're not supposed to be speaking your own mind. Your job is to implement the policies of an administration elected by the people of America. If you don't want to, your only option is to resign. I understood that and that's one of the reasons I resigned—to give myself the freedom to talk out.

There are a lot of people still in government service speaking out, but you've got to read between the lines. The senior military leaders in Iraq, what they've been saying is very different from what Donald Rumsfeld and the gang in Washington say. These guys are being honest and truthful about the lack of Iraqi battalions really ready for military work, the dangers the troops are under, the days when the military doesn't go out on the streets. They're signaling to America: We're up a creek on this one, guys, and you, the people of America, are going to have to help us out.

TD: Let's talk about [Colin Powell's chief of staff] Larry Wilkerson as an example. He assumedly left after the election when Colin Powell did, so almost a year has passed. He saw what he believed was a secret cabal running the government and it took him that long after he was gone to tell us about it. I'm glad he spoke out. But I wonder why there isn't a more urgent impulse to do so?

Wright: If you look at Dick Clarke [the President's former chief adviser on terrorism on the National Security Council], he had all the secrets from the very beginning and he retired in January 2003. Yet he didn't say anything for over a year and a half, until he published that book [*Against All Enemies*] in 2004. If he had gone public before the war started, that man could have told us those same secrets right then. So could [the National Security Council's senior director for combating terrorism] Randy Beers. I worked with both of them on Somalia, on Sierra Leone. I know these guys personally and it's like: Guys, why didn't you come forward then?

As you probably know, on the key issues of the first four years of the Bush administration, the State Department was essentially iced out. I mean, look at the Iraq War. Colin Powell and the State Department were just shoved aside and all State's functions put into the Department of Defense. Tragically, Colin Powell, who was trying to counsel Donald Rumsfeld behind the scenes that there weren't enough troops in Iraq, never stood up to say, "Hold it, guys, I'll resign if we don't get this under control so that logical functions go in logical organizations and you, the Defense Department, don't do post-combat civil reconstruction stuff. That's ours." He just didn't do it. To me, he was more loyal to the Bush family than he was to the country. His resignation was possibly the one thing that could have deterred the war. Then the people of America would really have looked closely at what was going on. But tragically he decided loyalty to the administration was more valuable than loyalty to the country. I mean, it breaks my heart to say that, but it's what really happened.

TD: So what is it that actually holds people back?

Wright: I think the higher up you go, the more common it is for people to retire, or maybe even resign, and not say what the reasons are, because they may hope to get back into government in a different administration. Dick Clarke had served every administration since George Washington and maybe he was looking toward being called back as a political appointee again. Sometimes such people don't speak out because they feel loyalty to the person who appointed them. Nobody appointed me to nothin', except the American people. I'm a career foreign service officer and I serve the American people. When an administration wasn't serving the best interests of the American people, I felt I had to stand up.

TD: And are you now pretty much a full-time antiwar activist?

Wright: [She laughs.] That's the way it's turned out.

TD: What, if anything, do you think your military career, your State Department career, and this . . . well, I can't call it a career . . . have in common?

Wright: Service to America. It's all just a continuation of a real concern I have about my country.

TD: And what would you say to your former compatriots still in the military and the State Department?

Wright: Many of the emails I received from Foreign Service officers said, I wish I could resign right now, but I've got kids in college, I've got mortgages, and I'm going to try really hard, by staying, to ameliorate the intensity of these policies. All I can say is that they must be in agony about not being able to affect policy. There have been plenty of early retirements by people who finally realized they couldn't moderate the policies of the Bush administration.

TD: What message would you send to the person you once were from the person you are now?

Wright: You trained me well.

TD: If in this room you had the thirty-five-year-old woman about to go into Grenada, as you did back in 1983, what would you want her to mull over.

Wright: I would say: You were a good Army officer and Foreign Service officer. You weren't blind to the faults of America. In many jobs, you tried to rectify things that were going badly and you succeeded a couple of times. My resignation wasn't the first time I spoke out. For instance, I was loaned, or seconded, from the State Department to the staff of the United Nations operation in Somalia and ended up writing a memo concerning the military operations the UN was conducting to kill a warlord named Addid. They started taking helicopters, standing off, and just blowing up buildings where they had intelligence indicating perhaps he was there. Well, tragically he never was, and here we were blowing up all these Somali families. Of course the Somalis were outraged and that outrage ultimately led to Blackhawk Down.

I wrote a legal opinion to the special representative of the Secretary General, saying the UN operations were illegal and had to stop. It was leaked to the *Washington Post* and I got in a bit of hot water initially, but ultimately my analysis proved correct. I was also a bit of a rabble-rouser on the utilization of women in the military back in the eighties, part of a small group of women who took on the Army when it was trying to reduce the career potentials of women. I ended up getting right in the thick of some major problems which ultimately cost the Army millions of dollars in the reassessment of units that had been given incorrect direct-combat probability codings. I was also part of a team which discovered that some of our troops had been looting private homes in Grenada. The Army court-martialed a lot of our soldiers for this violation of the law of land warfare. We used their example in rewriting how you teach the code of conduct and, actually, the Geneva Convention on the responsibility of occupiers.

TD: You know a good deal about the obligations of an occupying power to protect public and private property, partially because in the 1980s you were doing planning on the Middle East, right?

Wright: Yes, from 1982 to 1984, I was at Fort Bragg, North Carolina when the Army was planning for potential operations using the Rapid Deployment Force—what ultimately became the Central Command. One of the first forces used in rapid deployment operations was the 82nd Airborne at Fort Bragg. I was in the special operations end of it with civil affairs. Those are the people who write up the annexes to operations plans about how you interact with the civilian population, how you protect the facilities—sewage, water, electrical grids, libraries. We were doing it for the whole Middle East. I mean, we have operations plans on the shelf for every country in the world, or virtually. So we did one on Iraq; we did one on Syria, on Jordan, Egypt. All of them.

We would, for instance, take the UNESCO list of treasures of the world and go through it. Okay, any in Iraq? Yep. Okay, mark 'em, circle 'em on a map, put 'em in the op-plan. Whatever you do, don't bomb this. Make sure we've got enough troops to protect this. It's our obligation under the law of land warfare. We'd be circling all the electrical grids, all the oil grids, all the museums. So for us to go into Iraq and let all that looting happen. Well, Rumsfeld wanted a light, mobile force, and screw the obligations of treaties. Typical of this administration on any treaty thing. Forget 'em.

So everything was Katy-bar-the-door. Anybody could go in and rip up anything. Many of the explosives now being used to kill our troops come from the ammo dumps we did not secure. It was a total violation of every principle we had for planning military operations and their aftermath. People in the civil affairs units, they were just shaking their heads, wondering how in the hell this could have happened. We've been doing these operations plans forever, so I can only imagine the bitchin' and moanin' about—how come we don't have this civilian/military annex? It's in every other op-plan. And where are the troops, where are the MPs?

TD: If back in the early eighties you were planning to save the antiquities of every country in the Middle East, then obviously the Pentagon was also planning for a range of possible invasions in the region. Do you look back now and ask: What kind of a country has contingency plans to invade any country you can imagine?

Wright: One of the things you are likely to do at a certain point in your military career is operations plans. It did not then seem abnormal to me at all that we had contingency plans for the Middle East, or for countries in the Caribbean or South America. At that stage, I was not looking at the imperialism of the United States. I just didn't equate those contingency plans with empire-building goals. However, depending on how those plans are used, they certainly can be just that. Remember as well that this was in the days of the Cold War and, by God, that camouflaged a lot of stuff. You could always say: You never can tell what those Soviets are going to do, so you better be prepared anywhere in the world to defeat them.

TD: And we're still prepared anywhere in the world . . .

Wright: Well, we are and now, let's see, where are the Russians? [She laughs heartily.]

TD: Tell me briefly the story of your life.

Wright: I grew up in Arkansas, just a normal childhood. I think the Girl Scouts was a formative organization for me. It had a plan to it, opportunity to travel outside Arkansas, good goals—working on those little badges. Early State Department. Early military too. It's kind of interesting, the militarization of our society, how we don't really think of some things, and yet when I look back, there I was a little Girl Scout in my green uniform, and so putting on an Army uniform after college wasn't that big a deal. I'd been in a uniform before and I knew how to salute, three fingers. [She demonstrates.]

If you look, we now have junior ROTC in the high schools. We have child soldiers in America. We're good at getting kids used to those uniforms. And then there's the militarization of industries and corporations, the necessity every ten years to have a war because we need a new generation of weaponry. Corporations in the military-industrial complex are making lots of money off of new types of weaponry and vehicles.

TD: While you were in the military, did you have any sense that these wars were actually living weapons labs?

Wright: Particularly seeing the privatization after Gulf War I going into Somalia. All of a sudden, as fast as military troops were arriving, you had Halliburton and Kellogg, Brown, and Root in Somalia. They started saying, You need mess halls, oh, we'll do the mess halls for you. And it turned out they had staged a lot of their equipment in the Middle East after the Gulf War. So it was in Somalia lickety-split. The privatization of military functions is now so pervasive that the military can no longer function by itself, without the contractors and corporations. These contractors, these mercenaries really, are now fundamentally critical to the operations of the U.S. military.

TD: So a Girl Scout and . . .

Wright: In my junior year at the University of Arkansas, a recruiter came through town with the film, "Join the Army, See the World." I had been an education major for three years. Nurse, teacher, those were the careers for women. I didn't want any of it. So, in the middle of the Vietnam War, I signed

up to go to a three-week Army training program, just to see if
I liked it. And I found it challenging. Even though there were
protests going on all over America, I divorced myself from
what the military actually did versus what opportunities it
offered me. I hated all these people getting killed in Vietnam,
but I said to myself: I'm not going to kill anyone and I'm taking
the place of somebody who will be able to go do something
else. All these arguments that . . . now you look at it and go:
Oh my God, what did you do?

TD: Don't you think this happens now?

Wright: Absolutely! I sympathize with the people in the military
right now. The majority didn't sign up to kill anybody. You
always prayed that, whatever administration it was, it didn't go
off on some wild goose chase that got you into a war you personally thought was really stupid.

TD: Would you counsel a young woman now to go into the
military?

Wright: I think we will always have a military and I think the military is honorable service as long as the civilian leadership uses it
in appropriate ways and is very cautious about sending us to war.
And yes, I would encourage people to look at a military career,
but I would also tell them that, if they're sent to do something
they think is wrong, they don't have to stay in, though they may
have to take some consequences for saying, "Thank you very
much but I'm not going to kill anybody."

In fact, if I were recalled to active duty, which is possible . . .
I put myself purposely at the Retired Ready Reserve so that, if
there was ever an emergency and my country needed me, I could
be recalled, and in fact there are people my age, fifty-nine, who

are agreeing to be recalled. The ultimate irony would be resigning from my career in the diplomatic corps and then having the Bush administration recall me, because my specialty, civil affairs, reconstruction, is in really short supply. I'm a colonel. I know how to run battalions and brigades. I can do this stuff. But I would have to tell them, sorry, I refuse to be placed on active duty. And if they push hard enough, then I'd just have to be court-martialed and I'd go to Leavenworth. I will not serve this administration in the Iraq war which I firmly believe is an illegal war of aggression.

TD: You know, if someone had said to me back in the 1960s that a Vice President of the United States might go to Congress to lobby for a torture exemption for the CIA the way Dick Cheney has done, I would have said: This couldn't happen. Never in American history. I'm staggered by this.

Wright: Me, too. The other thing that's quite interesting is the number of women who are involved in it. There were something like eighty women I've identified, ranging from high officers to CIA contractors being used as interrogators in Guantánamo. Talking about things that will come back to bite us big time, this is it. And we are complicit, all of us, because, quite honestly, we're not standing out in front of the White House every single day, and every time that Vice President leaves throwing our bodies in front of his car, throwing blood on it. We need to get tough with these guys. They're not listening to us. They think we're a bunch of wimps. We've got to get tougher and tougher with them to show them we're not going to put up with this stuff.

TD: You've quoted Teddy Roosevelt as saying: "To announce that there must be no criticism of the President, or that we are to stand by the President, right or wrong, is not only unpatriotic and servile, but is morally treasonable to the American public." I was particularly struck by that word "servile." Do you want to talk about dissent for a moment?

Wright: Well, we shouldn't be hesitant about voicing our opinions, even in the most difficult of times which generally is when your nation is going to war and you're standing up to say, this isn't right. That's tough and, in fact, the first couple of months after I resigned, oh man, all that TV and nothing on but the war, and very few people wanted to hear me. It probably was a good four months before anybody even asked me to come speak about why I had dissented, and that was a little lonely. [She chuckles.]

TD: Any final thoughts?

Wright: We now have a two-and-a-half-year track record of being a very brutal country. We are the cause of the violence in Iraq. That violence will continue as long as we're there, and the administration maintains that we will be there until we win. That means to me that this administration is planning for a long-term siege in Iraq. It means that young men and women in America should be prepared for the draft because the military right now cannot support what this administration wants. In fact, yesterday I was talking to about ninety high school seniors in Fayetteville, Arkansas, a very Republican part of the United States. I said: Your parents may support this war, but how strongly do you feel about it? If it drags on for years and there's a draft, how many of you will willingly go? Only three put up their hands.

We are continuing down a very dangerous road. The United States and its citizenry are held in disdain in world opinion for not being able to stop this war machine. So one of the things I'm doing is ratcheting up my own level of response. A dear friend, Joe Palambo, a Vietnam veteran in Veterans for Peace who went to hear the President in Norfolk when he talked about terrorism, was recently cited in the newspapers this way: There was one protestor in the second row of the audience who stood up and railed against the President, saying: "You're the terrorist! This war is a war of terrorism!" Joe called me right after that happened and said, "Hey, Ann, I heard what you did in the Senate and I thought, I'm going to go do the same thing to the President."

I mean, we're going to dog these guys all over the country. Our Secretary of State, our Secretary of Defense, our Vice President, our President, our National Security Adviser, the head of the CIA, any of these people who are the warmongers, who are the murderers in the name of our country, wherever they go, the people of America need to stand up to them to say, "No! Stop! Stop this war. Stop this killing. Get us out of this mess." Because that's the only time they hear it, when we stand up in these venues. They don't come out to the street in front of the White House to see the hundreds of thousands of people who are protesting. They ignore that. But for those fifteen seconds, if you can stand up so that everybody in that audience sees that there's one person, or maybe even two or three . . . Who knows?

6. The Treasure, the Strongbox, and the Crowbar

Juan Cole

OCTOBER 17–18, 2005

The man who starts my every online day is standing at the door. He's small-framed with short, wavy hair and fragile-looking specs. Nattily dressed in a dark suit and tie, he apologizes, as he enters, for being so formally togged out on a Sunday morning. As it happens, I'm but a pit stop on the way to an afternoon TV interview at the PBS program *Great Decisions* on one of his specialties, Iran.

This is, of course, Juan Cole. His Web site, *Informed Comment*, first came on line in April 2002, almost a year before the Bush administration's invasion of Iraq. As he recalls his life back then, "I was just a Midwestern college professor. I taught my courses and wrote my articles about the Middle East. My interests were in religious institutions, religious movements, especially Shiite Islam and Sunni modernism. I knew where these movements came from. I knew the history of the Shiite clergy in Najaf back to the eighteenth century. And I had lived in the

Middle East off and on for a significant period of time. When my blog began, it was little more than gardening for me, a small hobby on the side to put up a few thoughts every once in a while, initially read by fifty to a hundred people a day." Now, it is counted among the top hundred blogs at Technorati.com, a site which follows such things, and may be one of the more linked to blogs on Earth. American reporters trapped in hotels in Baghdad read it regularly for the latest news from Iraq. The secret of his success? "I type fast," he says with a sly smile. "Seventy words a minute."

An "Army brat," with Arabic, Persian, and Urdu under his belt, a scholar who "can make something out of an Ottoman text," he teaches modern Middle Eastern history at the University of Michigan. He is exceedingly mild looking, mild-mannered, and quiet-spoken. Even his humor is hushed. He's ironic. The very name of his blog, he tells me, was meant as a quiet commentary on the "grandiose" blog titles people were choosing back in 2002. And yet, as anyone who reads his blog knows, his mind is anything but mild. As a reasonable man increasingly appalled by the Bush administration and American policy in the Middle East, he can be, and often is, an impressively fierce essayist.

As he settles into an easy chair in my living room to await breakfast on a day when nature has once again dealt a horrific blow to humanity—the Pakistani earthquake had just occurred—he proceeds to tell me much I didn't know about the history and plate tectonics of the region. When asked a question, he pauses to formulate his response. It's rare in our world, but you can actually *see* him think. If you were a student with a penny of sense in your head, this is the man you would want for your professor. In fact, an hour and a half after our interview begins, as I click off my tape recorders, I feel I've only scratched the surface. There are reams of questions still to be asked—perhaps on another day—and the first Tomdispatch two-part interview to type up.

Tomdispatch: Do you sleep? This is a question your readers wonder about. Take October fourth. You put up four posts, time-stamped between six and six-thirty A.M. By the time I'm up at seven you're always there.

Juan Cole: I'm a night owl. The way it works is this: The Arabic and Persian newspapers in the Middle East go up around ten or eleven P.M. our time, but they're the next day's newspapers. So basically it's like time travel. I get to see tomorrow's newspapers tonight.

TD: About the President's most recent global terror speech you wrote, "Mr. Bush, I don't recognize the world you paint." Could you start by laying out for us what's missing from our picture of Iraq—not just Bush's picture, but the mainstream media's?

Cole: It's not just from Iraq. It's our picture of the world. The United States is a peculiarly insular society. Most people here haven't traveled very much and our mass media, all television news of any significance, is controlled by about five corporations. We have a tradition in the State Department and our press corps of preferring generalists and being suspicious of deep expertise as a form of bias. So a journalist covering Iraq, who knows the Middle East well and knows Arabic, might well be seen as someone too entangled with the region to be objective. The American way of ensuring objectivity is to parachute generalists into a situation and have them depend on local informants. The whole theory of it is wrong. The BBC, for example, wouldn't dream of having most of its Middle Eastern coverage done by people who don't know Arabic.

Basically, the public is informed about things like the Middle East by generalist journalists who were in Southeast Asia or Russia last year, and by politicians and bureaucrats who were dealing with some other region last week. And then there's official Washington spin, and the punditocracy, the professional commentators, mainly in New York and Washington, who comment about the Middle East without necessarily knowing anything serious about it. Anybody who's lived in parts of the world under the microscope in Washington is usually astonished at how we represent them. You end up with an extremely persistent set of images that almost no actual information is able to make a dent in.

TD: Can you apply this to Iraq?

Cole: The famous instance is the interview Deputy Secretary of Defense Paul Wolfowitz gave to National Public Radio in February before the Iraq War. He said words to the effect that Iraq will be a better friend to the United States than Saudi Arabia had been. It shows you he was intending to replace Saudi Arabia with Iraq as a pillar of the U.S. security establishment in the Middle East. Saudis are Wahabis and they have sensitivities about their holy cities, Mecca and Medina. Iraq, he said, is a Shia society. It's secular. He juxtaposed Shia and secular. And then he added, it doesn't have the problem of having holy cities. The Washington power elite that planned out the invasion appears to have thought that Iraq was a secular society, including the Shiites amongst them, and they seem to have been unaware of Najaf and Kabala as among the holiest shrine cities in the world of Islam.

It's not a matter of stupidity on Wolfowitz's part. It's a matter of being uninformed. Willfully uninformed. He just believed whatever people like [long-time Iraqi expatriate politician and corrupt banker, now vice-premier] Ahmed Chalabi told him about Iraq. He probably hadn't read as much as a whole book on Iraq's modern history. Well, Iraq wasn't a secular society.

TD: You wrote in April 2002, considering American dreams of a post-Saddam Iraq, "A democratically elected government and a friendly government are not necessarily going to be the same thing, at least in the long run." This is where we are now and it was obviously very knowable a year before the invasion.

Cole: The International Institute at the University of Michigan asked me to write a pro-and-con piece about an Iraq war in January of 2003. Among the reasons I gave for not going to war were: a) if you overthrow the Baath regime and discredit secular Arab nationalism in Iraq, the Sunni Arab community may well gravitate toward more al-Qaeda types of identity; and b) if you invade Iraq and let loose popular politics, the Shiite Iraqis may well hook up with the Ayatollahs in Iran. These things were perfectly foreseeable. I think if you went back to the early 1990s and took a look at Dick Cheney's speeches, he voiced similar analyses.

TD: So what happened between then and March 2003, for Dick Cheney at least?

Cole: I think Dick must have found motives for an Iraq war that overrode his earlier concerns. We don't have transparent governance and therefore we're not in a position to know exactly what our Vice President's motives were, but clearly he became convinced that, whatever the validity of his earlier concerns, they were outweighed by other considerations.

TD: And your guess on those considerations?

Cole: My guess with regard to Cheney is that his experience in the energy sector and with Halliburton as CEO must have been influential in his thinking. For the corporate energy sector in the United States, Iraq must have been maddening. It was under those United Nations sanctions. It's a country that, with significant investment, might be able to rival Saudi Arabia as a producer of petroleum. Saudi Arabia can produce around eleven million barrels a day, if it really tries. Iraq before the war was producing almost three million barrels a day and, if its fields were explored and opened and exploited, it might be up to the Saudi level in twenty years. This could bring a lot of petroleum on the market. There would be opportunities for making money from refining. There might even be an opportunity, if you had a free-market regime in Iraq, for Western petroleum companies to go back to owning oil fields—something they haven't been able to do since the 1970s in the Middle East when most of these fields were nationalized. All that potential in Iraq was locked up.

The petroleum industry, structurally, is a horrible industry because it depends on constantly making good finds and being able to get favorable contracts for developing them, so that one is constantly scrambling for the next field. To have an obvious source of petroleum and energy in Iraq locked up under sanctions, and this Arab socialist regime with the government controlling everything, it must have just driven people crazy.

And you never knew when the sanctions might slip and Iraq might crank back up its production. If you're in the petroleum industry, what you'd like is to have a ten-year timeline for what the future's going to look like. What if Iraq was able to produce five million barrels a day? That would have an impact on prices. It would have an impact on the plans you might like to make. But you couldn't predict that. It was completely unknowable.

So Iraq was like a treasure in a strongbox. You knew exactly where it was; you knew what the treasure was; but you couldn't get at it. The obvious thing to do was to take a crowbar and strike off the strongbox lock. My suspicion is that, for someone like

Cheney, such considerations had a lot to do with his support for an Iraq war—and he was willing to take a chance on the rest of it, including the Shiites.

TD: The rest which he, unlike many of the others in the administration, already knew?

Cole: Oh, he knew it very well. Among all those people who planned out this war, Cheney and [Secretary of State Colin] Powell were knowledgeable about the situation on the ground in Iraq.

TD: What do you make then of the rest of them, their motivations?

Cole: When we as historians get access to all the documents and can figure out how this thing was planned and who supported it, I think we'll find that the Bush administration was a coalition of various forces and each part of the coalition had its own reasons for wanting to fight this war. The group most explored has been the neoconservatives, but I suspect they will bulk less large in our final estimation of the promotion of the war. They weren't in command positions for the most part. They were in positions to make an argument. They may also have been fall guys. When things started going bad, more stuff got leaked about what they had been saying than about others.

I suspect it will come out that George W. Bush had wanted an Iraq War since he was governor of Texas—"to take out Saddam," as he said. The various reasons he might have wanted this are undoubtedly complex. He had connections to the energy sector and so would be influenced by Cheney's kind of thinking, but there was a personal family vendetta too. You know, George Bush senior expected Saddam to fall after the Gulf War. By his own admission, he was very surprised when Saddam survived. I think he expected the Iraqi officer corps to—quote unquote—do the right thing, which tells you something about the American WASP elite, what their expectations are about politics. When someone fails miserably, they expect the rest of the elite to step in and remove the person. It didn't happen in Iraq and I think that was a blow to Bush family prestige. It may have been important for W to vindicate the family in that regard.

There were probably many motivations for the war, but the degree to which Bush himself has been a central, policy-making player somehow gets elided in American discourse. It's not as if he's a leaf blown by the wind. When the Bush presidency is finally examined from the primary documents, a lot of the things that are attributed to the number three man at the Pentagon may actually turn out to have been Bush's idea from the beginning, and something he pushed hard for.

His personal style is to play it by ear. He doesn't have patience for a lot of details. In Texas, he was used to calling together the Republican and Democratic state representatives to work out deals about this or that as they came up. That's his background as a policymaker, but the world is not like the Texas legislature. It's not a chummy club in which you can find compromises and go forward. The world is a much more complex and vicious place, and there are often incommensurate issues for which there is no acceptable compromise. Trying to run the world the way you run Texas is a big mistake.

As a set of organizations, the U.S. government has actually had a lot of experience in post-conflict situations. Bosnia. Kosovo. This is what a lot of people in the State Department and the Pentagon have been doing for the last twenty years. There are functional experts who may not know Bosnian or Arabic, but know about the need for policing after a war or about the need for sanitation and garbage collection. These people were giving advice about Iraq. I know for a fact that they were. But they were simply

ignored in the actual event. Somehow, the civilians in the Department of Defense sidelined all those experts and so the U.S. military was given no instructions about how to put Iraq back on its
feet after the war.

TD: Just to return to your strongbox image, the lock was busted
in March of 2003. Now, two and half years later, I'd like you to
take us on a little tour of Iraq as best you understand the situation there.

Cole: Okay, let's start from north to south. Three of Iraq's
eighteen provinces were heavily Kurdish and formed a confederacy called Kurdistan under the [post-Gulf War I Anglo-
American] no-fly zone. They were a kind of mini-state with a
regional parliament and prime minister. The U.S. military
never had much of a presence in the far north. The city of
Kirkuk was actually taken during the war by Kurdish fighters
with close U.S. air support—rather as [in 2001] many cities in
Northern Afghanistan had been taken by the Northern
Alliance. So the northern part of Iraq looked much more like
the Afghanistan War.

TD: Air support, the CIA, and tribal peoples, this had been a basic
style of American warfare since Laos in the 1960s.

Cole: Yes, that's how Kosovo was fought. That's how Afghanistan
was fought too, but it was especially significant here because the
Kurdish militia, the Peshmerga, which took Kirkuk, then formed
the police force for that contested city whose population includes
Turkmen, Arabs, and Kurds. The Kurds are probably close to
half now. A lot of them had been expelled by Saddam, but
they're coming back in large numbers. From all accounts I've

been able to get from people on the ground, the three provinces that are heavily Kurdish are doing very well.

TD: And are unoccupied?

Cole: There aren't many American troops there. Behind the scenes there have been some battles between the Kurdish forces and the Americans from time to time, some bombing of Kurdish positions when the Americans feel they're going too far, getting out of hand. But those have not been reported publicly. I've heard about them from people in Iraq. By and large, though, Kurdistan has not been occupied by the United States and economically seems to be doing very well. There's low unemployment and a lot of construction work.

On the other hand, the province of Kirkuk is potentially a powder keg. It could explode in a way that might have unfortunate consequences for all of Iraq and the region. Oil fields are around Kirkuk and the Kurds want those fields and the city for their Kurdistan federation. The Turkmen, traditionally dominant in the area but recently overwhelmed by the Kurds, resist this idea, and the Arabs Saddam settled up there are not happy about it either. The Kurds would get their way under ordinary circumstances, but the Turkmen are supported by Turkey; and northern Iraq is a mirror image of Turkey itself where the Kurds are a minority and the Turks a majority. If a kind of communal war broke out—and there is a lot of terrorism, people are assassinated almost every day—it would inflame passions of a regional sort. So one worries about Kirkuk.

And then you come to the Sunni Arab center. It's not true by the way that the problems in Iraq are only in four provinces. I figure, including Baghdad, about half of Iraqis live in the troubled parts of the country. The seven or eight provinces especially affected are in a condition of unconventional, low-intensity war. People who haven't lived in such a situation find it difficult to imagine what it's like, because the tendency in any reporting is to focus on the specific violent events that occur. But you're talking about an area in which maybe twelve million people live and most of them get up every day, go about their business, and don't encounter any violence. If you were living in Mosul, most days you might not see any violence with your own eyes. On the other hand, quite often there would be machine-gun fire in the distance. From time to time, there would be the sound of a bomb going off. This is how it is in Baghdad. This is why it's so wrong for Western reporters to parachute into Iraq, often embedded in U.S. military forces, and say, well, I saw the markets bustling and things seemed to be going on just fine. It's the constant drumbeat of violence over time that produces insecurity and fear, that affects investment, the circulation of money, the ability to employ people, people's willingness to send their children to school. This is something that's not visible to the naked eye.

So, in the center of the country, there's no guarantee of security. Basically, the Sunni Arab guerrilla movement wants to destabilize Iraq, force the U.S. military to withdraw, and, once it's gotten rid of them, hopes it can kill the politicians of the new government and make a coup. It's a classic guerrilla strategy used in Algeria and elsewhere.

TD: And what of the ongoing destruction of the country's infrastructure?

Cole: The guerrilla movement destroys infrastructure deliberately. Electricity facilities, petroleum pipelines, rail transport. And it deliberately baits the U.S. military in the cities, basing its fighters in civilian neighborhoods in hopes that a riposte will cause damage, because Iraqis, even urban ones, are organized by clan. Clan vendettas are still an important part of people's sense of honor. So when the American military kills an Iraqi, I figure they've made enemies of five siblings and twenty-five first cousins who feel honor-bound to get revenge. The Sunni Arab guerrilla movement has taken advantage of that sense of clan honor gradually to turn the population against the United States. Many more Sunni Arabs are die-hard opposed to the U.S. presence in Iraq now than was the case a year ago, and there were more a year ago than the year before that.

The U.S. has used bombing of civilian neighborhoods on a massive scale because the alternative is to send its forces in to fight close, hand-to-hand combat in alleyways in Iraq's cities and that would be extremely costly of U.S. soldiers' lives. It certainly would have turned the American public against the war really quickly.

TD: When the Bush administration was getting ready to launch its invasion, this was the great professed fear, the subject of a hundred predictive articles—being trapped in house-to-house urban warfare in the back streets of Baghdad, which is more or less where we are now.

Cole: It didn't happen in the course of the actual war because Saddam always mistrusted the military. He wasn't a military man himself; he was a failed law student and he would not allow the military into the capital. He made them stay outside, essentially to be massacred by the U.S. But the people who went underground from the Baath party and are mainly running the guerrilla movement have decided to use this tactic of basing themselves in cities. And it has succeeded. Even a city like Fallujah—the United States destroyed two-thirds of its buildings, emptied the city for a long time, and has been very careful about allowing people back in—is not secure. Every day there are mortar and bomb attacks against U.S. forces in that area. So it's certainly not the case that the U.S. has made any friends in Fallujah.

TD: In a recent post, you wrote of Baghdad: "Bush has turned one of the world's greatest cities into a cesspool with no order, little authority, and few services."

Cole: That's the image I get from people who are there and also visiting Arab journalists.

TD: If you go back to the neocons and their prewar vision, the world out there on the peripheries was a jungle world of failed states to which we were going to bring order. Isn't that what Iraq has become today?

Cole: Iraq is a failed state at the moment.

TD: Now just to continue the tour south . . .

Cole: The south is largely Shiite. Most of the areas have gradually been taken over, as far as I can tell, by the Supreme Council for Islamic Revolution in Iraq. The Supreme Council was a coalition of fundamentalist Shiite religious parties who fled Saddam's repression in 1980, based themselves in Teheran, received the patronage of Ayatollah Khomeini, and conducted essentially terrorist raids on Baath targets in Iraq from Iranian soil. They would come into Iraq through Basra, through the marshes, through Baquba in the east, and so gained supporters in those areas.

After the fall of Saddam, the Supreme Council came back

from Iran. Its leadership settled into Najaf and Basra. Their people would go out from the cities to small towns and villages and open political offices. They were very good grass-roots campaigners. It's not exactly clear to me how they pulled it off, but they won nine provinces in the January 30th elections.

The problem with the Shiite south was: After the war, the U.S. asked its coalition partners to garrison the south. These were small forces—Spanish, Italian, Ukrainian, Dutch, Polish— and often not very well integrated. So the south was this patch-work of multinational forces, and there were only eight or nine thousand British troops for Basra, which was a city of over a mil-lion, and Maysan, another half million. Local security was pro-vided, if at all, by neighborhood militias, and who was going to run those militias? The local Shiite religious political parties. Not surprisingly, when the elections came, they won. So now it's the Sadr movement and the Supreme Council that run Basra. It's Khomeini and Khomeini's stepson. Of course, liquor and video stores have been closed, and girls are being forced to veil, and the militias patrol the streets. Since their parties took over the civil government, they're now being admitted to the police force.

So that's how Basra's being run—by religious political par-ties the U.S. essentially helped put into power by having these elections that everybody in America was so excited about last January 30th. The elections were taken by most Americans as a political victory for Bush, but they didn't seem to pay any atten-tion to who was actually winning them on the ground in places like Basra. Now the British have a big problem. Their eight thousand troops have to deal with security forces and police heavily infiltrated by the paramilitaries of these groups. Of course, there have been increasing conflicts. And I'll tell you, in the long run, I don't think the British are going to win this one.

PART 2
THROWING GRENADES IN THE GLOBAL ECONOMIC COCKPIT

NOTE: *On September 22nd, 2005, Tomdispatch posted a piece by sociologist Michael Schwartz, "Why Immediate Withdrawal Makes Sense," which ended:*

"American withdrawal would undoubtedly leave a riven, impoverished Iraq, awash in a sea of weaponry, with problems galore, and numerous possibilities for future violence. The either/or of this situation may not be pretty, but on a grim landscape, a single reality stands out clearly: Not only is the American presence the main source of civilian casualties, it is also the primary contributor to the threat of civil war in Iraq. The longer we wait to withdraw, the worse the situation is likely to get—for the U.S. and for the Iraqis."

The next day, at his Informed Comment Web site, Juan Cole posted a response in which he wrote, "I just cannot understand this sort of argument," and then laid out the nature of his disagreement with it in some detail. This started several days of debate among various experts, scholars, and bloggers at his site (and elsewhere) which resulted in Cole rethinking his position somewhat and issuing an eloquent call for American ground troops to be withdrawn from Iraq.

This debate and discussion provided the basis for the second half of this interview. My own thoughts on withdrawal can be found in "Time of Withdrawal," a piece I wrote six months after the fall of Baghdad and updated as "Withdrawal on the Agenda" in June 2005.

Tomdispatch: Now I want to turn to the issue of withdrawal. I've been particularly impressed that, at your site, you post your own intellectual development, so to speak—and that includes putting up letters and essays by people who take you on. This is unbelievably rare. The reader can actually see a brain at work, regularly reassessing a changing situation. It's been especially true on the question of the withdrawal of American forces from Iraq. Having gone back recently to read your site's earliest months, it's obvious that you've become fiercer and angrier as time has gone on in relation to the Bush administration. You recently wrote a piece saying that U.S. ground troops must come out now, "for the good of Iraq, for the good of America." Would you discuss the development of your thoughts on this? Where are you now on the issue of withdrawal and how it might happen?

Juan Cole: The first thing I should say is I'm not under any illusion that it matters a great deal what I think on the subject.

TD: [Laughs.] Neither of us is exactly capable of withdrawing American troops from Iraq. I'm endlessly aware of this when people call for one plan or another. I think, wait a minute . . .

Cole: [Laughs.] When you're talking about the debates I hold with my readers and the way I put up critiques of my position, what academic life has to offer is open debate and being honest about your sources, about how you come to a conclusion. The whole point of my blog is to attempt to represent the life of the mind in a public forum. I view what I do as different from politics where you want to stay on message, stay on point. You want to put out an image, a position, and stick to it. You make fun of your opponent for waffling or being indecisive. But what serious thinker hasn't gone back and forth? You'd have to be crazy if you didn't consider other options than the one you initially started out with or if, over time, experience didn't sometimes cause you to take a different position.

You know, Whitman said: "Do I contradict myself? Very well, then I contradict myself, I am large, I contain multitudes." That's the American spirit, so I'm happy to debate these things, reveal my thinking, and let the world see how one intellectual concerned with the Middle East deals with the array of information that's coming at us over time.

Well, I'm now *really* worried about what the outcome in Iraq might mean for the Middle East, for the United States, and for the world. I'm *really, really* worried and I can think up some nightmare scenarios . . .

TD: Give me one . . .

Cole: Say the U.S. and its allies draw down their troops—and it's very clear, the allies are pfffft! Everybody's announced that, after the December 15th election, they're going to draw down. But if a withdrawal is done in the wrong way, or unwisely, here's what could happen:

You've already got this low-intensity sectarian war going on in a province like Babel. Twenty-two guys'll show up dead in the morning, bullets behind their ears, mafia-style. They'll be Shiites or they'll be Sunnis. So you know the two sides—at night, when the U.S. can't see them so well—are already fighting it out with each other. And it's over land. Babel province was traditionally heavily Shiite. Saddam expelled Shiites and brought in Sunnis. It was part of his planting of Sunnis.

TD: As in Kirkuk . . .

Cole: That was Arabization, this was Sunnitization. So let's say the U.S. is not around much anymore, what's going to happen if you have a whole brigade of Sunni fighters come down from Mahmudiyah and attack Hila? That sort of thing happened in Lebanon during the civil war. These neighborhood militias can become armies and leave their areas to wage war against other neighborhood militias that become armies. Now, if that started happening, and if the Sunni Arabs started to win, it's inevitable that the Revolutionary Guards will come across the border from Iran to help the Shiites. Iran's not going to sit by and allow Iraq's Shiites to be massacred. If that happened, the Saudis, the Jordanians, and the Syrian Sunnis are not going to stand by either and let Iranian Revolutionary Guards massacre Sunni Arabs in reprisal. They're going to come in. You could simultaneously be having Kurdish massacres of Turkmen which would bring Turkey in. So you could end up with a regional low-intensity war. Think of the Spanish Civil War.

Back in the 1980s, Saddam Hussein and Khomeini fought a war with one another for eight years, but on the whole they avoided hitting each other's oil facilities. Both understood that doing that would reduce their countries to fourth-world states. So there was a kind of mutually-assured-destruction doctrine between them, which is possible between states. But in the guerrilla war in Iraq, the Sunni guerrillas have already pioneered using pipeline sabotage and oil sabotage . . .

TD: I'm actually surprised that such sabotage has yet to make it to the Caspian pipelines or elsewhere.

Cole: Well, it could still spread. In August of 2004, when the Marines were fighting the Muqtada al-Sadr people in Najaf, the Sadrists in Basra did make threats to start pipeline sabotage in the south, which really would have crippled Iraq. In a regional guerrilla war, there would be a lot of impetus for Sunni guerrillas to hit the Iranian pipelines, and there are some Sunni tribes in the oil-producing areas of Iran who might be enlisted for this purpose. If the Saudis got involved, then the radical Shiites have an impetus to hit the Saudi pipelines, and the Saudi petroleum facilities are in a heavily Shiite area. Basically, what we've learned from Iraq is that petroleum is produced in a human-security environment in which powerful local forces want it to be produced. If some significant proportion of the local forces doesn't want it to be produced, they can spoil it.

TD: As in Nigeria . . .

Cole: We have seen this all over the world. We focus on states, but states can't provide security for hundreds of miles of pipeline. It's literally impossible. So think what you're talking about here. Something on the order of 80-84 million barrels of petroleum are produced every day in the world. Saudi Arabia produces 9 of that reliably, sometimes more. Iran produces 4. On a good day, Iraq used to produce almost 3. Now it's down to somewhere around 1.8 million. If you took all of that off the market, that's about a fifth of world petroleum production. Do you know what that's going to do to prices!

If you don't like three-dollar-a-gallon gasoline, you're going to really hate this kind of world I'm painting. I think the price shock would reduce economic growth globally, plunging some countries into recession or even depression. This would be a world-class catastrophe. And it's also not clear, once it starts, how you stop it.

TD: In this context, you still called recently for U.S. ground troops to be brought out now.

Cole: Because I'm not convinced that U.S. ground troops are preventing this kind of scenario from happening.

TD: So talk a little about your thinking on withdrawal.

Cole: Well, my concern is that U.S. ground troops are being used at the moment for things like the Fallujah operation, the Tal Afar operation, or now the Haditha operation. This essentially means using the troops to attack cities which are Sunni Arab (or in the case of Tal Afar, Sunni Turkmen). These are seen as bastions of the guerrilla movement and facilitators of the infiltration of foreign fighters into the country. To empty them of their populations, to flatten entire neighborhoods, to do extensive infrastructural and building damage to them, to reduce their inhabitants to tent dwellers and refugees, and maybe gradually let them back in to live in tents on the rubble of their former homes—this way of proceeding has no chance of success as an anti-insurgency tactic. People in other cities see this happening and they sympathize with their fellow Sunnis.

The hope for counterinsurgency would involve three things. Of course, you'd have to hit people who are blowing up innocent civilians. You'd have to try to stop that, but you'd also have to open backchannels to their political leadership and try to find ways to bring them into the system. And you have to convince the general population not to support them. Operations like Fallujah, Tal Afar, and Haditha might have some limited effect—I think not very much—in fighting the guerrilla movement. But they do not cause the political leadership to come in from the cold or the general Sunni population to think well enough about the U.S. and its Iraqi allies to start informing on that movement.

So things are only getting worse in the Sunni areas. People forget that a year ago, before the second Fallujah campaign, Mosul was being held up as a model. It had been governed by General [David H.] Petraeus. It seemed like it might be possible to woo the Sunni Arabs there. But during the Fallujah campaign Mosul exploded. Four thousand police resigned. Guerrillas en masse took over checkpoints throughout the city. There were

bombings and it never really has settled down again. As *al-Zaman*
[the *Times of Baghdad*] reported recently, Northern Mosul is now
essentially guerrilla-held territory.

TD: And after fifteen months on the job, Petraeus, who was also
responsible for "standing up" the Iraqi Army, has just been reas-
signed to the United States.

Cole: He's been replaced, which indicates to me that the whole
thing is not going very well. It may be that he was given an impossible job.

So, if the U.S. ground troops are going to be used in this way,
then they're just creating more guerrillas over time. I don't see
evidence of progress here but of deterioration. It's looking more
and more like Algeria in the early 1960s rather than the mid-50s
when the French were having some success against the guerrilla
movement in Algiers. Therefore, it seems to me, we ought to get
the ground troops out and stop using them this way to empty
cities, destroy neighborhoods, and pursue what is frankly a puni-
tive and scorched-earth policy towards the Sunni Arab population.

TD: I've been calling it the Carthaginian solution.

Cole: Yes, and in the context of modern guerrilla war it's possibly
the worst way to proceed. *But* unlike some of my friends to the
left of me—and I'm not sure it's even a left-right issue since the
libertarians feel the same way—I think it's really dangerous just
to up and leave altogether and allow Iraq to fall into civil war.
People say the most amazing things. Like, "Well, Iraq is already
in civil war, so why would it matter if we left?" No! No! No! This
is the stage before proper civil war. The difference is a matter of
scale. You have hundreds of people a week being killed by guerrilla violence in Iraq. That's different from thousands of people,

or tens of thousands, or hundreds of thousands. I mean we've seen it in other countries—Cambodia, Afghanistan, Congo—you can lose a fifth of the population in this kind of struggle. I think it's outrageous that people would say, "Let's just up and leave and let what happens happen." I know the Bush administration has mismanaged this thing so badly that one's tempted to say, let's get them away from this before they do any more damage, but do we want a genocide on our conscience?

I know one person who said, "Well, once we're out, whatever happens is not our responsibility." Is it really true? You can invade a country, overthrow its government, dissolve its military, and then walk away, and a million people die, and that's not your problem? I don't understand this way of thinking.

TD: Let me change the location of this to Washington for a minute. You noted recently that the Arab press referred to the antiwar demonstrators in Washington as "the American street" which I found amusing, and you also pointed out the virtual absence of Democratic legislators, except for some members of the Congressional Black Caucus, even marching in the demonstration, no less addressing it. When we're thinking about Iraq and the future, other than a rising popular opposition to the war (which comes from many places, including simple unhappiness that we're not winning), it seems as if the political opposition doesn't exist. To exaggerate only slightly, half the Democrats in Congress are still calling for sending more troops—which don't even exist—into Iraq. I was wondering what you made of this, given your recent call for getting American ground troops out?

Cole: Well, the first thing to say is that the Democratic Party is about as influential on Iraq policy as you and I are. Whatever position Democratic legislators took wouldn't necessarily be a policy position in the sense of having any hope of being implemented as long as Bush is in the White House. And I think they're fearful of looking weak on foreign policy . . .

TD: . . . .the result of which is that they become unbelievably weak . . .

JC: The strategy may be talk tough and let Bush fail.

TD: You recently called that "a dangerous strategy."

Cole: There's tremendous dissatisfaction in the country over the Iraq war and Bush foreign policy which could turn into grass-roots victories for Democratic candidates in 2006, if they could figure out how to address it and provide leadership on these issues. This is why I did one of my columns suggesting we turn to using Special Forces and air power to support Iraqi forces. Treat them like the Northern Alliance was treated during the Afghan War, even though I'm seeing this as an exit strategy rather than an entry strategy. I did this mainly to suggest that there are other stances the Democrats could take. You could say we need an exit strategy for Iraq that would be smart militarily and politically, and doesn't just involve 1975-style withdrawal from Vietnam with people hanging from helicopters but also doesn't involve being quiet and letting Bush dig his own grave. I think, first of all, that that's cowardly. Second, it's not good for the country not to have a debate and not to have leadership on the other side of an issue.

TD: Do you think Bush has dug his own grave?

Cole: I mean, this is one of the great foreign policy debacles of American history. There's an enormous amount at stake in the oil Gulf and Bush is throwing grenades around in the cockpit of the world economy. So I think he has dug his own grave with regard to Iraq policy. Most politics in the United States, though, focuses on domestic issues.

TD: Despite the usual centrality of domestic issues, I happen to think that, above all else, the war has driven the Bush people ever since the post-invasion period. When, for instance, you look at the latest AP/Ipsos poll, what's bothering the evangelicals now above all else? It's the war.

Cole: Yes, they are upset about what happened in Iraq because Bush made an alliance with the religious Shiites, which meant an alliance with Islamic fundamentalists who have now put a Koran veto on legislation in Iraq. You know, the evangelicals were dreaming big. They thought Iraq was going to be a missionary success, that they would make the Iraqis into Protestants. But any missionary who showed up in Iraq now, we'd soon be seeing him on video pleading for his life. None of their objectives with regard to Iraq have been achieved.

This is something, by the way, that the evangelicals have been dreaming of since the 1850s. It's how the American University in Beirut got there. The Presbyterian missions were the ones that originally tried to missionize the Middle East and they failed all along the line—and they continue to fail. The Bush moment was a moment in which those nineteenth century dreams of evangelical missionizing and imperial might being melded together were briefly revived. Now it's become clear to them that this is just not going to happen, so they're angry, they're disappointed. You can understand that.

7. You Can Do Anything with a Bayonet Except Sit on It

Mark Danner

FEBRUARY 26, 2006

On a cloudless day, the sky a brilliant, late-afternoon blue, my car winds its way up the Berkeley hills. Plum and pear trees in glorious whites and pinks burst into sight at each turn in the road. Beds of yellow flowers, trees hung with lemons, and the odd palm are surrounded by the green of a northern California winter, though the temperature is pushing seventy degrees. An almost perfectly full moon, faded to a tattered white, sits overhead. Suddenly, I take a turn and start straight up, as if into the heavens, but in fact toward Grizzly Peak before turning yet again into a small street and pulling up in front of a wooden gate. You swing it open and proceed down a picturesque stone path through the world's tiniest grove of redwoods toward the yellow stucco cottage that was only recently the home of Nobel-Prize-winning poet Czeslaw Milosz, but is now the home—as yet almost furniture-less—of journalist Mark Danner, who has said that, as a young writer in search of "a kind of moral clarity," he gravitated toward countries where "massacres and killings and torture happen, in the place, that is, where we find evil."

Danner greets me at the door which, thrown open, reveals a bay window with a dazzling vista of the Golden Gate Bridge and San Francisco Bay and through which the sun blazes goldenly. In a rumpled dark shirt and slacks, he ushers me out onto a stone patio. "This is where the deer hang out," he says and points to a small area just beyond our chairs where the grass is slightly pressed down. "They lie there contemplating me as I pace on the other side of the bay window. I feel like their Ping-Pong game."

Facing this peaceable kingdom, Danner has a slightly distracted, out-of-the-washer-but-not-the-drier look to him, except for his face, strangely unmarked, which would qualify as lighting up (even without the sun). He beams in such a welcoming way and there is in him something—in this setting at least—that makes it almost impossible to believe he has reported from some of the least hospitable, most dangerous spots on the planet over the last decades: Haiti in the 1980s, war-torn Yugoslavia in the 1990s, and Iraq, which he's visited three times in recent years, among other spots. He has covered the world for the *New Yorker*, the *New York Times Magazine*, and especially the *New York Review of Books*.

Danner is now an expert on the torture practices of the U.S. military, the CIA, and the Bush administration (and his primer on the subject, *Torture and Truth: America, Abu Ghraib and the War on Terror*, is a must for any bookshelf). A professor at the Graduate School of Journalism at the University of California, Berkeley, his cup of tea seems to be dicey American foreign-policy situations. His book-writing career began with a now-classic volume, *The Massacre at El Mozote*, in which he traveled to El Salvador for the exhumation of an infamous site where over

750 Salvadorans were massacred by U.S. trained troops during Ronald Reagan's first year in office. A new book of his recent writings, *The Secret Way to War*, is due out in April.

We seat ourselves and turning away from the slowly sinking sun, simply plunge in.

Tomdispatch: I wanted to start with an area of expertise for you, torture policy. For me, the Bush administration's decision to enter this arena so quickly after 9/11 was a reach for power. If you can torture, you can do anything.

Mark Danner: When you look at the record, the phrase I come back to, not only about interrogation but the many other steps that constitute the Bush state of exception, state of emergency, since 9/11 is "take the gloves off." We hear this again and again. The interesting thing about that phrase is the implication that before we had the gloves on, that the laws and principles that constitute our belief not only in democracy but in human rights left the country vulnerable. The U.S. adherence to the Geneva Conventions, the U.S. record of treating prisoners humanely that goes back to George Washington, laws like the FISA law passed to restrict the government's power to surveil its citizens—all of these constitute the gloves on American power and 9/11 signaled to those in power that the system with "the gloves on" was insufficient to protect Americans. That seems to be their belief.

As you know, very shortly after 9/11, the then-White House counsel [Alberto Gonzales] proposed to President Bush that provisions of the Geneva Conventions had been rendered obsolete, even quaint, by this quote "new paradigm." The Geneva Conventions, the Convention against Torture, and the federal statutes against torture—these undertakings by the U.S.—represented restrictions that would unduly hobble the country in fighting the war on terror and, by extension, threatened the existence of the

United States. And I think that's where torture—"extreme interrogation" is the euphemism—goes to the heart of the reaction against the way this country has observed human rights in the past, a reaction in a way against law itself. What we have here is a conflict between legality and power.

Torture is a very direct route from human rights, which is to say, restricted power, to unleashed power. We see a movement here backwards from ideals that were at the root of this country's founding during the enlightenment: the restriction of government power and the conviction that human beings had certain inherent rights, one of which was the freedom from cruel and inhuman treatment. Under this way of looking at the matter, those enlightenment ideals embodied in the Declaration of Independence and the Constitution, which were given to Americans, were extended through the Geneva Conventions, through the Convention against Torture, to all people—and the administration, in pushing extreme interrogation, in going from a secret abuse of power to a public one . . .

TD: Wasn't it really less an abuse of power than a proclamation of power?

Danner: Exactly. In what I've started to call Bush's state of exception, we've now reached the second stage. Many of these steps, including extreme interrogation, eavesdropping, arresting aliens—one could go down a list—were taken in relative or complete secrecy. Gradually, they have come into the light, becoming matters of political disputation; and, insofar as the administration's political antagonists have failed to overturn them, they have also become matters of accepted practice, which is where I think we are now. As we sit here, we are approaching the two-year anniversary of the publication of the Abu Ghraib photographs. It would have been the very unusual observer, on seeing those photographs in April 2004, who would have predicted two years later that extreme interrogation would, in effect, have become accepted within the CIA. And though the Senate passed an amendment that forbade it, the President replied with a signing statement that essentially reserved his right to violate that amendment according to his supposed powers as commander-in-chief.

In effect, the President claims to believe that his wartime powers give him carte blanche to break the law in any sphere where he decides national security is involved. An added element is the elevation of Samuel Alito to the Supreme Court. The only countervailing power we've seen since 9/11 really lay in the June 2004 Supreme Court detention decisions. In one of them, Justice O'Connor declared that the President's power in wartime was not a blank check. Now, she's been replaced by an admitted believer in a "unitary executive." It was Alito when he was at the Justice Department who strongly pushed the strategy of presidential signing statements as a way to mitigate congressional assertions of power.

TD: Weren't you struck by the fact that, of all the things top Bush officials did, their urge toward torture, toward taking the gloves off, was first and fastest? It was an impulse at the top.

Danner: I think that's an interesting way to put it, an impulse at the top. The President and the Vice President have said that, after 9/11, they asked the national security and law enforcement bureaucracies to come to them with proposals. What should the U.S. do? Look, it's time to take the gloves off and every one of you has to show me the way to do it. General [Michael] Hayden said in an interview just the other night that, with the NSA eavesdropping program, he was responding to a request from the White House.

TD: Wasn't it Rumsfeld, when they were "interviewing" John Walker Lindh, the American Taliban, in Afghanistan, who actually told the interrogators to take the gloves off?

Danner: According to a *Newsweek* report, Rumsfeld had someone essentially telephone the interrogators: Do what you have to do. Go as far as you have to go.

TD: Torture hasn't exactly been absent from U.S. government policy in our lifetimes, but one difference, it seems to me, is the degree to which our leaders have been involved. I think Rumsfeld was getting reports on the Lindh interrogation by the hour.

Danner: When we look at the techniques used by the CIA, these things go back a ways. Alfred McCoy and others have written about this. These techniques of torture, developed in the 1950s and 1960s, are reappearing. There is one very important difference: the explicit official approval and the determination to defend these techniques in the case of public exposure and public controversy. And torture has survived its exposure—a critical difference. The clear evidence of intent at the very top of the government is also striking. At a certain point, of course, you have to get into the realm of the psycho-political, which is a very mushy realm.

TD: Let's do it anyway.

Danner: The central question here is: Why did we have the kind of response we did after 9/11? The Bush administration, which professed itself so strong on national security, had let the United States suffer the most catastrophic attack on its territory in history. We have to remind ourselves of the effect of this. Remember, their major security programs were the Strategic Defense Initiative and confronting China. They thought that terrorism, which they didn't care about, was a matter for sissies. Like humanitarian intervention, the threat posed by non-state actors—and many other concerns of the previous administration—all this stuff was, as they saw it, a kid's view of national security, so they ignored it. And afterwards they knew very well that reports existed showing how they had ignored it, most notably the PDB [Presidential Daily Briefing] that was famously entitled "Bin Laden determined to strike in U.S." This was a very human thing. Having proclaimed how strong they were on national security, they were attacked. I think that accounted, to some degree, for the ferocity of the counterattack. You don't need to get too deep to see that. When you look at this idea of the gloves coming off, the implication is very much exculpatory. They're saying, in effect: Before the gloves were on, so we weren't able to detect and prevent this attack.

General Hayden has explicitly said, had this [NSA warrantless eavesdropping] program been in place, we would have prevented 9/11. There's no evidence of that, but when you talk about the psycho-political roots of this stuff, I think it's very revealing. It also dovetails with the concerns of several prominent officials, especially Rumsfeld and Cheney, that the government had been unduly hobbled during the late Vietnam War era. Cheney has said this explicitly. We're talking about the War Powers Resolution, which was passed in 1973. FISA is out of the same complex of political concerns, though it was passed under Carter.

TD: They chafed under FISA in the Reagan era.

Danner: Oh, indeed they did. Then there were the Church and Pike hearings of the mid-1970s, which, in their view, disabled the

CIA. So part of this has to do with righting wrongs that they believe were committed in an earlier and very traumatic time in their lives. Rumsfeld was Secretary of Defense just after the Vietnam War. Cheney was chief of staff in a White House that was under siege. So history is coming back to haunt this era in a personal and vivid way.

TD: You've often quoted a piece in which reporter Ron Suskind is told by an unidentified senior administration official that he's in the "reality-based community," after which that official says something striking: "We're an empire now and when we act we create our own reality."

Danner: I think that quote is immensely revealing. It underlines their policies in all kinds of areas, their belief that the overwhelming or preponderant power of the United States can simply change fact, can change truth. It is quite indicative of their policy of public information inside the United States. They don't care about people who read the *New York Times*, for instance. I use that as a shorthand. They don't care about people concerned with facts. They care about the broader arc of the story. We sit here constantly citing facts—that they've broken this or that law, that what they originally said turns out not to be true. None of this particularly interests them.

What interests them is the larger reality believed by the 50.1 percent that they need to govern. Kenneth Duberstein said this recently—he was chief of staff to Ronald Reagan—that this administration is unique in that they govern with 50.1 percent. He was referring not to elections but to popularity while governing. His notion was that Reagan would want to get 60–65 percent backing him, while the Bush people want a bare majority, which means they have a much more extremist policy because they're appealing to the base. It makes them very hard-knuckle when approaching politics, simply wanting the base plus one.

On empire, what's unusual about this administration isn't only its focus on power, but on unilateralism. It's the flip side of isolationism. The notion that alliances, economic or political, and international law inevitably hinder the most powerful nation. You know, the image of the strings around Gulliver. They said in the National Security Strategy of the United States, the 2005 version, that rivals will continue to challenge us using the strategies of the weak including "international fora, judicial processes, and terrorism." They're associating terror and asymmetric warfare with international law as similar ways to blunt the overwhelming power of the United States. That represents an attitude toward international law and institutions that, I think, is a real and dramatic break from past practice in the United States. In our history, certainly recently, there's just no comparison to them—no government anywhere near as radical.

TD: They're really extreme American nationalists, though you can't use that word in this country.

Danner: That's true, and they combine with this belief in great-power America an almost nativist distrust of international institutions. That's the difference between Truman America and this regime in its approach to foreign policy. They put international institutions in a similar class with terrorism—that is, weapons of the weak.

TD: Weapons of mass interference.

Danner: I should add that, in my view, the era of neocon leadership is clearly coming to an end. The impression that they were ever entirely in control is wrong in any event and the vanguard of the neocons has obviously been blunted by the great failure of Iraq—because their assumption of preponderant American power turned out not to be true. Napoleon had this wonderful line that you can do anything with a bayonet except sit on it. Military power is good for blowing things up; it's good for destroying things. It's not good for building a new order. It takes a great deal more power, skill, and patience to construct an enduring order in Iraq. The United States doesn't have sufficient power; it doesn't have the skill; and we know it doesn't have the patience. One part of the axis of evil has been occupied—you can think of it as the part of the axis that has sacrificed itself to make way for the greater freedom (freedom from attack, freedom perhaps to build nuclear weapons) of North Korea and Iran. Although I think the U.S. has dealt with Iran rather cleverly in the last few months, they're playing a very weak hand. After all, the use of military force against Iran is now out of the question in large part because of the disaster next door in Iraq and the way Iran's hand has been strengthened by that disaster.

TD: Here's my hesitation: If these people are pushed to the wall, I could construct a scenario for you, I believe, in which Iran, crazy as it might seem, could be hit.

Danner: The difference we have on this just has to do with how willing we are to imagine the utter irrationality of the administration. When I look at Iran now, the upside of a military strike of a kind that they could do, with aerial bombardment, and the downside of such a step seems obviously to be so wildly out of proportion, I can't believe even they would take that step.

TD: You've talked about our current American world as one of "frozen scandal," an interesting phrase. When you first used it, we were in the Downing Street Memo scandal and nothing was happening. Now, we're immersed in the NSA and other scandals and nothing is happening . . .

Danner: The icebergs are floating by. I've used the phrase to indicate that a process of scandal we've come to know, with an expected series of steps, has come to an end. Before, you had, as step one, revelation of wrongdoing by the press, usually with the help of leaks from within an administration. Step two would be an investigation which the courts, often allied with Congress, would conduct, usually in public, that would give you an official version of events. We saw this with Watergate, Iran-Contra, and others. And finally, step three would be expiation—the courts, Congress, impose punishment which allows society to return to some kind of state of grace in which the notion is, look we've corrected the wrongdoing, we can now go on. With this administration, we've got revelation of torture, of illegal eavesdropping, of domestic spying, of all kinds of abuses when it comes to arrest of domestic aliens, of inflated and false weapons of mass destruction claims before the war, of cronyism and corruption in Iraq on a vast scale. You could go on. But no official investigation follows.

TD: You get revelation and repetition.

Danner: Yes, R and R. It's been three years since the invasion and occupation of Iraq and there's been no official investigation of how the administration made use of intelligence to suggest that the intelligence agencies were certain Iraq had weapons of mass destruction. Now, the consequence of this is that we live with the knowledge of these scandals, published in newspapers, magazines, books, but we get no official acknowledgement of wrongdoing and no punishment. Perhaps in the end a handful of people will be punished . . .

TD: . . . minor figures . . .

Danner: . . . who were silly enough to get themselves caught—for example, the military police whose images appear in the Abu Ghraib digital pictures. The actual policymakers responsible for the change in interrogation policy will suffer no punishment whatsoever. In fact, they're still in their jobs. None of the investigations has reached them. Even the people who actually carried on the interrogations themselves we know very little about.

TD: You've interviewed some interrogators, haven't you?

Danner: Indeed, and I've had from them accounts of some of the things that were done. The great problem in the Age of Frozen Scandal is that it's as if we're this spinning wheel, constantly confirming facts that we already knew, so the revelations become less and less effective in causing public outrage. The public begins to become inured to it, corrupted in its turn.

TD: I'm going to suggest something grimmer. In what's likely to be the dirtiest election any of us has experienced, if the Democrats actually took one house of Congress in November 2006 and begin to investigate, I think you'd enter the era of frozen investigation. The administration will claim commander-in-chief rights.

Danner: That's a good prediction. The Bush administration is already stonewalling extremely timid Republican-led committees when it comes to the response to Hurricane Katrina or NSA eavesdropping. If the Democrats do take control of a house of Congress and mount real investigations, on the one hand, they'll be very circumspect because they'll be concerned about jeopardizing their chances in the elections of 2008. On the other hand, you'll have the overwhelming claim of commander-in-chief power which could completely handcuff investigations.

TD: I came across this sentence today in a piece on the Plame case. "A spokesman for Cheney would not comment for this story, saying the investigation into the leak was ongoing. The spokesman refused to give her name."

Danner: [laughs] A secret spokesman.

TD: So you've got secrecy, lying, and a third thing you've brought up before, a bizarre kind of frankness. I was wondering if you could talk about that.

Danner: There's been an interesting ambivalence in the administration when it comes to all these actions they've taken in the name of national security—between the impulse to deny and stonewall and the impulse to come forward and very boldly assert that they took such actions in the name of national security. You see it in eavesdropping, where Karl Rove has clearly indicated a preference for declaring, in a very clever response to the NSA revelation, "If al-Qaeda is talking to someone in the United States we want to know about it. Apparently some Democrats don't." Which is basically to say: If you're concerned about this, you're weakening the United States. All this human rights, Fourth Amendment stuff is so much hooey.

In essence, this is an assault on the Bill of Rights. The Bill of Rights is in the Constitution because the framers understood that a lot of these rights, especially when under pressure in wartime, are not particularly popular. So they were put in permanently, so as not to be subject to majority control or majority abnegation. It's politics of the most savagely bare-knuckle and dangerous kind when you use that gap between the country's precepts as embodied in the Constitution and the fact that many of these become unpopular in time of war to destroy your political opponents, which is what this administration does.

There are many in the administration who want to come out four-square for these things. You saw that impulse also with interrogation. They could have come out after Abu Ghraib—there were hints of this—and said, "Yes, there are a few bad apples, but yes, we use extreme interrogation, we do it to defend the country." And if they'd done this, they might have pumped up a majority who would, for example, have supported waterboarding.

When I talk about these matters, there's an ambivalence on my part as well because one becomes extremely upset that they're lying in public and doing these things in secret and denying them; but, on the other hand, I fear the kind of populist technique they could use if they declared these policies openly to rally support for themselves.

All this, of course, begs the question of a second attack. It's the assumption of many people that a second attack would punch through everything, that there'd be a much more explicit assumption of powers.

TD: And do you believe this?

Danner: It's quite possible, sure. If it had happened a year after 9/11, I think that's exactly what would have occurred. Now that time has passed, I'm not so sure. They're in a much more defensive political position. It depends on what kind of attack it was, whether it was an attack of a kind that they should have anticipated —that is, one where it was at least conceivable that they should have prevented it.

TD: It's always dangerous to predict the future, but can you imagine, in quite another direction, this administration imploding or unraveling?

Danner: Well, as in so many things, Yogi Berra had it right: I never make predictions, especially about the future. When it comes to raw political power, the ramrod backbone of the administration is clearly national security. 9/11 restored to the Republican Party what they had lost with the end of the Cold War—this persistent advantage in national security. If there is one thing this administration has done brilliantly, ruthlessly, efficiently, it's making political use of its war on terror. It remains to be seen whether they can go to that well one more time in the 2006 election. There is an opportunity for the Democratic Party, exactly because Americans, after four years of it, are tired of this rhetoric and they've been enlightened by the Iraq war, the response to Hurricane Katrina, and the Medicare debacle among other things to the general incompetence of the administration and to its corruption.

Could the administration unravel? The notion many people on the left are putting forward about a move toward impeachment—it's hard for me to imagine that. First of all, we're coming to a point in the political calendar where Democrats, as at the time of Iran-Contra, are not going to want impeachment to get in the way of retaking the White House in 2008. Democrats also saw what impeachment did to the Republican Party in 1998. For the first time in memory in an off-year election in a President's second term, the Republicans lost seats—leading, as you'll remember, to the abrupt fall of Newt Gingrich. On the other hand, if the Democrats did take one house of Congress this November, I think there are a number of areas where an investigation could hurt this administration severely, and it's hard to predict what the Bush people's reaction would be if they found themselves the target of aggressive congressional committees actually investigating officials who faced being charged, convicted, and sent to jail. Even with Congress actually doing its job, we would confront the central political reality of our time: Terrorism has embedded itself in our political system, which is to say that fear has become the most lucrative political emotion and the administration would retain a considerable power to promote fear. It has the power to suggest that an attack on the national security bureaucracy is an attack on the safety of the people.

TD: I'd like to turn to Iraq now by backing up to an earlier moment in your career, a terrible massacre in El Salvador in the 1980s, whose aftermath you reported on, a massacre by Salvadoran troops trained and backed by the United States. Could you compare that early age of Reagan moment to today, given that so much of the cast of characters has turned out to be the same, including . . .

Danner: . . . Elliott Abrams . . .

TD: . . . and Cheney, Rumsfeld, Negroponte, and any number of others. I'd also like you to consider a more general question: How does the U.S. get up to its elbows in blood so regularly?

Danner: Oh boy . . . When I look back at the massacre at El Mozote, which happened at the beginning of the Reagan administration, what sticks out is the way it served to signal the renewed determination—of the incoming Reagan officials and the newly defiant Salvadoran military—to draw a line at Salvador and not let that so-called advance of communist interests within the hemisphere continue.

When I compare now and then, I think of the power of a determined government to deny the facts and, if it is ruthless, to make its denials stick. Because what reverberates now about El Mozote is that two reporters, Raymond Bonner and Alma Guillermoprieto, from the *New York Times* and the *Washington Post*, got to that massacre site within a few weeks and filed stories. These were published on the front pages of the two most powerful news-papers in the country . . .

TD: . . . far more so then than now.

Danner: Exactly. At a time of real dominance by the *Times* and *Post*, and the administration came forward, denied the massacres took place, and was able to make its views stick. And remember we knew that the death squads were being run out of the Sal-vadoran government; that the American embassy knew all about this; that it was the public policy of the American government that this shouldn't be happening and that aid would be cut off if it was. But every time a new outrage took place, the press oblig-ingly reported the denial of the administration, the denial of the embassy in San Salvador that, in fact, they knew anything about the connection of the death squads and the government the United States was supporting.

That leads me to a conclusion I came to then: that in many stories it's not the information, it's the politics. It's not that we were lacking information. It's that, when that information came out, it was denied and those in power were able to impose their view of reality. Political power decided what reality was, despite clear information to the contrary. When I look at our time I see that phenomenon writ large. It's gone way beyond a massacre in a relatively obscure Central American country. It's gone to poli-cies and statements that led the United States to invade a country that had not attacked us, to torture prisoners and deny we're doing it even when clear evidence says that we are, to domestic spying in which the government is clearly breaking the law and the President declares that he will continue to do so. In all these cases, it's not the information, it's the politics. This is a hard thing for journalists to admit because the model of journalistic behavior in our era is Watergate. It's very hard for journalists to come to grips with the reality that wrongdoing can indeed be exposed, and continue to be exposed again and again with no result, in a kind of tortuous eternal return.

TD: Apply this to Iraq. You've been to Iraq three times. It must be startling to arrive in this described land and see the actual country.

Danner: One of the striking things about going to Iraq is the extraordinarily large chasm between what people know about the story here and what the story actually is. First of all, the lurid, security-imposed landscape of the country is very hard to convey to people here: the miles of concrete blast walls, the miles of barbed wire, the constant fear in driving around and trying to report, and the absolute, constant accompaniment of death. Most of the killings in Iraq are not reported here and yet American viewers think that they're seeing the war when what they're seeing is a television reporter doing a stand-up on the roof of a heavily guarded hotel behind blast walls and barbed wire and countless armed guards, who may or may not have exited that hotel that day. Many reporters are doing extraordinary jobs under horrific conditions, but those conditions make adequate reporting, as we know it, nearly impossible.

The result is that the Iraq we see is a tiny, tiny sliver of a very complex, very violent reality, and the constant repetition of the bad news, of the continual deaths there, has been absorbed by the news system of the United States. By that I mean, whereas ten deaths might have made the front page of the paper or been not quote "a tell" but an actual filmed report on a network newscast, now it takes more death than that. The country and the news media are gradually absorbing how badly the war has gone so that the normal pace of death there which, had we predicted it before the war, would have been a horrible outcome—an outcome that, had we known, no one would have supported the war in the first place—this horrible outcome has become the baseline that we take for granted.

For the story to occupy the news space, a particularly catastrophic attack is necessary. Today in the *New York Times*, there was a striking report about the steady upsurge in the number of attacks since the beginning of the insurgency. This has been inexorable, which shows that the insurgency is growing more formidable, despite all these reports about American and Iraqi successes in the war. That story appeared on page A12. It wasn't even news. Accompanying it was a piece about the failure of infrastructure in Iraq. Though the United States has put roughly $16 billion of American money into the Iraqi infrastructure, the number of hours of average electricity available to an inhabitant of Baghdad has gone from twenty-four hours to four. All the figures on infrastructure point downward, so that if you're an Iraqi, you have seen your standard of living steadily decline under the Americans even as you now have a much greater chance of being kidnapped or killed or blown up in an explosion or having your children kidnapped. Very little of this gets through to Americans. In fact, the story has generally been migrating off the front pages and becoming a small version of Orwell's famed distant and never-ending war between East Asia and Oceania.

I think it's widely known at the top of the administration that Iraq is a failure. It's also been recognized by many that, in strategic terms, the Iraq war could turn out to be a catastrophe because it's essentially created a Shia Islamist government sympathetic to Iran and, among other things, made it impossible for the U.S. to adequately pressure Iran on the nuclear issue. The result of this occupation is going to be a reversal of fifty years of American policy in the Gulf, which has been a reliance on the Sunni autocracies in the area. That policy had an awful lot wrong with it; its support of those autocracies over many decades certainly helped lead to al-Qaeda and its epigones. The fact is, though, that the Bush administration has essentially overthrown that policy with nothing to put in its place.

TD: You've written, "I think I became a writer in part because I found that yawning distance between what I was told and what I could see to be inescapable." Now, that yawning gap is available to everybody. And we're in a strangely demobilized moment, it seems to me. I was wondering: If you're a reporter, what's the story now? Remind me?

Danner: Thank you, Tom, for putting a deeply depressing point in such a deeply depressing way. I congratulate you on that, and indeed that yawning gap is now available to everyone and it's debilitating partly because one is perilously close to arriving at the conclusion that reality doesn't matter. When I look at the pieces on the inside pages of the papers about the stealing of funds in Iraq by American officials, when I realize that no one is likely to be punished for this, I think of the novels of [Milan] Kundera, of his vivid descriptions of what it was like to live in Eastern Europe in the 1950s and 60s—in the Soviet system where everyone realized the corruption, the abuse of power, the mediocrity of the government, the yawning gap between what was said and what was really going on, but no one could do anything about it.

TD: Are we in a kind of Brezhnev moment?

Danner: I'm not sure I would go so far as that because a Brezhnev moment means we're talking about a system that has reached its geriatric debility. I'm by no means saying that the U.S. now is equivalent to Eastern Europe back then, but there is a similarity in this gap between what you know is true and officially recognized reality—and in the fact that that gap cannot be breached. On the other hand, the fall in Bush's approval ratings, and especially the catastrophic decline in the all-important do-you-think-the-country-is-on-the-right-track question shows that this has had a broad effect among a lot of people. And I take some comfort from that.

The Democrats are doing very well in a generic poll about who you would want to run the country. This doesn't mean the mid-term elections will turn out that way, of course. It does mean people have not been so dulled by fear as not to see that the war has been a mistake and that the administration has done a very bad job when it comes to, say, Katrina or the Medicare program. At the end of the day, the problem is that there needs to be a political alternative that is in some way viable and believable—and the political elite that opposes this administration has been unable to formulate a believable program in opposition to it.

At the heart of this is the problem of national security. Since the end of the Vietnam War, in poll after poll the American people say they trust Republicans more than Democrats to pro-tect them. This is a cliché of polling. At this particular time, it's been made worse by a paradox. If, with great skill, the Democ-rats attack the Republican handling not just of the Iraq war but of the more general war on terror—and the Bush administration has been brilliant in connecting those two—if the Democrats suc-ceed in doing this, they are, in effect, igniting the overwhelming political emotion of fear. And the Republicans have been very successful in using fear; fear, whatever its cause, seems to benefit the Republicans and the self-described strong leadership they offer. Their basic strategy in the 2004 election was to say: Elect this guy Kerry with his surfboard, and he's going to get you killed. Enough people were willing to believe that then. It's unclear whether that old snake oil will still have as many willing buyers. I tend to doubt it.

TD: As dusk settles in, let me end this way: You've reported on some countries in horrific situations over the years. You wrote somewhere that in State Department parlance they are called TFN, totally fucked-up nations. Your mother, when you come home, has a tendency to say, "Can't you go someplace nice for a change?" So here we are on this patio, the sun going down, the Golden Gate Bridge in the background. This looks nice. My question is: Is it nice, or are you now reporting from and teaching in a TFN?

Danner: [laughs heartily] Oh, you mean, this is just a mask, a sunny, picturesque mask over what is, in reality, a totally fucked-up nation? Actually, to reach the point of being a TFN, I think we have a long way to go. We're at a very low point in the political evolution of this country. I've certainly not lived under an administration as radical in its techniques, its methods, and its beliefs as this one. I've seen nothing like it in my lifetime.

It's a difficult time for those of us who care about the truth and who don't believe, as I think this administration does, that the truth is actually determined by what those in power think. I take comfort from the fact that a lot of people don't believe that.

There are two borderline dangers here. One is to go off into a state of political debility in which you think that none of this matters. To hell with politics, let's try to live our lives. And that's a very natural response, to kind of bow out of political engagement, but I think that would be very wrong and very harmful. The other risk is to equal the administration in their exaggerations and their distortions, in their stunning lack of fidelity to what is happening. To exaggerate, to overstate, to alter the truth in the cause of a political goal—this, I think, is very tempting . . . very tempting. When you see Fox News existing as it does, you want something of the same on the other side. But I don't think that's my job and I'm glad it's not the job of a lot of writers and journalists out there.

You asked a little while ago what reporters should do in a time like this. I think it's immensely important that people continue, with great determination, to report what is true, to investigate things like the NSA story, to make a record of all of this. Because, at the end of the day, that is what reporters do, and that is why their work is so valuable—so, if you'll forgive this word, sacred. They try to tell what actually happened.

As I leave him at the now dark doorway and head up the stone steps to my car, he calls, "Watch out for the deer! They tend to be up there at this time of night!"

8. Cold Warrior in a Strange Land

Chalmers Johnson

MARCH 21, 2006

As he and his wife Sheila drive me through downtown San Diego in the glare of mid-day, he suddenly exclaims, "Look at that structure!" I glance over and just across the blue expanse of the harbor is an enormous aircraft carrier. "It's the USS *Ronald Reagan*," he says, "the newest carrier in the fleet. It's a floating Chernobyl and it sits a proverbial six inches off the bottom with two huge atomic reactors. You make a wrong move and there goes the country's seventh largest city."

Soon, we're heading toward their home just up the coast in one of those fabled highway traffic jams that every description of Southern California must include. "We feel we're far enough north," he adds in the kind of amused tone that makes his company both alarming and thoroughly entertaining, "so we could see the glow, get the cat, pack up, and head for Quartzsite, Arizona."

Chalmers Johnson, who served in the U.S. Navy and now is a historian of American militarism, lives cheek by jowl with his former service. San Diego is the headquarters of the 11th Naval District. "It's wall to wall military bases right up the coast," he comments. "By the way, this summer the Pentagon's planning the largest naval concentration in the Pacific in the post-World War II period! Four aircraft-carrier task forces—two from the Atlantic and that's almost unprecedented—doing military exercises off the coast of China."

That afternoon, we seat ourselves at his dining-room table. He's seventy-four years old, crippled by rheumatoid arthritis and bad knees. He walks with a cane, but his is one of the spriest minds in town. Out the window I can see a plethora of strange, oversized succulents. ("That's an Agave attenuata," he says. "If you want one, feel free. We have them everywhere. When the blue-gray Tequila plant blooms, its flower climbs seventy-five feet straight up! Then you get every hummingbird in Southern California.") In the distance, the Pacific Ocean gleams.

Johnson is wearing a black T-shirt that, he tells me, a former military officer and friend brought back from Russia. ("He was amused to see hippies selling these in the Moscow airport.") The shirt sports an illustration of an AK-47 on its front with the inscription, "Mikhail Kalashnikov" in Cyrillic script, and underneath, "The freedom fighter's friend, a product of the Soviet Union." On the back in English, it says, "World Massacre Tour" with the following list: "The Gulf War, Afghanistan, Vietnam, Angola, Laos, Nicaragua, Salvador, Lebanon, Gaza Strip, Karabakh, Chechnya . . . To be continued."

Johnson, who served as a lieutenant (jg) in the Navy in the early 1950s and from 1967–1973 was a consultant for the CIA, ran the Center for Chinese Studies at the University of California, Berkeley for years. He defended the Vietnam War ("In that, I was distinctly a man of my times . . ."), but is probably the only person of his generation to have written, in the years since, anything like this passage from the introduction to his book *Blowback:* "The problem was that I knew too much about the international Communist movement and not enough about the United States government and its Department of Defense . . . In retrospect, I wish I had stood with the antiwar protest movement. For all its naiveté and unruliness, it was right and American policy wrong."

Retired, after a long, provocative career as a Japan specialist, he is the author of the prophetic *Blowback: The Costs and Consequences of American Empire*, published in 2000 to little attention. After 9/11, it became a bestseller, putting the word "blowback," a CIA term for retaliation for U.S. covert actions, into common usage. He has since written *The Sorrows of Empire, Militarism, Secrecy, and the End of the Republic.* ("As an academic subject, the American Empire is largely taboo," he tells me. "I'm now comfortably retired, but I had a successful academic career. I realize that young academics today will take up the subject and start doing research on aspects of our empire only if they've got some cover. They need somebody to go first. I've had some of my former graduate students say, 'Look, you're invulnerable. If you won't take the lead, why do you expect us to go do a research project on the impact of American military whorehouses on Turkey.' I mean, let's face it, it's a good subject!")

He is just now completing the final volume of his *Blowback Trilogy*. It will be entitled *Nemesis*.

Sharp as a tack, energetic, and high-spirited, by turns genuinely alarmed and thoroughly sardonic, he's a talker by nature. Our encounter is an interview in name only. No one has ever needed an interviewer less. I do begin with a question that had been on my mind, but it's hardly necessary.

Tomdispatch: Let's start with a telltale moment in your life, the moment when the Cold War ended. What did it mean to you?

Chalmers Johnson: I was a cold warrior. There's no doubt about that. I believed the Soviet Union was a genuine menace. I still think so.

There's no doubt that, in some ways, the Soviet Union inspired a degree of idealism. There are grown men I admire who can't but stand up if they hear the *Internationale* being played, even though they split with the Communists ages ago because of the NKVD and the gulag. I thought we needed to protect ourselves from the Soviets.

As I saw it, the only justification for our monster military apparatus, its size, the amounts spent on it, the growth of the Military-Industrial Complex that [President Dwight] Eisenhower identified for us, was the existence of the Soviet Union and its determination to match us. The fact that the Soviet Union was global, that it was extremely powerful, mattered, but none of us fully anticipated its weaknesses. I had been there in 1978 at the height of [Soviet leader Leonid] Brezhnev's power. You certainly had a sense then that no consumer economy was present. My colleagues at the Institute for the USA and Canada were full of: Oh my god, I found a bottle of good Georgian white wine, or the Cubans have something good in, let's go over to their bar; but if you went down to the store, all you could buy was vodka.

It was a fairly rough kind of world, but some things they did very, very well. We talk about missile defense for this country. To this day, there's only one nation with a weapon that could penetrate any missile defense we put up—and that's Russia. And we still can't possibly match the one they have, the Topol-M, also known as the SS-27. When [President Ronald] Reagan said he was going to build a Star Wars, these very smart Soviet weaponmakers said: We're going to stop it. And they did.

As [Senator] Daniel Moynihan said: Who needs a CIA that couldn't tell the Soviet Union was falling apart in the 1980s, a $32 billion intelligence agency that could not figure out their economy was in such awful shape they were going to come apart as a result of their war in Afghanistan and a few other things.

In 1989, [Soviet leader] Mikhail Gorbachev makes a decision. They could have stopped the Germans from tearing down the Berlin Wall, but for the future of Russia he decided he'd rather have friendly relations with Germany and France than with those miserable satellites Stalin had created in Eastern Europe. So he just watches them tear it down and, at once, the whole Soviet empire starts to unravel. It's the same sort of thing that might happen to us if we ever stood by and watched the Okinawans kick us out of Okinawa. I think our empire might unravel in a way you could never stop once it started.

The Soviet Union imploded. I thought: What an incredible vindication for the United States. Now it's over and the time has come for a real victory dividend, a genuine peace dividend. The question was: Would the U.S. behave as it had in the past when big wars came to an end? We disarmed so rapidly after World War II. Granted, in 1947 we started to rearm very rapidly, but by then our military was farcical.

In 1989, what startled me almost more than the [Berlin] Wall coming down was this: As the entire justification for the Military-Industrial Complex, for the Pentagon apparatus, for the fleets around the world, for all our bases came to an end, the United States instantly—pure knee-jerk reaction—began to seek an alternative enemy. Our leaders simply could not contemplate dismantling the apparatus of the Cold War.

That was, I thought, shocking. I was no less shocked that the American public seemed indifferent. And what things they did do were disastrous. George Bush, the father, was President. He instantaneously declared that he was no longer interested in Afghanistan. It's over. What a huge cost we've paid for that, for creating the largest clandestine operation we ever had and then just walking away, so that any Afghan we recruited in the 1980s in the fight against the Soviet Union instantaneously came to see us as the enemy—and started paying us back. The biggest blowback of the lot was, of course, 9/11, but there were plenty of them before then.

I was flabbergasted and felt the need to understand what had happened. The chief question that came to mind almost at once, as soon as it was clear that our part of the Cold War was going to be perpetuated—the same structure, the same military Keynesianism, an economy based largely on the building of weapons— was: Did this suggest that the Cold War was, in fact, a cover for something else; that something else being an American empire intentionally created during World War II as the successor to the British Empire?

Now that led me to say: Yes, the Cold War was not the clean-cut conflict between totalitarian and democratic values that we had claimed it to be. You can make something of a claim for that in Western Europe at certain points in the 1950s, but once you bring it into the global context, once you include China and our two East Asian wars, Korea and Vietnam, the whole thing breaks down badly and this caused me to realize that I had some rethinking to do. The wise-ass sophomore has said to me—this has happened a number of times—"Aren't you being inconsistent?" I usually answer with the famous remark of John Maynard Keynes, the British economist, who, when once accused of being inconsistent, said to his questioner, "Well, when I get new information, I rethink my position. What, sir, do you do with new information?"

A personal experience five years after the collapse of the Soviet Union also set me rethinking international relations in a more basic way. I was invited to Okinawa by its governor in the wake of a very serious incident. On September 4, 1995, two Marines and a sailor raped a twelve-year-old girl. It produced the biggest outpouring of anti-Americanism in our key ally, Japan, since the Security Treaty was signed [in 1960].

I had never been to Okinawa before, even though I had spent most of my life studying Japan. I was flabbergasted by the thirty-two American military bases I found on an island smaller than Kauai in the Hawaiian Islands and the enormous pressures it put on the population there. My first reaction as a good Cold Warrior was: Okinawa must be exceptional. It's off the beaten track. The American press doesn't cover it. It's a military colony. Our military has been there since the battle of Okinawa in 1945. It had all the smell of the Raj about it. But I assumed that this was just an unfortunate, if revealing, pimple on the side of our huge apparatus. As I began to study it, though, I discovered that Okinawa was not exceptional. It was the norm. It was what you find in all of the American military enclaves around the world.

TD: The way we garrison the planet has been essential to your rethinking of the American position in the world. Your chapters on Pentagon basing policy were the heart of your last book, *The Sorrows of Empire*. Didn't you find it strange that, whether reviewers liked the book or not, none of them seemed to deal with your take on our actual bases? What do you make of that?

Johnson: I don't know why that is. I don't know why Americans take for granted, for instance, that huge American military reservations in the United States are natural ways to organize things. There's nothing slightly natural about them. They're artificial and expensive. One of the most interesting ceremonies of recent times is the brouhaha over announced base closings. After all, it's perfectly logical for the Department of Defense to shut down redundant facilities, but you wouldn't think so from all the fuss.

I'm always amazed by the way we kid ourselves about the

influence of the Military-Industrial Complex in our society. We use euphemisms like supply-side economics or the Laffer Curve. We never say: We're artificially making work. If the WPA [Works Progress Administration of the Great Depression] was often called a dig-holes-and-fill-'em-up-again project, now we're making things that blow up and we sell them to people. Our weapons aren't particularly good, not compared to those of the great weapons makers around the world. It's just that we can make a lot of them very rapidly.

TD: As a professional editor, I would say that when we look at the world, we have a remarkable ability to edit it.

Johnson: Absolutely. We edit parts of it out. I mean, people in San Diego don't seem the least bit surprised that between here and Los Angeles is a huge military reservation called Camp Pendleton, the headquarters of the First Marine Division. I was there myself back in the Korean War days. I unfortunately crossed the captain of the LST-883 that I was serving on. We had orders to send an officer to Camp Pendleton and he said, "I know who I'm going to send." It was me. [He laughs.] And I'll never forget it. The world of Marine drill sergeants is another universe.

In many ways, as an enthusiast for the natural environment, I am delighted to have Pendleton there. It's a *cordon sanitaire*. I spent a little time with its commandant maybe a decade ago. We got to talking about protecting birds and he said, "I'm under orders to protect these birds. One of my troops drives across a bird's nest in his tank and I'll court martial him. Now, if that goddamn bird flies over to San Clemente, he takes his chances." Even then I thought: That's one of the few things going for you guys, because nothing else that goes on here particularly contributes to our country. Today, of course, with the military eager to suspend compliance with environmental regulations, even that small benefit is gone.

TD: So, returning to our starting point, you saw an empire and . . .

Johnson: . . . it had to be conceptualized. Empires are defined so often as holders of colonies, but analytically, by empire we simply mean the projection of hegemony outward, over other people, using them to serve our interests, regardless of how their interests may be affected.

So what kind of empire is ours? The unit is not the colony, it's the military base. This is not quite as unusual as defenders of the concept of empire often assume. That is to say, we can easily calculate the main military bases of the Roman Empire in the Middle East, and it turns out to be about the same number it takes to garrison the region today. You need about thirty-eight major bases. You can plot them out in Roman times and you can plot them out today.

An empire of bases—that's the concept that best explains the logic of the seven hundred or more military bases around the world acknowledged by the Department of Defense. Now, we're just kidding ourselves that this is to provide security for Americans. In most cases, it's true that we first occupied these bases with some strategic purpose in mind in one of our wars. Then the war ends and we never give them up. We discovered that it's part of the game; it's the perk for the people who fought the war. The Marines to this day believe they deserve to be in Okinawa because of the losses they had in the bloodiest and last big battle of World War II.

I was astonished, however, at how quickly the concept of empire—though not necessarily an empire of bases—became acceptable to the neoconservatives and others in the era of the younger Bush. After all, to use the term proudly, as many of them did, meant flying directly in the face of the origins of the United States. We used to pride ourselves on being as anti-imperialist as anybody could be, attacking a king who ruled in such a tyrannical manner. That lasted only, I suppose, until the Spanish-American War. We'd already become an empire well before that, of course.

TD: Haven't we now become kind of a one-legged empire in the sense that, as you've written, just about everything has become military?

Johnson: That's what's truly ominous about the American empire. In most empires, the military is there, but militarism is so central to ours—militarism not meaning national defense or even the projection of force for political purposes, but as a way of life, as a way of getting rich or getting comfortable. I guarantee you that the first Marine Division lives better in Okinawa than in Ocean-side, California, by considerable orders of magnitude. After the Wall came down, the Soviet troops didn't leave East Germany for five years. They didn't want to go home. They were living so much better in Germany than they knew they would back in poor Russia.

Most empires try to disguise that military aspect of things. Our problem is: For some reason, we love our military. We regard it as a microcosm of our society and as an institution that works. There's nothing more hypocritical, or constantly invoked by our politicians, than "support our boys." After all, those boys and girls aren't necessarily the most admirable human beings that ever came along, certainly not once they get into another society where they are told they are, by definition, doing good. Then the racism that's such a part of our society emerges very rapidly—once they get into societies where they don't understand what's going on, where they shout at some poor Iraqi in English.

TD: I assume you'd agree that our imperial budget is the defense budget. Do you want to make some sense of it for us?

Johnson: Part of empire is the way it's penetrated our society, the way we've become dependent on it. Empires in the past—the Roman Empire, the British Empire, the Japanese Empire—helped to enrich British citizens, Roman citizens, Japanese citizens. In our society, we don't want to admit how deeply the making and selling of weaponry has become our way of life; that we really have no more than four major weapons manufacturers—Boeing, Lockheed Martin, Northrop Grumman, General Dynamics—but these companies distribute their huge contracts to as many states, as many congressional districts, as possible.

The military budget is starting to bankrupt the country. It's got so much in it that's well beyond any rational military purpose. It equals just less than half of total global military spending. And yet here we are, stymied by two of the smallest, poorest countries on Earth. Iraq before we invaded had a GDP the size of the state of Louisiana and Afghanistan was certainly one of the poorest places on the planet. And yet these two places have stopped us.

Militarily, we've got an incoherent, not very intelligent budget. It becomes less incoherent only when you realize the ways it's being used to fund our industries or that one of the few things we still manufacture reasonably effectively is weapons. It's a huge export business, run not by the companies but by foreign military sales within the Pentagon.

This is not, of course, free enterprise. Four huge manufacturers with only one major customer. This is state socialism and it's keeping the economy running not in the way it's taught in any economics course in any American university. It's closer to what John Maynard Keynes advocated for getting out of the Great Depression—counter-cyclical governmental expenditures to keep people employed.

The country suffers from a collective anxiety neurosis every time we talk about closing bases and it has nothing to do with politics. New England goes just as mad over shutting down the Portsmouth Naval Shipyard as people here in San Diego would if you suggested shutting the Marine Corps Air Station. It's always seen as *our* base. How dare you take away *our* base! Our congressmen must get it back!

This illustrates what I consider the most insidious aspect of our militarism and our military empire. We can't get off it any more. It's not that we're hooked in a narcotic sense. It's just that we'd collapse as an economy if we let it go and we know it. That's the terrifying thing.

And the precedents for this should really terrify us. The greatest single previous example of military Keynesianism—that is, of taking an economy distraught over recession or depression, over people being very close to the edge and turning it around— is Germany. Remember, for the five years after Adolf Hitler became chancellor in 1933, he was admired as one of the geniuses of modern times. And people *were* put back to work. This was done entirely through military Keynesianism, an alliance between the Nazi Party and German manufacturers.

Many at the time claimed it was an answer to the problems of real Keynesianism, of using artificial government demand to reopen factories, which was seen as strengthening the trade unions, the working class. Capitalists were afraid of government policies that tended to strengthen the working class. They might prove to be revolutionary. They had been often enough in that century. In this country, we were still shell-shocked over Bolshevism; to a certain extent, we still are.

What we've done with our economy is very similar to what Adolf Hitler did with his. We turn out airplanes and other weapons systems in huge numbers. This leads us right back to 1991 when the Soviet Union finally collapsed. We couldn't let the

Cold War come to an end. We realized it very quickly. In fact, there are many people who believe that the thrust of the Cold War even as it began, especially in the National Security Council's grand strategy document, NSC68, rested on the clear understanding of late middle-aged Americans who had lived through the Great Depression that the American economy could not sustain itself on the basis of capitalist free enterprise. And that's how—my god—in 1966, only a couple of decades after we started down this path, we ended up with some 32,000 nuclear warheads. That was the year of the peak stockpile, which made no sense at all. We still have 9,960 at the present moment.

Now, the 2007 Pentagon budget doesn't make sense either. It's $439.3 billion . . .

TD: . . .not including war . . .

Johnson: Not including war! These people have talked us into building a fantastic military apparatus, and then there was that famous crack [Clinton Secretary of State] Madeleine Albright made to General Colin Powell: "What's the point of having this superb military you're always talking about if we can't use it?" Well, if you want to use it today, they charge you another $120 billion dollars! [He laughs.]

But even the official budget makes no sense. It's filled with weapons like Lockheed Martin's F-22—the biggest single contract ever written. It's a stealth airplane and it's absolutely useless. They want to build another Virginia class nuclear submarine. These are just toys for the admirals.

TD: When we were younger, there were always lots of articles about Pentagon boondoggles, the million-dollar military monkey wrench and the like. No one bothers to write articles like that any more, do they?

Johnson: That's because they've completely given up on decent, normal accounting at the Pentagon. Joseph Stiglitz, the Nobel Prize–winning economist, and a colleague at Harvard have put together a real Pentagon budget which, for the wars we're fighting right now, comes out to about $2 trillion. What they've added in are things like interest on the national debt that was used to buy arms in the past. Turns out to be quite a few billion dollars. Above all, they try to get a halfway honest figure for veterans' benefits. For this year, it's officially $68 billion, which is almost surely way too low given, if nothing more, the huge number of veterans who applied for and received benefits after our first Gulf War.

We hear on the nightly news about the medical miracle that people can be in an explosion in which, essentially, three 155 millimeter shells go off underneath a Humvee, and they survive through heroic emergency efforts. Barely. Like Bob Woodruff, the anchor person from ABC News. The guy who saved his life said, I thought he was dead when I picked him up. But many of these military casualties will be wards of the state forever. Do we intend to disavow them? It leads you back to the famous antiwar cracks of the 1930s, when Congressmen used to say: There's nothing we wouldn't do for our troops—and that's what we do, nothing.

We almost surely will have to repudiate some of the promises we've made. For instance, Tricare is the government's medical care for veterans, their families. It's a mere $39 billion for 2007. But those numbers are going to go off the chart. And we can't afford it.

Even that pompous ideologue Donald Rumsfeld seems to have thrown in the towel on the latest budget. Not a thing is cut. Every weapon got through. He stands for "force transformation" and we already have enough nuclear equipment for any imaginable situation, so why on Earth spend anything more? And yet the Department of Energy is spending $18.5 billion on nuclear weapons in fiscal year 2006, according to former Senior Defense Department Budget Analyst Winslow Wheeler, who is today a researcher with the Center for Defense Information.

TD: Not included in the Pentagon budget.

Johnson: Of course not. This is the Department of Energy's budget.

TD: In other words, there's a whole hidden budget . . .

Johnson: Oh, it's huge! Three-quarters of a trillion dollars is the number I use for the whole shebang: $440 billion for the authorized budget; at least $120 billion for the supplementary warfighting budget, calculated by Tina Jones, the comptroller of the Department of Defense, at $6.8 billion per month. Then you add in all the other things out there, above all veterans' care, care of the badly wounded who, not so long ago, would have added up to something more like Vietnam-era casualty figures. In Vietnam, they were dead bodies; these are still living people. They're so embarrassing to the administration that they're flown back at night, offloaded without any citizens seeing what's going on. It's amazing to me that [Congressman] John Murtha, as big a friend as the defense industry ever had—you could count on him to buy any crazy missile-defense gimmick, anything in outer space—seems to have slightly woken up only because he spent some time as an old Marine veteran going to the hospitals.

Another person who may be getting this message across to the public is Gary Trudeau in some of his *Doonesbury* cartoons. Tom, I know your mother was a cartoonist and we both treasure Walt Kelly, who drew the *Pogo* strip. How applicable is Pogo's most famous line today: "We have met the enemy and he is us."

PART 2:
WHAT EVER HAPPENED TO CONGRESS?

Tomdispatch: You were discussing the lunacy of the 2007 Pentagon budget . . .

Chalmers Johnson: What I don't understand is that the current defense budget and the recent Quadrennial Defense Review (which has no strategy in it at all) are just continuations of everything we did before. Make sure that the couple of hundred military golf courses around the world are well groomed, that the Lear jets are ready to fly the admirals and generals to the Armed Forces ski resort in Garmisch in the Bavarian Alps or the military's two luxury hotels in downtown Seoul and Tokyo.

What I can't explain is what has happened to Congress. Is it just that they're corrupt? That's certainly part of it. I'm sitting here in California's 50th district. This past December, our congressman Randy Cunningham confessed to the largest single bribery case in the history of the U.S. Congress: $2.4 million in trinkets—a Rolls Royce, some French antiques—went to him, thanks to his ability as a member of the military subcommittee of the House Appropriations Committee to add things secretly to the budget. He was doing this for pals of his running small companies. He was adding things even the Department of Defense said it didn't want.

This is bribery and, as somebody said the other day, Congress comes extremely cheap. For $2.4 million, these guys got about $175 million in contracts. It was an easy deal.

The military is out of control. As part of the executive branch, it's expanded under cover of the national security state. Back when I was a kid, the Pentagon was called the Department of War. Now, it's the Department of Defense, though it palpably has nothing to do with defense. Hasn't for a long time. We even have another department of the government today that's concerned with "homeland security." You wonder what on Earth do we have that for—and a Department of Defense, too!

The government isn't working right. There's no proper supervision. The founders, the authors of the Constitution, regarded the supreme organ to be Congress. The mystery to me—more than the huge expansion of executive branch powers we've seen since the neoconservatives and George Bush came to power—is: Why has Congress failed us so completely? Why are they no longer interested in the way the money is spent? Why does a Pentagon budget like this one produce so little interest? Is it that people have a vested interest in it, that it's going to produce more jobs for them?

I wrote an article well before Cunningham confessed called "The Military-Industrial Man" in which I identified a lot of what he was doing, but said unfortunately I didn't know how to get rid of him in such a safe district. After it appeared on the *Los Angeles Times* op-ed page, the paper got a couple of letters to the editor from the 34th district in downtown LA saying, I wish he was my congressman. If he'd bring good jobs here, I wouldn't mind making something that just gets blown up or sunk in the ground like missile defense in Alaska. I mean, we've already spent $100 billion on what amounts to a massive high-tech scarecrow. It couldn't hit a thing. The aiming devices aren't there. The tests fail. It doesn't work. It's certainly a cover for something much more ominous—the expansion of the Air Force into outer space or "full spectrum dominance," as they like to put it.

We need to concentrate on this, and not from a partisan point of view either. There's no reason to believe the Democrats would do a better job. They never have. They've expanded the armed forces just as fast as the Republicans.

This is the beast we're trying to analyze, to understand, and it seems to me today unstoppable. Put it this way: James

Madison, the author of our Constitution, said the right that controls all other rights is the right to get information. If you don't have this, the others don't matter. The Bill of Rights doesn't work if you can't find out what's going on. Secrecy has been going crazy in this country for a long time, but it's become worse by orders of magnitude under the present administration. When John Ashcroft became attorney general, he issued orders that access to the Freedom of Information Act should be made as difficult as possible.

The size of the black budget in the Pentagon has been growing ever larger during this administration. These are projects no one gets to see. To me, one of the most interesting spectacles in our society is watching uniformed military officers like General Michael Hayden, former head of the National Security Agency, sitting in front of Congress, testifying. It happened the other day. Hillary Clinton asked him: Tell us at least approximately how many [NSA warrantless spying] interventions have you made? "I'm not going to tell you" was his answer. Admiral Jacoby, head of the Defense Intelligence Agency, was asked directly about a year ago, are we still paying Ahmed Chalabi $340,000 a month? And his reply was, "I'm not going to say."

At this point, should the senator stand up and say: "I want the U.S. Marshall to arrest that man." I mean, this is contempt of Congress.

TD: You're also saying, of course, that there's a reason to have contempt for Congress.

Johnson: There is indeed. You can understand why these guys do it. Richard Helms, the Director of the CIA back in 1977, was convicted of a felony for lying to Congress. He said, no, we had nothing to do with the overthrow of [Chilean President] Salvador Allende when we had everything to do with it. He gets a suspended sentence, pays a small fine, walks into the CIA building at Langley, Virginia, and is met by a cheering crowd. Our hero! He's proudly maintained the principles of the secret intelligence service, which is the private army of the president and we have no idea what he's doing with it. Everything they do is secret. Every item in their budget is secret.

TD: And the military, too, has become something of a private army . . .

Johnson: Exactly. I dislike conscription because it's so easily manipulated, but I do believe in the principle of the obligation of citizens to defend the country in times of crisis. Now, how we do that is still an open question, but at least the citizens' army was a check on militarism. People in the armed forces knew they were there involuntarily. They were extremely interested in whether their officers were competent, whether the strategy made sense, whether the war they might have to fight was justified, and if they began to believe that they were being deeply lied to, as in Vietnam, the American military would start to come apart. The troops then were fragging their officers so seriously that General Creighton Abrams said, we've got to get them out of there. And call it Vietnamization or anything else, that's what they did.

I fear that we're heading that way in Iraq. You open the morning paper and discover that they're now going to start recruiting down to level four, people with serious mental handicaps. The terrible thing is that they'll just be cannon fodder.

It's not rocket science to say that we're talking about a tragedy in the works here. Americans aren't that rich. We had a trade deficit in 2005 of $725.8 billion. That's a record. It went up almost 25 percent in just over a year. You can't go on not making things, fighting these kinds of wars, and building weapons that are useless. Herb Stein, when he was chairman of the council of economic advisers in a Republican administration very famously said, "Things that can't go on forever don't."

TD: So put our problems in a nutshell.

Johnson: From George Bush's point of view, his administration has achieved everything ideologically that he wanted to achieve. Militarism has been advanced powerfully. In the minds of a great many people, the military is now the only American institution that appears to work. He's enriched the ruling classes. He's destroyed the separation of powers as thoroughly as was possible. These are the problems that face us right now. The only way you could begin to rebuild the separation of powers would be to reinvigorate the Congress and I don't know what could shock the American public into doing that. They're the only ones who could do it. The courts can't. The President obviously won't.

The only thing I can think of that might do it would be bankruptcy. Like what happened to Argentina in 2001. The richest country in Latin America became one of the poorest. It collapsed. It lost the ability to borrow money and lost control of its affairs, but a great many Argentines did think about what corrupt presidents had listened to what corrupt advice and done what stupid things during the 1990s. And right now, the country is on its way back.

TD: But superpower bankruptcy? It's a concept nobody's really explored. When the British empire finally went, we were behind them. Is there somebody behind us?

Johnson: No.

TD: So what would it mean for us to go bankrupt? After all, we're not Argentina.

Johnson: It would mean losing control over things. All of a sudden, we would be dependent on the kindness of strangers, looking for handouts. We already have a $725 billion trade deficit; the largest fiscal deficit in our history, now well over 6 percent of GDP. The defense budgets are off the charts and don't make any sense, and don't forget that $500 billion we've already spent on the Iraq war—every nickel of it borrowed from people in China and Japan who saved and invested because they would like to have access to this market. Any time they decide they don't want to lend to us, interest rates will go crazy and the stock exchange will collapse.

We pour about $2 billion a day just into servicing the amounts we borrow. The moment people quit lending us that money, we have to get it out of domestic savings and right now we have a negative savings rate in this country. To get Americans to save 20 percent of their income, you'd have to pay them at least a 20 percent interest rate and that would produce a truly howling recession. We'd be back to the state of things in the 1930s that my mother used to describe to me—we lived in the Arizona countryside then—when someone would tap on the rear door and say, "Have you got any work? I don't want to be paid, I just want to eat." And she'd say, "Sure, we'll find something for you to do and give you eggs and potatoes."

A depression like that would go on in this country for quite a while. The rest of the world would also have a severe recession, but would probably get over it a lot faster.

TD: So you can imagine the Chinese, Japanese, and European economies going on without us, not going down with us.

Johnson: Absolutely. I think they could.

TD: Don't you imagine, for example, that the Chinese bubble economy, the part that's based on export to the United States might collapse, setting off chaos there too?

Johnson: It might, but the Chinese would not blame their government for it. And there is no reason the Chinese economy shouldn't, in the end, run off domestic consumption. When you've got that many people interested in having better lives, they needn't depend forever on selling sweaters and pajamas in North America. The American economy is big, but there's no reason to believe it's so big the rest of the world couldn't do without us. Moreover, we're kidding ourselves because we already manufacture so little today—except for weapons.

We could pay a terrible price for not having been more prudent. To have been stupid enough to give up on infrastructure, health care, and education in order to put eight missiles in the ground at Fort Greeley, Alaska, that can't hit anything. In fact, when tested, sometimes they don't even get out of their silos.

TD: How long do you see the dollar remaining *the* international currency? I noticed recently that Iran was threatening to switch to Euros.

Johnson: Yes, they're trying to create an oil bourse based on the Euro. Any number of countries might do that. Econ 1A as taught in any American university is going to tell you that a country that runs the biggest trade deficits in economic history must pay a penalty if the global system is to be brought back into equilibrium. What this would mean is a currency so depreciated no American could afford a Lexus automobile. A vacation in Italy would cost Americans a wheelbarrow full of dollars.

TD: At least it might stop the CIA from kidnapping people off the streets of Italy in the style to which they've grown accustomed.

Johnson: [Laughs.] Their kidnappers would no longer be staying in the Principe di Savoia [a five-star hotel] in Milano, that's for sure.

The high-growth economies of East Asia now hold huge amounts in American treasury certificates. If the dollar loses its value, the last person to get out of dollars loses everything, so you naturally want to be first. But the person first making the move causes everyone else to panic. So it's a very cautious, yet edgy situation.

A year ago, the head of the Korean Central Bank, which has a couple of hundred billion of our dollars, came out and said: I think we're a little heavily invested in dollars, suggesting that maybe Dubai's currency would be better right now, not to mention the Euro. Instantaneous panic. People started to sell; presidents got on the telephone asking: What in the world are you people up to? And the Koreans backed down—and so it continues.

There are smart young American PhDs in economics today inventing theories about why this will go on forever. One is that there's a global savings glut. People have too much money and nothing to do with it, so they loan it to us. Even so, as the very considerable economics correspondent for the *Nation* magazine, William Greider, has written several times, it's extremely unwise for the world's largest debtor to go around insulting his bankers. We're going to send four aircraft-carrier task forces to the Pacific this summer to intimidate the Chinese, sail around, fly our airplanes, shoot off a few cruise missiles. Why shouldn't the Chinese say, let's get out of dollars. Okay, they don't want a domestic panic of their own, so the truth is they would do it as subtly as they could, causing as little fuss as possible.

What does this administration think it's doing, reducing taxes when it needs to be reducing huge deficits? As far as I can see, its policies have nothing to do with Republican or Democratic ideology, except that its opposite would be traditional, old Republican conservatism, in the sense of being fiscally responsible, not wasting our money on aircraft carriers or other nonproductive things.

But the officials of this administration are radicals. They're crazies. We all speculate on why they do it. Why has the President broken the Constitution, let the military spin virtually out of control, making it the only institution he would turn to for anything—another Katrina disaster, a bird flu epidemic? The whole thing seems farcical, but what it does remind you of is ancient Rome.

If a bankruptcy situation doesn't shake us up, then I fear we will, as an author I admire wrote the other day, be "crying for the coup." We could end the way the Roman Republic ended. When the chaos, the instability become too great, you turn it over to a single man. After about the same length of time our republic has been in existence, the Roman Republic got itself in that hole by inadvertently, thoughtlessly acquiring an empire they didn't need and weren't able to administer, that kept them at war all the time. Ultimately, it caught up with them. I can't see how we would be immune to a Julius Caesar, to a militarist who acts the populist.

TD: Do you think that our all-volunteer military will turn out to be the janissaries of our failed empire?

Johnson: They might very well be. I'm already amazed at the degree to which they tolerate this incompetent government. I mean the officers know that their precious army, which they worked so hard to rebuild after the Vietnam War, is coming apart again, that it's going to be ever harder to get people to enlist, that even the military academies are in trouble. I don't know how long they'll take it. Tommy Franks, the general in charge of the attack on Baghdad, did say that, if there were another terrorist attack in the United States comparable to 9/11, the military might have no choice but to take over. In other words: If we're going to do the work, why listen to incompetents like George Bush? Why take orders from an outdated character like Donald Rumsfeld? Why listen to a Congress in which, other than John McCain, virtually no Republican has served in the armed forces?

I don't see the obvious way out of our problems. The political system has failed. You could elect the opposition party, but it can't bring the CIA under control; it can't bring the military-industrial complex under control; it can't reinvigorate the Congress. It would be just another holding operation as conditions got worse.

Now, I'll grant you, I could be wrong. If I am, you're going to be so glad, you'll forgive me. [He laughs.] In the past, we've had clear excesses of executive power. There was Lincoln and the suspension of *habeas corpus*. Theodore Roosevelt virtually invented the executive order. Until then, most presidents didn't issue executive orders. Roosevelt issued well over a thousand. It was the equivalent of today's presidential signing statement. Then you go on to the mad Presbyterian Woodrow Wilson, whom the neocons are now so in love with, and Franklin Roosevelt and his pogrom against Americans of Japanese ancestry. But there was always a tendency afterwards for the pendulum to swing back, for the American public to become concerned about what had been done in its name and correct it. What's worrying me is: Can we expect a pendulum swing back this time?

TD: Maybe there is no pendulum.

Johnson: Today, Cheney tells us that presidential powers have been *curtailed* by the War Powers Act [of 1973], congressional oversight of the intelligence agencies, and so on. This strikes me as absurd, since these modest reforms were made to deal with the grossest violations of the Constitution in the Nixon administration. Moreover, most of them were stillborn. There's not a president yet who has acknowledged the War Powers Act as legitimate. They regard themselves as not bound by it, even though it was an act of Congress and, by our theory of government, unless openly unconstitutional, that's the bottom line. A nation of laws? No, we are not. Not anymore.

TD: Usually we believe that the Cold War ended with the Soviet Union's collapse and, in essence, our victory. A friend of mine put it another way. The United States, he suggested, was so much more powerful than the USSR that we had a greater capacity to shift our debts elsewhere. The Soviets didn't and so imploded. My question is: Are we now seeing the delayed end of the Cold War? Perhaps both superpowers were headed for the proverbial trash bin of history, simply at different rates of speed?

Johnson: I've always believed that they went first because they were poorer and that the terrible, hubristic conclusion we drew—that we were victorious, that we won—was off the mark. I always felt that we both lost the Cold War for the same reasons —imperial overstretch, excessive militarism, things that have been identified by students of empires since Babylonia. We've never given Mikhail Gorbachev credit. Most historians would say that no empire ever gave up voluntarily. The only one I can think of that tried was the Soviet Union under him.

TD: Any last words?

Johnson: I'm still working on them. My first effort was *Blowback.* That was well before I anticipated anything like massive terrorist attacks in the United States. It was a statement that the foreign-policy problems—I still just saw them as that—of the first part of the twenty-first century were going to be left over from the previous century, from our rapacious activities in Latin America, from our failure to truly learn the lessons of Vietnam. *The Sorrows of Empire* was an attempt to come to grips with our militarism. Now, I'm considering how we've managed to alienate so many rich, smart allies—every one of them, in fact; how we've come to be so truly hated. This, in a Talleyrand sense, is the sort of mistake from which you can't recover. That's why I'm planning on calling the third volume of what I now think of as "The Blowback Trilogy," *Nemesis*. Nemesis was the Greek goddess of vengeance. She also went after people who became too arrogant, who were so taken with themselves that they lost all prudence. She was always portrayed as a fierce figure with a scale in one hand—think, Judgment Day—and a whip in the other . . .

TD: And you believe she's coming after us?

Johnson: Oh, I believe she's arrived. I think she's sitting around waiting for her moment, the one we're coming up on right now.

9. A World at 36/7 Speed

Katrina vanden Heuvel

APRIL 20, 2006

You enter the nondescript grey building off a small street just east of Union Square, ride an oh-so-slow elevator up to the eighth floor, and pass into the offices of the *Nation* magazine, which just turned 141 years old. It is housed in a vast space. Imagine something between an enormous loft and an old press room with a warren of open, half-walled cubicles clustered at its heart and filled with toiling interns, fact-checkers, and assisters of various sorts. Around the rim of the room, the editors have their offices.

Behind a modest expanse of glass, Katrina vanden Heuvel, editor, publisher, and part-owner of the magazine, is at her desk, her phone headset on, deep in conversation. In our speeded-up media world in which reporters are constantly sent onto TV as pundits just to get a little attention for increasingly desperate newspapers, vanden Heuvel—remarkably composed in any talk-show setting—has become the branded face of her magazine.

On her desk is a half-full in-box, but only, as it happens,

because the rest of the desk is bursting with papers, stacks of them, one of which half-obscures her as she talks. Turning, she spots me at the door. Clad in a black jacket and dark slacks, she rises with a welcoming smile. She's smaller than you might imagine from the television screen and, refreshingly, lacks any evident sense of self-importance.

Her office is neat as a pin, clean as a whistle—unless you check out the surfaces which are chaos itself: the desk, a riot of paper; the bookshelves, stuffed not only with books but with nesting dolls of every sort, including a Mikhail Gorbachev one, a box of "revolutionary finger puppets," and lots of framed photos. Every inch of the small coffee table near which she seats us is stacked with books, except where a Santa nesting doll ("I did an interview with a Russian journalist and he gave me this") resides near a Talking Clinton doll (with two buttons on its base, one labeled "funny," the other "inspiration").

I settle onto the sofa, place my two little tape recorders precariously atop one of the piles of books, and we begin. Her voice is soft and low, but the minute she starts speaking her face lights with animation and energy fills her small frame.

Tomdispatch: Tell me something about your daily life at the magazine. I'm sure you're understaffed, under-everythinged. But what's it like to spend a day as the *Nation*'s editor and publisher, beginning to end?

Katrina vanden Heuvel: I begin the day by reading from three to five papers. By then I'm already so agitated . . . [She laughs.] Anyway, I start with the *Washington Post*, then I do the *New York Times*, then parts of the *Financial Times* or the *Wall Street Journal*, *USA Today*, the *Los Angeles Times*, and the *Guardian*. Then I look at the Web. I'll read Tompaine, Commondreams, Romenesko, Tomdispatch, Juan Cole, Alternet, the Huffington

Post, James Wolcott's blog, Jay Rosen's PressThink, sometimes Josh Marshall's Talking Points Memo or the Daily Kos. Just kind of absorbing as much as I can. Then the trick is to be an editor who's outraged by what's going on, but remains humane and sane as a watchdog.

So you begin the week by thinking about what the lead editorial will be. That's short term. On Monday, you read the galleys of the articles section for the upcoming issue. You're on the phone talking to writers who are part of our community about what's on their mind and, of course, trying to find new writers. Then there's the rest of *Nation* life. Talking to our Web editor about what's going to lead the site, using our little radio studio to do a weekly one-minute *Nation* commentary for Air America, hammering out the details of the magazine's first-ever student journalism conference.

Then I'll write a blog entry, or a short riff for our new magazine blog, the Notion, or something for the *Guardian*'s new blog, Comment Is Free, or maybe I'll talk to an editor here about a special issue like the one we're doing on media this summer. I'll speak with people who want me to talk at media or political events. I just got a call from [Sen.] Dick Durbin's office, asking if I'd be on a conference call tomorrow about the new Democratic security strategy.

Then there are the little, unexpected things that arise. We publish a piece that outrages a corporation or a lobbyist, so we get a letter threatening libel action. That can take half a day. That's when you feel like you're in a political campaign because you're tamping something down. So your plans for that day are pfftttt. And then there's television. I did TV this Sunday, but if it's during the work week, I'll usually only do it at the end of the day or at 7:15 on one of the morning shows.

There are so many regular tasks. There's checking out the cover. Our production manager comes in every Wednesday and says, "Here's the final cover," but during the course of the week you decide what that cover and the headlines are going to be, which second, third, fourth stories to feature on it, and then you work it out with your cover designers. I'm also replying to one hundred or more emails in the course of a day. And then there's the *Nation* cruise, now entering its eighth year, which is an important part of our bottom line. Today, I literally sent a letter to Noam Chomsky asking if he would be on it, and I met with the woman who's kind of the in-house cruise director.

And then people just come through. I have a delegation of Spanish socialists passing through next week. Ben Cohen was in a few days ago to talk about his True Majority project and a sane defense budget. The Reverend Jesse Jackson, Jr., just called and I asked if he'd come talk to us at our weekly Thursday editorial meeting. Then I deal with my mother, who leaves me a voicemail almost every night because she stays up till three in the morning watching C-Span. She leaves me messages like [her already low voice drops to a breathy whisper]: "This man, this military lawyer, I can't remember his exact name, who's standing up for the rights of detainees, he makes me proud to be an American! I know I never say that . . ." [She laughs.] And I've got a fourteen-year-old daughter who's a basketball fanatic. It's March Madness, and like any good American outfit, the *Nation* has its pool. Last night I watched the Duke-UConn women's semi-finals with Nika [her daughter Nicola]. And then there's the twice-a-year editorial board meeting this Friday and all the planning that goes into it. And tomorrow, I'll be introducing a Tom Hayden-Laura Flanders conversation at the Strand [book store]. So there's that piece of it.

TD: At least, I assume you're not having to spend too much time worrying about what's going to be in your next issue—thanks to George Bush.

vanden Heuvel: No, absolutely not. We have a story meeting tomorrow. We often have too many things in the pipeline or planned out, but sometimes what's really important is the ability to rip up the magazine. Hurricane. New Orleans. That's obvious. There was a period of two or three weeks where we were just going with Katrina. Recently, on the other hand, we had Mike Davis on the aftermath of New Orleans and that had been in the works for quite a while.

TD: Multiply this by every day and your life must have that flooded feeling?

vanden Heuvel: Yes, but like you, I would hate to have work that wasn't meaningful, especially because these last years have been so devastating. Maybe this isn't the healthiest thing to say, but the ability to come to work and just be so engaged, maybe it allows me to suppress some of that personal emotion of devastation I might feel otherwise.

TD: Something I learned from Studs Terkel years ago was that action engenders hope. You can't be hopeful just by thinking or wishing, not in bad times anyway.

vanden Heuvel: I know that every day I have to be engaged here and sometimes what's frustrating is that you get so sidelined. One thing that truly frustrates me is sectarian disputes. They detract from the energy that should be going into the larger project. There's also a humbling quality to this job, because there's such an enormity to the outrages. Sometimes, trying to follow all of this closely, your head feels flooded. I'm following so many things and I find I know just a little bit about everything. It's like: How do you put it all together? It's like: When will people understand! Those are the thoughts that roll through your mind.

TD: Does the magazine feel like a hard-to-fit jigsaw puzzle each week?

vanden Heuvel: There is that quality sometimes: Where do you put it, what do you choose, what are we going to highlight? Then there are weeks when you feel like you've gotten it, or others when you know you've done something no other publication in America is going to do. Sometimes, though, frustration lies in the feeling that you just can't convey the enormity of, say, the Bush administration's unitary executive theory. How do you convey that no previous administration I know of has so openly, so brazenly, on so many fronts tried to subvert the Constitution, that what we're living through is a crisis that may bode the death knell of our democracy. Why aren't people jumping up and down? Anyway, that's where the quality of flooding hits and you just get overwhelmed. Then, throw in the Internet, which moves with such ferocious speed and allows for such quick interventions, it all just moves 36/7.

TD: That's a new phrase for me. My knowledge stops at 24/7 . . .

vanden Heuvel: It's just that the Internet is expanding so exponentially that it's not even as confined as the 24/7 cable-media culture.

TD: I feel it every day.

vanden Heuvel: Well, no wonder. You're at the edge of the abyss!

TD: I think I may be.

vanden Heuvel: For the *Nation*, there's the hope of both being able to harness the pace and power of the Internet and then being a little bit more thoughtful, doing some deeper reporting, longer form thinking in the magazine.

TD: In time terms, I suspect it goes: Internet, newspaper, magazine, book. I mean each one is a step back in time with the Internet closest to this second; you know, the most pounding.

vanden Heuvel: I think that's right and we're trying to harness almost all of those elements—from our Web site to Nation Books.

TD: [Laughs.] It's like a little empire.

vanden Heuvel: We're an anti-imperialist empire.

TD: You know, a Mexican political cartoonist once said to me that the period of the one-party state was a great shame for Mexicans, but for cartoonists it was like paradise; there was so much material they were like pigs in slop. And I was thinking how appropriate this was for both the *Nation* and, in a much smaller way, Tomdispatch. We're in the worst period in anyone's memory, but for us, weirdly, it's all manna from Hell. In these terms, how does the *Nation's* recent success strike you?

vanden Heuvel: Our circulation has increased by about 70% in the last six years and that certainly reflects this horrifying political and cultural moment, but it's also that we were poised to take it on when others were intimidated, fearful. In a sense, we were there to do it because it's in our genes. I mean, these are *really* bad times, but this country has gone through bad times before. The *Nation* has been around for 141 years and seen it all. So it was as if the core animating principles of this magazine just came into play: fierce independence, defense of the constitution, defense of democracy, first amendment rights, rule of law and of international law, civil rights, civil liberties, economic justice. All of those things kicked in and allowed us to say: Hey, we have to defend these principles and not just be pragmatic—and especially not be fearful.

TD: You were here on September 11, 2001. How quickly did you sense that this was the *Nation*'s moment?

vanden Heuvel: I'd say within a week. Of course, we grappled with what millions of Americans grappled with. As journalists and editors, we had to speak for something larger than ourselves, but we were also people and we're in New York City. We were only a mile away. So there was this sense of shock, of trauma, personal and political; but very quickly we understood that, while we had to speak to that human pain, we also had to speak to the dangers we saw, the almost instantaneous attempt to shut down a real discussion. In the days that followed, it became even clearer that we were going to be one of the few media outlets willing to raise tough questions. We had a range of views at this magazine, but we understood pretty quickly that there was going to be a fierce backlash against those who would stand outside the conformity. Fortunately, there was an extraordinary community of people here and a team of dedicated editors. I was fortunate to have Jonathan Schell, Richard Falk, David Cole, and so many others to draw on.

TD: Imagine that if an oppositional public, the magazine, and the Democratic Party form the points of a triangle, then one of the weird aspects of the post-9/11 moment was the way the Democratic Party disappeared as an oppositional party, if it ever was one. Along with the Bush disaster, don't you think that the disaster of the Democrats drove people to you? After all, people who want to oppose the moment have to look somewhere . . .

vanden Heuvel: Absolutely. First of all, this has always been an independent magazine. We're not, by any measure, part of the Democratic Party, but there was indeed this void, this vacuum, and not only in the media. Where were the voices, the alternatives? Where were people speaking up?

I have to dissent a little, though, when people speak about the Democratic Party as if it were a monolith. There's a really good congressman from Massachusetts named Jim McGovern, no relationship to [former Senator George] McGovern, who once told me that if we were in Europe, the Democratic Party would be about eight parties. We have a system that doesn't allow the full parameters of debate inside what, since at least New Deal days, has essentially been a coalition party. It's easy to forget that there were a few Democrats speaking up and some of them were in our pages: Dennis Kucinich, John Conyers, and Barbara Lee, to name three.

In fact, part of what we want to do is make sure our readers understand that there are still some courageous voices inside the Party—and then, of course, outside the Democratic Party there were many courageous voices in this country and the world community, who wondered what exactly was going on. To give voice to that was very important.

But that said, we grew because people were frustrated with the Democrats and because the mainstream media was so vapid. What still frustrates me, Tom, is that there's not enough sense in the world of what I would call the other America. This is a divided country. At this point, years after 9/11, places like the *Nation* probably speak for a majority view on certain issues like the war. But what mattered here from the beginning was making people understand that there was more than just a monologue in this country—which you might have doubted if you spent your time watching TV news and reading mainstream papers.

TD: Here's a quote from Richard Wirthlin, Reagan's pollster.

Recently he spoke of seeing the beginning of "a decisive turn in public opinion" against the Iraq war. "It is hard for me to imagine any set of circumstances," he said, "that would lead to an enhancement of the public support that we have seen. It is more likely to go down, and the question is how far and how fast." It mystifies me at such a moment that, out of crass self-interest, the Democratic Party still isn't ready to run against the Iraq War.

vanden Heuvel: There is a political calculation infused with cowardice on the part of the Democratic leadership to this day. They seem to want to sit back and let this administration and its debacle in Iraq crumble on their own. That doesn't say much about convictions or morality in politics, but that, I believe, has been the strategy. It mystifies me that you don't have a party willing to become a tribune, not just of antiwar sentiment, but of sanity. Of course, for many, our politics has become little more than an investment. The money in politics dovetails with the Democratic unwillingness to take bold stands—not only on war and peace but also on the terrible morality and slash-and-burn economics of the corporate agenda—as well as with the urge to cut to the center, wherever they think the center might be (though I doubt it's where too much of the Democratic Party thinks it is). What a moment to seize, right? But they blew it once in 2002 at the midterm elections, when they just kind of backed off. Why not again? So many of them don't have the courage of their convictions . . .

TD: They may not have the convictions, forget the courage.

vanden Heuvel: There's one Russ Feingold for every twenty-five, that's the problem.

TD: I was actually going to turn to Feingold's censure motion . . .

vanden Heuvel: And look at how his party ran away from that! What's so interesting is that the contempt for, the willingness to ignore, the base—which is an odd word—becomes somewhat harder with the coming of age of the Internet, with the net roots.

TD: Net roots?

vanden Heuvel: The grassroots manifested on the net. It's a fairly new phrase. It's sites like the *Daily Kos* and it's the ability to galvanize communities. One wishes that the net roots were being paid attention to because of their convictions and their ideas, but I think their ability to raise money is what really got the Democrats' attention. Still, that's where you may see the base, which is so far out ahead of the political leadership, exert some influence over the Party. That, to me, is hopeful, though one also hopes that the net roots don't become a new establishment, new gatekeepers.

TD: Can you imagine a future oppositional party in the U.S.?

vanden Heuvel: I wish that our votes were counted differently and our districts proportioned differently, because the structural limitations on the ability to have third-party politics frustrate me; but I do think you can build a more oppositional structure within the Democratic Party. I really do and that's where we're seeing some possibilities. There are good efforts underway around this country to build a farm team of true progressive elected officials for the long term and there's also hope in what's now called "progressive federalism." Federalism used to scare progressives, and for good reason, because it meant abusing civil rights and the like. But now, when you have gridlock in Washington, there's a lot going on in states. Three hundred seventy-five-plus communities passing resolutions opposing the Patriot Act. States raising the minimum wage. City councils passing "bring them home now" resolutions. It's all small, but if we measure our accomplishments by we've-gotta-change-the-world-overnight standards, we're all going to go back to bed . . .

TD: As Americans tend to do when things don't work out reasonably quickly . . .

vanden Heuvel: Yes, the paralysis factor is great. I think what we need to do is keep at it. Before people are going to jump over to the other side of the river, you need to give them a sense of what can be. The other day a loyal *Nation* associate—one of the 29,000 who contribute a little to the magazine every year above and beyond the subscription price—wrote me, "Let's have some stories about our victories . . . about the triumph of the human spirit over great obstacles." It was that spirit that moved me last year to start a series on the Web called "Sweet Victories." I hoped that bringing attention to often small but still sweet triumphs— electoral victories, organizing efforts, protests and boycotts, new ideas, new organizations, new initiatives—would maintain a sense of hope and inspiration in a dark time. I also wanted to say, hey, here's some news that is too often off the mainstream media radar screen.

TD: So what kind of a relationship do you see the magazine having with the liberal wing of the Democratic Party?

vanden Heuvel: One manifestation of just that was—not very sexy admittedly—an issue we did at the time of the President's State of the Union address, where we asked twenty leading members of the progressive caucus, the largest in the House, to write their alternative State of the Union. I can see building a relationship with those members of the House and a few in the Senate who care about the grass roots, who care about democracy. All of those members are for economic and social justice and against the war. We forget that a majority of the Democrats in the House did vote against the war resolution and a hundred-plus members of the House are now in favor of getting out, which means you have something to work with. So I don't give up.

TD: We're heading toward what looks like an immensely impoverished presidential race in 2008. What do you make of it and, of course, of Hillary?

vanden Heuvel: It drives me crazy. First of all, I have terrible Clinton fatigue. The idea of Bush, Clinton, Bush, Clinton—1988 to 2012 or beyond . . . But I don't begin with the personalities. I think there are three issues that matter in such an election. There's the Constitution—defend it; there's Iraq—get out of it; there's universal health care—pass it. Hillary Clinton on the Constitution, not there. On the war and universal health care, terrible. It is not shaping up, Tom, to be a great moment in American political history, even though it should be since it's one of the most fluid we've experienced, right? I think it's the first time since 1952 that we don't have an incumbent VP or President in the race. It should be wide open. The frustration about what you call this impoverished race is leading some good people to seek new faces, unusual ones who would run in 2008. Some see the new Al Gore as a political leader who would give Hillary a run for her money. And I hear through the grapevine that a group is urging Bill Moyers to run. That would be interesting.

TD: I always believed the Bush administration stood a reasonable chance of imploding. My wife called me—like the people labeled "premature anti-fascists" when we finally got into World War II —a premature optimist, which I was. I was wrong on my time scheme, but probably by this midterm election, certainly by the presidential election of 2008, we'll be standing in the ruins of Bush-land.

vanden Heuvel: Oh, in the rubble. Deep rubble.

TD: . . . and what a strange moment, for so relatively little to be happening.

vanden Heuvel: At the national political level. It's a measure of the downsized politics of excluded alternatives we live with. It really is. There's a lot going on, just not in inside-the-Beltway politics and that, again, is a measure of how limited the ability of our system is to express the real range of views in this country. I do think there's a cynical calculus on the part of the Democrats that, as the Bush people implode, they will stand aside—certainly in 2006—not take too many chances and try to pick up the pieces. Now, to be fair, in the history books, if you go back and look, all Newt Gingrich's Contract-with-America stuff didn't really emerge until late in 1994. So there's a little bit of a mythology about the need to unveil alternative policies before elections.

What's so interesting right now is how much ferment there is on the conservative side of the aisle, because these people in the White House are not real conservatives. They're extremists. I don't call them "radical" because it's a term I like. What I don't like—and you must feel this, too—is: So William Buckley finally speaks up, right, and Francis Fukuyama speaks up . . . Suddenly, people are saying, "Oh, this is extraordinary!" And, you know, we've been slogging away for four years. Where is the accountability? Where is there any notion of people standing up and saying not, "You were right," because it's so ugly what's happened, but: "God, you understood the debacle this would be early on!" There's something in our culture that accords people like a Buckley or a George Will or an Andrew Sullivan more credibility when they finally change their minds. Hell, the *Nation* called for Donald Rumsfeld's resignation in April 2003. But maybe it's just a case of the pundits giving plaudits to each other.

TD: We're actually in a weird conversion moment, don't you think? One conversion after another on the right. A very American conversion moment in which all memory of what actually happened before is blanked out.

vanden Heuvel: Gore Vidal had the great line, the United States of Amnesia, and there is this quality in our country. Someone once said, history is to a nation what memory is to an individual and, boy, this country is not on a good track. What's exciting, on the other hand, is something you've documented at Tomdispatch, which is people inside government institutions where it's so bad, so extreme what's happened, people who might otherwise have been quiet, being stirred up to say something, to oppose the Bush administration, to push back. And that's when someone like a Sy Hersh always says that you begin to see the leaks.

TD: Let's turn to the media for a moment. For 141 years the *Nation* has lost money and had to throw itself on the kindness of strangers, yet it seems in many ways stronger than a lot of our megalith media institutions today.

vanden Heuvel: First of all, we've been known for two things over all those years, our ability to speak truth to power and our ability to not make a profit. [She laughs.] But we've finally broken even. Just barely. I think this year it's actually a $5,000 profit. Maybe it's because we sort of know what we stand for, because we believe in conviction. I mean it's a moment for that, whereas the more bland media institutions are having a really hard time of it in this environment where there are many more media outlets. As compared to media in many other countries where there's real dissent, debate all across the spectrum, it seems to me we're arguing over a remarkably narrow bandwidth here in the U.S.

TD: Most regular media outlets are experiencing the flight of readers from print. You're experiencing the opposite. Your circulation is what?

vanden Heuvel: About 200,000. Of course, the Internet has become a vehicle for us, too. Last year we got 30,000 subscriptions to the magazine over the Internet! Through it, we're reaching an audience that might not otherwise be exposed to the *Nation*'s views. We have readers in a lot of cities around this country, but not a lot in the middle of Nevada—and you do reach people like that via the Internet. We're aware that we increasingly need to offer the *Nation* in different modes, even if print remains the anchor. I do think a powerful interest in print will stay with us—just as when paperback books came out, people predicted the demise of hardcovers. In the end, I think they'll prove complementary forms.

TD: It says something about the moment and about the necessity of branding in the TV version of the media world, but out there your face is something like the *Nation* right now.

vanden Heuvel: I'll tell you why I do TV. Because there are very few opportunities for people on the left or progressives to speak to a broader audience, to reach people, and eighty percent of Americans still get their news from television. What's frustrating, of course, is how little time there is to say anything on TV. Still, as long as you come with the views you express in your real day job and you don't check your integrity at the door, it's an opportunity to say a few things you just don't hear in this mainstream media wasteland. Now, the shouting shows I do less of—I think they're a disservice to our nation—and there are a few people I won't do TV with anymore like Ann Coulter because I do think you debase yourself. But judging from some of the emails I get, viewers out there will hear something from me that they feel and believe, but they're living in a place where they don't hear it much and so they may think they're wacko or deviant. And in the last year, I've been getting more and more emails from viewers who say I'm a conservative, which I find somehow encouraging. What's odd in this opinionated TV landscape, which for the most part has not been a contribution to our political culture, is that they're seeking opinionated voices and there are so many bland voices in the media that they come to the *Nation*.

John Edwards has this line about two Americas. I think there are three, four, five media Americas, many levels of news, and that, on or off the Internet, you can certainly find what you want if you seek it in this country. But, believe me, if you talked with someone about the issues you follow, who listened to talk radio, watched CNN for five minutes a day, and read his or her local paper for a few minutes, you'd understand how badly served by our media so many people are.

TD: Do you feel there's a ceiling on the *Nation* audience?

vanden Heuvel: I think we could easily be at 250,000 and that was kind of a pipedream not so many years ago. Arthur Carter, a former publisher and general partner of this place, once made the mistake of saying, "Oh, easy million." Well, never say never is how I feel about that figure now.

TD: You wrote in one of your blog entries, "History hasn't ended, but the American Century may have." Do you really think so?

vanden Heuvel: I think it has and there's displaced fear and anxiety about that among the elite as well as ordinary people, which is finding channels in dangerous xenophobic politics and a messianic Christianization of our political culture, not to speak of a more general growing religiosity. Just on the basic raw statistics of economic power, America is not the superpower it was and that's even before we know what the debacle in Iraq will really mean, not just for American power but for the American psyche. Remember, after Vietnam came twenty-five or thirty years of reckoning with what America had become. I think we're going to see that after Iraq, if and when it ends.

The rise of India and China will certainly mean a very different global geopolitical order. The United States will have a powerful place in it, but it will not be the American Century. One issue that excites me in this regard—and that we want to do more about at the magazine—one that progressives should take heart from is this: It's now pretty well recognized that the neo-liberal economic project was vastly oversold—to workers in our country, to the world's poor. In this spirit, I don't see how one can't be encouraged by the developments in Latin America in recent years, where U.S. dominance is really being contested and whole countries are taking themselves out of the IMF [International Monetary Fund] frame of corporate-led economic development.

TD: Any final words?

vanden Heuvel: Just that these are some times. Everyone does their little thing and I think . . . I just hope . . . it makes a difference. One last thing: Our mainstream media does a real disservice to us all, because I do believe that this is a more progressive country than is understood. On some of the fundamental core issues, people don't want this kind of messianic, militaristic policy. They just want to be secure and have some kind of principled foreign policy. They want universal health care. They want an end to the war. With virtually no political leadership, I think people seek a saner, more decent country than our elected representatives offer and the mainstream media paint. And this blue/red divide they're always harping on, I don't like it. This is a much more complicated country than they imagine. One of our passionate readers, for instance, is the mayor of Salt Lake City. There's more complexity and more decency and more generosity of spirit here than is generally allowed in the kind of 36/7 media culture we live in.

She walks me out into the warren that is the Nation. *"Take care," she says and, hands together in a little prayer-like gesture, half-nods, half-bows, offers me a lovely smile, and is gone. When I look back a moment later, she's already seated at that desk partially obscured by a stack of papers, her head set on, deep in conversation.*

10. Humanity's Ground Zero

Mike Davis

MAY 9, 2006

His short hair and mustache are heavily flecked with grey, but he still retains the stocky, powerful build of a butcher's son, who once, long ago, hauled animal carcasses for his father in the San Diego suburb of El Cajon. At a moment's notice, he puts you in his four-wheel drive and takes you out to San Diego's McMansion exurbs or down to the Mexican border and right up to the new, controversial triple fence just being erected (where you have a passing run-in with the Border Patrol). He is the tour guide of your dreams, a walking encyclopedia of whatever is strange and riveting about Southern California. No object on the landscape seems to escape comment, brief description, or analysis. The bridge on the Interstate you drive across somewhere in the desert lands far out of town is the highest poured-concrete one in the country. The military vessels of every sort that crisscross San Diego's blue harbor are identified and discussed, including the stealth landing craft of the Navy SEALs. ("The Navy has more toys out here!")

A small lecture on the local real-estate market follows the complaint that "all anybody talks about these days in San Diego is real-estate values!" Each military base and reservation you pass is carefully pointed out. "People here don't notice the wall-to-wall military. They don't see the death all around them, the killing platforms. They just edit it all out." And every now and then, an odd memory from earlier days surfaces. ("The only good thing about growing up in San Diego was Navy-town and its cheap movie theaters. It was a teenage paradise.") Sitting shotgun in his car, you can't help but be aware that you are watching a dazzling—if everyday—performance from a polymath who seems never to have forgotten a thing.

His modest house is at the edge of one of San Diego's poorest neighborhoods which you get a brief spin through—with a passing discussion of local graffiti thrown into the bargain. His small living room, where we set up my tape recorders, is dominated by a giant, multi-colored plastic playhouse for his two year-old twins, James and Cassandra (or Casey). To interview him in this house is to be surrounded by a world of revolutionary history. No wall, no nook or cranny, not even the bathroom, is lacking its revolutionary poster. (*Camarada! Trabaja y Lucha por la Revolution!*) All around you feet threaten to stamp on Russian plutocrats, giant hands to smash the German exploiting class, while you are urged to "Vote Spartacus!" in 1919.

Mike Davis, whose first book about Los Angeles, *City of Quartz*, burst into bestsellerdom and put him on the map as this country's most innovative urban scholar, has since written about everything from the literary destruction of LA to Victorian holocausts of the nineteenth century and the potential avian flu pandemic of our own moment. He has most recently turned his restless, searching brain upon the global city in a new book,

Planet of Slums, whose conclusions are so startling that I thought they should be the basis for our conversation.

We create a makeshift spot in the living room, my tape recorders between us, and begin. Davis has in him something of the older, nearly lost American tradition of the autodidact. In a tribal world, he would certainly have been any tribe's storyteller of choice. Midway through our interview, which is largely an inspired monologue, we are suddenly interrupted by weeping from elsewhere in the house. Casey has awoken from her nap upset. He quickly excuses himself, returning moments later with a collapsed, still sniffling, dark-haired little girl in pink pants and shirt on his shoulder. Under his ministrations she perks up, then sits up, then begins to talk, hardly less volubly (though slightly less comprehensibly) than her father. Soon she is seated inside the large plastic house, engaging both of us in a game of "big bad wolf." When she wanders off, perhaps twenty minutes later, he turns back to me and, before I can cue him on the interview (I've just checked his last words), he picks up in mid-sentence exactly where he left off and just rolls on.

Tomdispatch: I was hoping you would start by telling me how you came to the subject of the city.

Mike Davis: I came to the city by the most parochial path, which was studying Los Angeles, and I came to LA because, having been a sixties new leftist and having invested a lot of time in studying Marxism, I thought radical social theory could explain just about anything. But it struck me that the supreme test would be understanding Los Angeles.

Maybe I shouldn't say this, but almost everything I've written about other cities has grown, at least in part, out of my LA project. For instance, investigating the tendency toward the militarization of urban space and the destruction of public space in

Los Angeles has led me to explore similar trends as a global phenomenon. Interest in suburban Los Angeles got me considering
the fate of older suburbs across the country and then the emergent politics of edge cities. So, in this consistently parochial way,
the world emerged from Los Angeles which, in my original
project, was a mosaic of about 450 individual pieces.

Let me explain: Back in the 1950s, when county welfare
agencies were worried that war veterans moving into new suburbs had no sense of place, it did this big study of how many
actual life-worlds there were in Greater Los Angeles and came to
the conclusion that people lived in about 350 communities—
small towns, neighborhoods, suburbs. (Now, there are maybe
500 of these.) Behind my strategy for doing Los Angeles lay the
thought that each of these constituent pieces had an entirely
local, totally eccentric story to tell about itself, but also refracted
some important aspect of the larger whole. I literally believe I
could spend several lifetimes telling a story in each of these places
about Los Angeles; so that was my methodology. I suppose in the
process I only became an urbanist because people started calling
me that. I've never actually considered myself a historian, sociologist, political economist, or urban theorist.

TD: So do you have a name for yourself?

Davis: Like some of the other survivors of the New Left, I thought
of myself as an organizer, as doing power-structure or political
analysis. Almost everything I've written or thought about corre-
sponds in some insane way to what, in my mind at a given
moment, seems to be the imperative from a strategic or tactical
standpoint—as if I were still answerable to the SDS National
Council or the Chicago office of the IWW.

And this was all part of the strategic puzzle I addressed in

City of Quartz. LA was at a critical cusp in its history. Globalization had reorganized its economy, rewiring it in dramatic ways, and many people were being left behind. Yet the city had—and still has—this incredible, protean potential for better things, for progressive politics, for surprising activism. At the time, I wanted to write a book that was usable by a new generation of activists, while trying to figure out how to look at a place like Los Angeles whose fantasy self has been embodied materially in its structure. It's a city that lives its images.

TD: And then the riots of 1992 burst out, no?

Davis: . . .and I tried to understand them as a direct consequence of the globalization process. Some people were victors, some losers. It was also a fact that globalization ultimately came to South-central LA in the form of the transnational drug industry. That was the only form of globalization which ever put any money on those streets. The successor volume to *City of Quartz* was to be a history of the Rodney King riots, told on a neighborhood by neighborhood basis—the only narrative strategy that could possibly grasp the complexity of the events. Almost by accident, I had access to some of the key protagonists. I knew, for example, the mother of the guy who went to prison for almost killing the truck driver. I was also friends with the family of Dewayne Holmes, the principle instigator of the gang truce in Watts.

I hoped to weave these stories together with neighborhood histories to explain an uprising that was simultaneously a justifiable explosion of rage at the police, a postmodern bread riot, and a pogrom against Asian shop owners. But my ambition encountered crisis on two fronts. I could never find sufficient moral ground to loot people's lives for my narrative purposes or to assume the right to tell their stories. At the same time, I found the project too emotionally harrowing. The lives of my friends and acquaintances were filled with so much difficulty and pain, so much sadness and frustration. To live that with them—and this was a time when I was working several jobs and about to become a single parent to a teenager—this, I decided, was not what I could do. I had what I thought was an extraordinary design for a book in mind, but I couldn't find either the clear conscience or emotional stamina to write it.

Fortunately, natural disasters were added to my project—and the riot book morphed into *Ecology of Fear*, a study of the fetishism of disaster in Southern California where the natural gets seen in social terms (with coyotes and mountain lions compared to street gangs), while social problems (like street gangs) are seen as natural events ("feral and wilding youth"). *Ecology of Fear* was about the inability of Anglo-American civilization ever to completely understand the metabolism of the actual Mediterranean world it lives in—a misunderstanding that constitutes the very essence of Southern California.

In essence, I retreated to science and shifted from the microscale of biographies to the macro-scale of plate tectonics and El Niño. Science was my first love and I ended up writing that book largely in the geology library at Cal Tech rather than in the living rooms of people I knew in South and Central LA.

TD: If we jump fifteen years to your newest book, *Planet of Slums*, with its vast urban canvas, can we imagine that you're now taking your marching orders from some global central committee? And can you launch us on the subject of our slumifying planet today?

Davis: Stunningly enough, classical social theory, whether Marx, Weber, or even Cold War modernization theory, none of it anticipated what's happened to the city over the last thirty or forty years. None of it anticipated the emergence of a huge class, mainly of the young, who live in cities, have no formal connection with the world economy, and no chance of ever having such a connection. This informal working class isn't the lumpenproletariat of Karl Marx and it isn't the "slum of hope," as imagined twenty or thirty years ago, filled with people who will eventually climb into the formal economy. Dumped into the peripheries of cities, usually with little access to the traditional culture of those cities, this informal global working class represents an unprecedented development, unforeseen by theory.

TD: Just lay out some of the figures on the slumification of the planet.

Davis: Only in the last few years have we been able to see urbanization clearly on a global scale. Previously, the data was untrustworthy, but the United Nations Habitat has made heroic efforts involving new data bases, household surveys, and case studies to establish a reliable baseline for discussing our urban future. The report it issued three years ago, *The Challenge of Slums*, is as pathbreaking as the great explorations of urban poverty in the nineteenth century by Engels or Mayhew or Charles Booth or, in the United States, Jacob Riis.

By its conservative accounting, a billion people currently live in slums and more than a billion people are informal workers, struggling for survival. They range from street vendors to day laborers to nannies to prostitutes to people who sell their organs [for transplant]. These are staggering figures, even more so since our children and grandchildren will witness the final build-out of the human race. Sometime around 2050 or 2060, the human population will achieve its maximum growth, probably at around 10 to 10.5 billion people. Nothing as large as some of the earlier apocalyptic predictions, but fully 95 percent of this growth will occur in the cities of the south.

TD: In essence, in the slums . . .

Davis: The entire future growth of humanity will occur in cities, overwhelmingly in poor cities, and the majority of it in slums.

Classical urbanization via the Manchester/Chicago/Berlin/ Petersburg model is still occurring in China and a few other places. It's important to note, though, that the urban industrial revolution in China precludes similar ones in other places. It absorbs all the capacity for light manufacturing goods—and increasingly everything else. In China and a few adjacent economies, you still see city growth with an industrial motor. Everywhere else it's occurring largely without industrialization; even more shockingly, often without development in any sense. Moreover, what were, historically, the great industrial cities of the south—Johannesburg, Sao Paulo, Mumbai, Bello Horizonte, Buenos Aires—have all suffered massive deindustrialization in the last twenty years, absolute declines in manufacturing employment of 20–40 percent.

The mega-slums of today were largely created in the 1970s and 1980s. Before 1960, the question was: Why were Third World cities growing so slowly? There were, in fact, huge institutional obstacles to fast urbanization then. Colonial empires still restricted entry to the city, while in China and other Stalinist countries, a domestic passport system controlled social rights and so internal migration. The big urban boom comes in the 1960s with decolonization. But then, at least, revolutionary nationalist states were claiming that the state could play an integral role in the provision of housing and infrastructure. In the seventies, the state begins to drop out, and with the 80s, the age of structural adjustment, you have the decade of going backwards in Latin America, and even more so in Africa. By then, you had sub-Saharan cities growing at faster velocities than Victorian industrial cities in their boom periods—but shedding formal jobs at the same time.

How could cities sustain population growth without economic development in the textbook sense? Or, to put it differently, why didn't Third World cities explode in the face of these contradictions? Well, they did to some extent. At the end of the eighties and in the early nineties, you have anti-debt riots, IMF [International Monetary Fund] riots, all across the world.

TD: Are the '92 LA riots part of that?

Davis: Because Los Angeles combines features of a Third World as well as a First World city, it fits into the global pattern of unrest. What was invisible to LA's policymakers and leaders at the time, but obvious on the streets was the impact of the most severe recession since 1938 in Southern California—from which the worst damage wasn't to the aerospace industry (though that was much written about at the time), but to the city's poor and immigrant neighborhoods. In a year—where I lived downtown—a vacant hillside populated by a handful of homeless, middle-aged black males suddenly had 100, 150 young Latinos camped out. They had been day laborers or dishwashers six months before.

If the detonating event was the Rodney King atrocity and the accumulated grievances of black youth in a community where global employment meant crack cocaine, it became a more complex, larger-scale event because of the widespread looting in Latino neighborhoods where people were hungry and living at the edge of homelessness.

TD: How did policymakers and leaders globally interpret what was happening in the cities?

Davis: The discovery by the World Bank, developmental economists, and big NGOs in the 1980s that, despite the almost total abdication of the role of the state in planning and providing housing for poor urban dwellers, people were still somehow finding shelter, squatting, surviving, leading to the rise of a bootstrap school of urbanization. Give poor people the means and they'll build their own houses and organize their own neighborhoods. This was, in part, an entirely justifiable celebration of rank-and-file urbanism. But in the World Bank's hands, it became a whole new paradigm: The state is done; don't worry about the state; poor people can improvise the city. They just need some micro-loans . . .

TD: . . . and high-interest micro-loans at that.

Davis: Yes, that's right, and then poor people would miraculously create their own urban worlds, their own jobs.

Planet of Slums is intended to follow up the UN *Challenge* report, which alerted us that the global urban unemployment crisis was coequal to climate change as a threat to our collective future. Admittedly an armchair journey to cities of the poor, it is an attempt to synthesize a vast specialist literature on urban poverty and informal settlement. Two fundamental conclusions emerged.

First, the supply of free land for squatting had ended, in some cases a long time ago. The only way you can build a shack on free land now is to choose a place so hazardous that it will have no market value whatsoever. This increasing wager with disaster is what squatting has become. So, for instance, if I were to take you a few miles south and across the border to Tijuana you'd see almost immediately that land which once made up squatters' neighborhoods is now being sold, sometimes even subdivided and developed. Very poor people in Tijuana are squatting in the traditional fashion only at the edges of ravines and in streambeds where their houses will collapse in a couple of years. This is true all over the Third World.

Squatting has been privatized. In Latin America, it's called "pirate urbanization." Where, twenty years ago, people would have occupied vacant land, resisted eviction, and eventually been recognized by the state, they now pay high prices for small parcels of land or, if they can't afford it, rent from other poor people. In some slums, the majority of dwellers aren't squatters, they're renters. If you went to Soweto [in Johannesburg, South Africa], you'd see that people fill their backyards with shanties which they rent. The major survival strategy of millions of poor urban dwellers, who have been in the city long enough to have a little property, is to subdivide it and become landlords to yet poorer people, who sometimes subdivide and rent to others. So a fundamental safety valve, this much romanticized frontier of free urban land, has largely ended.

The other major conclusion concerns the informal economy—the ability of poor people to improvise livelihoods through unrecorded economic activity like street vending, day labor, domestic service, or even subsistence crime. If anything, economic informality has been romanticized more than squatting, with vast claims about the ability of micro-entrepreneurship to leverage people out of poverty. Yet scores of case studies from around the world show ever more people squeezed into a limited number of survival niches: Too many rickshaw wallahs, too many street vendors, too many African women turning their shanties into shabeens to sell liquor, too many people taking in laundry, too many people queued up at work sites.

TD: In a way, aren't you saying that the former Third World is being turned into something like the Three Hundredth World?

Davis: What I'm saying is that the two principle mechanisms for accommodating the poor to cities in which the state long ago ceased to invest have reached their limits just when we're looking forward to two generations of continued high-speed growth in poor cities. The ominous but obvious question is: What lies beyond that frontier?

TD: Here's a quote from *Planet of Slums:* "With a literal great wall of high-tech border enforcement blocking large-scale migration to the rich countries, only the slum remains as a fully franchised solution to the problem of warehousing this century's surplus humanity."

Davis: The two major poor cities of nineteenth century Europe that fit our present model were Dublin and Naples, but nobody saw them as the future; and the reason there weren't more Dublins and Naples was, above all, the safety valve of the Atlantic emigration. Today, most of the south is, in fact, blocked from migrating. There's simply no precedent, for instance, for the kinds of borders Australia and Western Europe have constructed, essentially designed for total exclusion—except for a limited flow of high-skill labor. The American border with Mexico has historically been of a different kind. It acts as a dam to regulate the supply of labor, not to close it off completely. But more generally, for people in poor countries today, there aren't the options poor Europeans had back then.

Inexorable forces are expelling people from the countryside and that population, made surplus by the globalized economy, piles up in the slums, on city peripheries that are neither countryside, nor really city, and that urban theorists have difficulty wrapping their minds around.

In the United States, we would call them exurbia, but exurbs here are quite a different phenomena. If you look at American cities, the most striking thing is that exurban settlement—people who commute to edge cities from the former countryside are now living in McMansions on ever larger lots with more SUVs parked in front. They're making the traditional fifties Levittown suburb, with its ticky-tacky homes, its little cubicles of consumption, look environmentally efficient. In other words, as middle-class people move farther out, their environmental footprint goes up two or three shoe sizes.

The other side of this is the poorest people shoehorned into the most dangerous sites on tumbling hillsides, next to toxic waste dumps, living in flood plains, leading to every year's rising toll from natural disasters—less a measure of changing nature than the desperate wagers poor people have to make. In the large cities of the Third World, you do have the flight of some of the rich to gated communities far out in the suburbs, but what you mainly have is two-thirds of the slum dwellers of the world piled up in a kind of urban no-man's land.

TD: You've called this "existential ground zero."

Davis: It is, because it's urbanization without urbanity. An example of this is the case of the radical Islamist group that attacked Casablanca a few years ago—about 15 or 20 poor kids who grew up in the city but were in no sense part of it. They were born on the edge, not in traditional working-class and poor neighborhoods that support a fundamentalist Islam but not a nihilist one, or they were expelled from the countryside but never integrated into the city. In their slum worlds, the only kind of society or order was provided by mosques or Islamicist organizations.

According to one account, when these kids attacked the city, some of them had never been downtown before and this, for me, became a metaphor for what is happening across the world: a generation consigned to the urban dumping grounds, and not just in the poorest, most savage cities either.

Take Hyderabad, India's high-tech showcase, a city of 60,000 software workers and engineers where people duplicate the California lifestyle in Santa Clara Valley-like suburbs and you can go to Starbucks. Well, Hyderabad is surrounded by endless exterior slums, several million people. There are more rag pickers than software engineers. Some of these urban dwellers consigned to pick over the scraps of the high-tech economy had been expelled from more centrally located slums, torn down to make room for the research parks of the new middle class.

PART 2:
THE IMPERIAL CITY AND THE CITY OF SLUMS

TD: It occurs to me that, in Baghdad, the Bush administration has managed to create a weird version of the urban world you describe in *Planet of Slums*. There's the walled imperial Green Zone in the center of the city with its Starbucks and, outside it, the disintegrating capital as well as the vast slum of Sadr City—and the only exchange between the two is the missile-armed helicopters going one way and the car bombs heading the other.

Davis: Exactly. Baghdad becomes the paradigm with the breakdown of public space and ever less middle ground between the extremes. The integrated Sunni/Shia neighborhoods are rapidly being extinguished, not just by American action now, but by sectarian terror.

Sadr City, at one point named Saddam City, the Eastern

quadrant of Baghdad, has grown to grotesque proportions—two million poor people, mainly Shia. And it's still growing, as are Sunni slums by the way, thanks now not to Saddam but to disastrous American policies toward agriculture into which the U.S. has put almost no reconstruction money. Vast farmlands have been turned back into desert, while everything focused, however unsuccessfully, on restoration of the oil industry. The crucial thing would have been to preserve some equilibrium between countryside and city, but American policies just accelerated the flight from the land.

Of course, Green Zones are gated communities of a kind, the citadel within the larger fortress. You see this, too, emerging across the world. In my book, I counterpoised this to the growth of the peripheral slums—the middle class forsaking its traditional culture, along with the central city, to retreat into off-worlds with themed California lifestyles. Some of these are incredibly security conscious, real fortresses. Others are more typical American-style suburbs, but all of them are organized around an obsession with a fantasy America, and particularly the fantasy California universally franchised through TV.

So the *nouveau riche* in Beijing can commute by freeway to gated subdivisions with names like Orange County and Beverly Hills—there's a Beverly Hills in Cairo too, and a whole neighborhood themed by Walt Disney. Jakarta has the same thing— compounds where people live in imaginary Americas. These proliferate, emphasizing the rootlessness of the new urban middle class across the world. With this goes an obsessiveness about getting things as they are in the TV image. So you have actual Orange County architects designing "Orange County" outside Beijing. You have tremendous fidelity to the things the global middle class sees on television or in the movies.

TD: Just to leap to the other Bush urban project, something a little like this seems to be happening in New Orleans, no?

Davis: Absolutely. Unfortunately much of the white upper class in New Orleans would prefer to live in a totally phony, theme-park version of the historical New Orleans rather than confront the real task of reconstructing the city or living with an African-American majority. People's expectations of authenticity have long lost any reference point in reality. In *Ecology of Fear*, I pointed out how Universal Studios had extracted from Los Angeles its icons, miniaturized them, and put them in one gated, secure place called City Walk. And then you substitute going there—or the Las Vegas equivalent—for actually visiting the city. You visit the city's theme park, which is essentially a mall. If you had a casino, you'd have the full experience. In this process, the poor are increasingly cut off from access to the culture and public space of the city, while the wealthy voluntarily abdicate it to withdraw into what is now a generic universal space that differs little from country to country. The middle ground is falling apart.

But there are still big differences between culture zones and continents. In Latin America, what's most frightening is the degree of political polarization that occurs, the ferocity of middle-class resistance to the demands of the poor. Chavez has to get Cuban doctors, because he can only get a handful of Venezuelan doctors to work in the slums. The Middle East is very different. In Cairo, for instance, where the state has withdrawn or is too corrupt to provide essential services, the need is met by Islamic professionals. The Muslim Brotherhood has taken over the association of doctors, the association of engineers. Unlike the Latin American middle class, mobilizing just to preserve its privilege, it's organized to provide services, a parallel civil society, for the poor. Part of that arises from the Koranic obligation to tithe, but it's a striking difference with important effects on the life of the city.

TD: I want to take a brief side trip. The book you wrote before *Planet of Slums* was *The Monster at Our Door* on the avian flu and

I realize, as we talk, that it's thematically linked to *Planet of Slums* because it's also about a kind of planetary slumification— of agriculture.

Davis: A Dickensian world of Victorian poverty is being recreated, but on a scale that would have staggered the Victorians. So, naturally, you wonder whether the preoccupation of the Victorian middle classes with the diseases of the poor isn't returning as well. Their first reaction to epidemics was to move to Hampstead, to flee the city, to try to separate from the poor. Only when it was obvious that cholera was sweeping from the slums into middle-class areas anyway, did you get some investment in minimum sanitation and the public-health infrastructure. The illusion today, as in the nineteenth century, is that we can somehow separate ourselves, or wall ourselves off, or take flight from the diseases of the poor. I don't think most of us realize the huge, literally explosive concentrations for potential disease that exist.

More than twenty years ago, the leading infectious disease researchers in a series of volumes warned about new and reemerging diseases. Globalization, they observed, was causing planetary environmental instability and ecological change likely to shift the balance between humans and their microbes in a way that could bring about new plagues. They warned as well of the failure to create a disease-monitoring or public-health infrastructure commensurate with globalization.

In my book, I looked at the relationship between the pervasive global slum, everywhere associated with sanitation disasters, with classical conditions favoring the rapid movement of disease through human populations; and on the other side, I focused on how the transformation of livestock production was creating entirely new conditions for the emergence of diseases among animals and their transmission to humans.

Influenza is an important paradigm for infectious disease. Its ancient reservoir lies in the uniquely productive agricultural system of southern China with its long, intimate ecological association among wild birds, domestic birds, pigs, and humans. As for bird flu: On the one hand, you've created optimal conditions in the modern world for its spread; on the other hand, even the growth of poor cities has been increasing the demand for protein in people's diets and this demand can no longer be met by traditional protein sources; it's met by industrialized livestock production.

What that means quite simply is the urbanization of live-stock. Instead of fifteen or twenty chickens in someone's yard and a couple of hogs on the farm, we're talking about, around Bangkok for instance, a chicken-raising belt very similar to what you'd find in Arkansas or northwestern Georgia—millions of chickens living in warehouses, in factory farms. Bird densities like this have never existed in nature and they probably favor, according to epidemiologists I've talked to, maximum virulence, the accelerated evolution of diseases.

At the same time, wetlands around the world have been degraded and water diverted, usually for the sake of irrigated agriculture, displacing migratory wild birds to irrigated fields, rice paddies, farms. And all of this—the livestock revolution, the growing urban demand particularly for chicken (now the number two protein meat source on the planet), the growth of slums, the degradation of wetlands—has happened with particular speed in the last ten to fifteen years; and all of it we were warned about a generation ago by experts on infectious disease. This is ecological disorder of a very radical kind and it has changed the ecology of influenza and the conditions under which animal diseases pass to humans. It's also happened at a time when public health in much of the urban Third World has declined. One of the consequences of structural adjustment in the 1980s was to force hundreds of thousands of doctors, nurses, and public-health workers to emigrate, leaving Kenya or the Philippines to work in England or Italy.

This is a formula for biological disaster and avian flu is the second pandemic of globalization. It's very clear now that HIV/AIDS emerged at least partially through the bush-meat trade, as West Africans were forced to turn to bush meat because European factory ships were vacuuming up all the fish in the Gulf of Guinea, the major traditional source of protein in urban diets. There's also a hypothesis, with a lot of circumstantial evidence, that HIV probably reached a critical mass in Kinshasha [in the Congo], a great city that is the ultimate current example of what happens after the state collapses or withdraws.

So HIV, avian flu, SARS—another disease that emerged from the bush-meat trade, this time in the cities of southern China, and spread around the world with frightening speed. This is the future of disease . . .

TD: . . . and slumification.

Davis: Yes, disease in a world of slums. Something like the avian flu's spread to humanity is almost inevitable, given the combination of the global slum and large-scale shifts in the ecology of humans and animals. What's more troubling than the mere threat of a disease like avian flu, though, is the reaction to it—an immediate hoarding of vaccines and anti-virals, an exclusive focus on protecting the health of populations in a handful of rich countries which also monopolize the production of these lifeline medicines. In other words, the almost reflexive abandonment of the poor without a second thought. If avian flu happened not this year, but five years from now, the difference would be in the degree of protection in the United States, Germany, or England. The poor would be in the same place, particularly Africans who are most at risk because the HIV holocaust creates a population optimally susceptible to other infections.

TD: So that's one potential exchange between the imperial city and the slum city. The other virulent exchange is of violence, our wars on terror, drugs, whatever. I mean if you think about Vietnam and then Iraq, the jungle quite literally becomes the slum city in the annals of modern war.

Davis: Without minimizing the explosive social contradictions still stored up in the countryside, it's clear that the future of guerrilla warfare, insurrection against the world system, has moved into the city. Nobody has realized this with as much clarity as the Pentagon, or more vigorously tried to grapple with its empirical consequences. Its strategists are way ahead of geopoliticians and traditional foreign-relations types in understanding the significance of a world of slums . . .

TD: . . . and of global warming.

Davis: Yes, because they realize the potential instability it will create and also perhaps imagine advantageous shifts in the balance of power in its wake.

What the U.S. has demonstrated in recent years is an extraordinary ability to knock out the hierarchical organization of the modern city, to attack its crucial infrastructures and nodes, to blow up the TV stations, take out the pipelines and bridges. Smart bombs can do that, but simultaneously the Pentagon discovered that this technology isn't applicable to the slum periphery, to the labyrinthine, unmapped, almost unknown parts of the city which lack hierarchies, lack centralized infrastructures, lack tall buildings. There's really quite an extraordinary military literature trying to address what the Pentagon sees as the most novel terrain of this century, which it now models in the slums of Karachi, Port au Prince, and Baghdad. A lot of this goes back to the experience of Mogadishu [in 1993], which was a big shock to the United States and showed that traditional urban war-fighting methods don't work in the slum city.

TD: . . . Although nobody mentions that, while a small number of American soldiers were killed in the streets of Mogadishu and we were shocked, an unknown but vast number of Somalis also died, in the hundreds at least.

Davis: Well, you can commit carnage on a huge scale; you can kill thousands of people. What you lack the ability to do is surgically take out the crucial nodes because they hardly exist; because you're dealing neither with a hierarchical spatial system, nor generally with hierarchical organizations. I'm not sure the National Security Council understands this, but many military thinkers certainly do. If you read studies from the Army War College, for example, you discover a different geopolitics from that embraced by the Bush administration. The war-planners don't emphasize axes of evil or over-arching conspiracies, instead they stress the terrain—the sprawling peripheral slum and the opportunities it provides to a miscellany of opponents—drug barons, al-Qaeda, revolutionary organizations, religious cults—to carve out fiefdoms. As a result, Pentagon theorists are studying architecture and urban-planning theory. They're using GIS technology and satellites to fill in missing knowledge, because the state usually knows very little about its own slum peripheries.

The question of the exchange of violence between the city of slums and the imperial city is linked to a deeper question—the question of agency. How will this very large minority of humanity that now lives in cities but is exiled from the formal world economy find its future? What is its capacity for historical agency? The traditional working class—as Marx pointed out in the *Communist Manifesto*—was a revolutionary class for two reasons: because it had no stake in the existing order, but also because it was centralized by the process of modern industrial production. It possessed enormous potential social power to go on strike, simply shut down production, take over the factories.

Well, here you have an informal working class with no strategic place in production, in the economy, that has nonetheless discovered a new social power—the power to disrupt the city, to strike at the city, ranging from the creative nonviolence of the people in El Alto, the vast slum twin of La Paz, Bolivia, where residents regularly barricade the road to the airport or cut off transport to make their demands, to the now universal use of car bombs by nationalist and sectarian groups to strike at middle-class neighborhoods, financial districts, even green zones. I think there's much global experimentation, trying to find out how to use the power of disruption.

TD: I'll tell you what I suspect may be the greatest of disruptive powers—the power to disrupt global energy flows. Poor people with minimal technology are capable of doing that across the thousands of miles of unguardable pipeline on this planet.

Davis: In that sense, you already see elements of an emergent campaign. In the last month alone, there was an attempted car bombing of Saudi Arabia's major oil facility and the first car bombing in the Niger Delta in Nigeria. It didn't hurt anybody, but it did raise the stakes.

TD: You end *Planet of Slums* on this note: "If the empire can deploy Orwellian technologies of repression, its outcasts have the gods of chaos on their side."

Davis: And chaos is not always a force for bad. The worst case scenario is simply when people are silenced. Their exile becomes permanent. The implicit triaging of humanity occurs. People are assigned to die and forgotten about in the same way we forget about the AIDS holocaust or become immune to famine appeals.

The rest of the world needs to be woken up and the slum poor are experimenting with a huge variety of ideologies, platforms, means of using disorder—from almost apocalyptic attacks on modernity itself to avant-garde attempts to invent new modernities, new kinds of social movements. But one of the fundamental problems is that, when you have so many people fighting for jobs and space, the obvious way to regulate them is through the emergence of godfathers, tribal chieftains, ethnic leaders, operating on principles of ethnic, religious, or racial exclusion. This tends to create self-perpetuating, almost eternal wars among the poor themselves. So, in the same poor city, you find a multiplicity of contradictory tendencies—people embracing the Holy Ghost, or joining street gangs, or enlisting in radical social organizations, or becoming clients of sectarian or populist politicians.

TD: Just a last observation: You're often thought of as an apocalypt, a prophet of hopeless, catastrophic doom, but almost everything you write is actually about the human contribution to catastrophe, the way we refuse to come to grips with the realities of our world; and so, to my mind, your work always has an element of use and of hope in it. After all, if it's a human contribution, it's also obviously something that we could humanly avoid or deal with differently.

Davis: Well, my obligation is to try to be as clear-sighted and honest as possible about my beliefs, the ideas I'm compelled to hold from my research and observation—and from my limited life experience. I feel no obligation to sweeten any of this with dollops of so-called optimism. Somebody once denounced *Ecology of Fear* for its almost erotic enjoyment of apocalypse, which said to me that it was either badly written or badly read; because, for instance, in one chapter about the literature of apocalypse in Los Angeles, I make clear that the enjoyment of apocalypse usually tends to be a kind of racist voyeurism.

But finally it's important to remember the true meaning of apocalypse in the Abrahamic religions, which is, ultimately, in the end time, at the end of history, the revelation of history's real text, real narrative, not the one written by the ruling classes, by the scribes of power. It's the history written from below. That's why I've always had a great interest in the religions of the oppressed, why I've given—some people think uncritical—attention to phenomena like Pentecostalism.

TD: So is our collective future simply likely to be a downhill ride to destruction?

Davis: The city is our ark in which we might survive the environmental turmoil of the next century. Genuinely urban cities are the most environmentally efficient form of existing with nature that we possess because they can substitute public luxury for private or household consumption. They can square the circle between environmental sustainability and a decent standard of living. I mean, however big your library is or vast your swimming pool, it'll never be the same as the New York Public Library or a great public pool. No mansion, no San Simeon, will ever be the equivalent of Central Park or Broadway.

One of the major problems, however, is: We're building cities without urban qualities. Poor cities, in particular, are consuming the natural areas and watersheds which are essential to their functioning as environmental systems, to their ecological sustainability, and they're consuming them either because of destructive private speculation or simply because poverty pours over into every space. All around the world, the crucial watersheds and green spaces that cities need to function ecologically and be truly urban are being urbanized by poverty and by speculative private development. Poor cities, as a result, are becoming increasingly vulnerable to disaster, pandemic, and catastrophic resource shortages, particularly of water.

Conversely, the most important step toward coping with global environmental change is to reinvest—massively—in the social and physical infrastructures of our cities, and thereby reemploy tens of millions of poor youth. It should haunt us that Jane Jacobs—who saw so clearly that the wealth of nations is created by cities not nations—should have devoted her last, visionary book to the specter of a coming dark age.

11. The Delusions of Global Hegemony

Andrew Bacevich

MAY 23, 2005

I wait for him on a quiet, tree and wisteria-lined street of red-brick buildings. Students, some in short-sleeves on this still crisp spring morning, stream by. I'm seated on cold, stone steps next to a sign announcing the Boston University Department of International Relations. He turns the corner and advances, wearing a blue blazer, blue shirt and tie, and khaki slacks and carrying a computer in a black bag. He's white haired, has a nicely weathered face, and the squared shoulders and upright bearing of a man, born in Normal, Illinois, who attended West Point, fought in the Vietnam War, and then had a twenty-year military career that ended in 1992.

Now a professor of history at Boston University, he directs me to a spacious, airy office whose floor-to-ceiling windows look out on the picturesque street. A tasseled cap and gown hang on a hook behind the door—perhaps because another year of graduation is not far off. I'm left briefly to wait while he deals with an anxious student, there to discuss his semester mark. Soon enough though, he seats himself behind a large desk with a cup of coffee and prepares to discuss his subjects of choice, American militarism and the American imperial mission.

Andrew Bacevich is a man on a journey—as he himself is the first to admit. A cultural conservative, a former contributor to such magazines as the *Weekly Standard* and the *National Review*, a former Bush Fellow at the American Academy in Berlin, he discovered sometime in the 1990s that his potential conservative allies on foreign policy had fallen in love with the idea of the American military and its imagined awesome power to change the world. They had jumped the tracks and left him behind. A professed cold warrior, in those years he took a new look at our American past—and he's not stopped looking, or reconsidering, since.

What he discovered was the American empire, which became the title of a book he published in 2002. In 2005, his fierce, insightful book on American dreams of global military supremacy, *The New American Militarism, How Americans Are Seduced by War*, appeared. It would have been eye-opening no matter who had written it, but given his background it was striking indeed.

Forceful and engaged (as well as engaging), Bacevich throws himself into the topic at hand. He has a barely suppressed dramatic streak and a willingness to laugh heartily at himself. But most striking are the questions that stop him. Just as you imagine a scholar should, he visibly turns over your questions in his mind, thinking about what may be new in them.

He takes a sip of coffee and, in a no-nonsense manner, suggests that we begin.

Tomdispatch: In a *Los Angeles Times* op-ed, you said the revolt of the retired generals against Secretary of Defense Rumsfeld represented the beginning of a search for a scapegoat for the Iraq War.

I wondered whether you also considered it a preemptive strike against the Bush administration's future Iran policy.

Andrew Bacevich: The answer is yes. It's both really. Certainly, it's become incontrovertible that the Iraq War is not going to end happily. Even if we manage to extricate ourselves and some sort of stable Iraq emerges from the present chaos, arguing that the war lived up to the expectations of the Bush administration is going to be very difficult. My own sense is that the officer corps—and this probably reflects my personal experience to a great degree—is fixated on Vietnam and still believes the military was hung out to dry there. The officer corps came out of the Vietnam War determined never to repeat that experience and some officers are now angry to discover that the Army is once again stuck in a quagmire. So we are in the early stages of a long argument about who is to be blamed for the Iraq debacle. I think, to some degree, the revolt of the generals reflects an effort on the part of senior military officers to weigh in, to lay out the military's case. And the military's case is: We're not at fault. They are; and, more specifically, he is—with Rumsfeld being the stand-in for [Vietnam-era Secretary of Defense] Robert McNamara.

Having said that, with all the speculation about Bush administration interest in expanding the Global War on Terror to include Iran, I suspect the officer corps, already seeing the military badly overstretched, doesn't want to have any part of such a war. Going public with attacks on Rumsfeld is one way of trying to slow whatever momentum there is toward an Iran war.

I must say, I don't really think we're on a track to have a war with Iran any time soon—maybe I'm too optimistic here [he laughs]—but I suspect even the civilian hawks understand that the United States is already overcommitted, that to expand the war on terror to a new theater, the Iranian theater, would in all likelihood have the most dire consequences, globally and in Iraq.

TD: Actually, I was planning to ask about your thoughts on the possibility of an Iranian October surprise.

Bacevich: You mean, attacking Iran before the upcoming fall election? I don't see Karl Rove—because an October surprise would be a political ploy—signing off on it. I think he's cunning, calculating, devious, but not stupid. With the President's popularity rating plummeting due to unhappiness with the ongoing war, it really would be irrational to think that yet another war would turn that around or secure continued Republican control of both houses of Congress.

TD: It seems that way to me with gas assumedly soaring to $120 a barrel or something like that . . .

Bacevich: Oh gosh, oh my gosh, yes . . .

TD: But let me throw this into the mix, because I've seen no one mention it: If you look at the list of retired commanders who came out against Rumsfeld, they're all from the Army or Marines. We always say the military is overextended, but only part of it is—and I note the absence of admirals or anybody connected to the Air Force.

Bacevich: That's a good point. One could argue that the revolt of the generals actually has a third source. If the first source is arguing about who's going to take the fall for Iraq and the second is trying to put a damper on war in Iran, the third has to do with Rumsfeld's military transformation project. To oversimplify, transformation begins with the conviction that the military since the end of the Cold War has failed to adapt to the opportunities and imperatives of the information age. Well before 9/11, the central part of Rumsfeld's agenda was to "transform"—that was his word—this old Cold-War-style military, to make it lighter, more agile, to emphasize information technology and precision weapons.

Well, if you're in the Air Force, or you're a Navy admiral, particularly one in the aviation community, that recipe sounds pretty good. It sounds like dollars, like programs being funded. But if you're in the Army or the Marine Corps, becoming lighter and more agile sounds like cutting divisions or like getting rid of tanks and artillery; it sounds like a smaller Marine Corps.

Both the initial stage of the Afghanistan War and the invasion of Iraq were specifically designed by Rumsfeld as projects to demonstrate what a transformed military could do. Hence, his insistence on beginning the Iraq War without a major build-up, on invading with a relatively small force, on having the ground intervention accompany the air campaign rather than having a protracted air campaign first as in the first Gulf War. All the literature about both Afghanistan and Iraq now shows that the war-planning process was filled with great civil/military tension. The generals argued, "Mr. Secretary, here's the plan; we want to do a Desert Storm Two against Iraq," and Rumsfeld kept replying, "I want something smaller, think it over again and get back to me"—reflecting his intention to demonstrate his notion of how America will henceforth fight its wars.

Well, now we can see the outcome and it's at best ambiguous. That is to say, the early stages of Afghanistan and Iraq proved to be smashing successes. The smaller, agile forces performed remarkably well in demolishing both the Taliban and the Baath Party regime; but in both cases, genuine victory has proven enormously elusive. This gets us to the third basis for the generals' gripe. When they talk about Rumsfeld's incompetence and micromanagement, they're arguing against the transformation project and on behalf of those services which have footed most of the bill.

TD: Just to throw one other thing into the mix, if there were a campaign against Iran, it would be a Navy and Air Force one.

Bacevich: It would *begin* with a Navy and Air Force campaign, but it wouldn't end that way. If the Army generals could be assured that we know exactly where the Iranian nuclear program is, that we have the targeting data and the munitions to take it out . . . Well, that would be one thing, but we don't have that assurance. From the Army and Marine Corps perspective, an air attack might begin a war with Iran, but the war would not end there. As is the case in both Afghanistan and Iraq, some sort of ugly aftermath would be sure to follow and the Navy and the Air Force aren't going to be there, at least not in large numbers.

TD: What about the Iraq War at present?

Bacevich: There are a couple of important implications that we have yet to confront. The war has exposed the limited depth of American military power. I mean, since the end of the Cold War we Americans have been beating our chests about being the greatest military power the world has ever seen. [His voice rises.] Overshadowing the power of the Third Reich! Overshadowing the Roman Empire!

Wait a sec. This country of 290 million people has a force of about 130,000 soldiers committed in Iraq, fighting something on the order of 10–20,000 insurgents and a) we're in a war we can't win, b) we're in the fourth year of a war we probably can't sustain much longer. For those who believe in the American imperial project, and who see military supremacy as the foundation of that empire, this ought to be a major concern: What are we going to do to strengthen the sinews of American military power, because it's turned out that our vaunted military supremacy is not what it was cracked up to be. If you're like me and you're quite skeptical about this imperial project, the stresses imposed on the military and the obvious limits of our power simply serve to emphasize the imperative of rethinking our role in the world so we can back away from this unsustainable notion of global hegemony.

Then, there's the matter of competence. I object to the generals saying that our problems in Iraq are all due to the micromanagement and incompetence of Mr. Rumsfeld—I do think he's a micromanager and a failure and ought to have been fired long ago—because it distracts attention from the *woeful* performance of the senior military leaders who have really made a hash of the Iraq insurgency. I remember General Swannack in particular blaming Rumsfeld for Abu Ghraib. I'll saddle Rumsfeld with about 10 percent of the blame for Abu Ghraib, the other 90 percent rests with the senior American military leaders in Baghdad . . .

TD: General Ricardo Sanchez signed off on it . . .

Bacevich: Sanchez being number one. So again, if one is an enthusiast for American military supremacy, we have some serious thinking to do about the quality of our senior leadership. Are we picking the right people to be our two, three, and four-star commanders? Are we training them, educating them properly for the responsibilities that they face? The Iraq War has revealed some major weaknesses in that regard.

TD: Do you think that the neocons and their mentors, Rumsfeld and the Vice President, believed too deeply in the hype of American hyperpower? Ruling groups, even while manipulating others, often seem to almost hypnotically convince themselves as well.

Bacevich: That's why I myself tend not to buy into the charge that Bush and others blatantly lied us into this war. I think they believed most of what they claimed. You should probably put believe in quotes, because it amounts to talking yourself into it. They believed that American omnipotence, as well as know-how and determination, could imprint democracy on Iraq. They really believed that, once they succeeded in Iraq, a whole host of ancillary benefits were going to ensue, transforming the political landscape of the Middle East. All of those expectations were bizarre delusions and we're paying the consequences now.

You know, the neoconservatives that mattered were not those in government like Douglas Feith or people on the National Security Council staff, but the writers and intellectuals outside of government who, in the period from the late seventies through the nineties, were constantly weaving this narrative of triumphalism, pretending to insights about power and the direction of history. Intellectuals can put their imprint on public discourse. They can create an environment, an atmosphere. When the events of September 11, 2001, left Americans shocked and frightened and people started casting about for an explanation, a way of framing a response, the neoconservative perspective was front and center and had a particular appeal. So these writers and intellectuals did influence policy, at least for a brief moment.

TD: Here's something that puzzles me. When I look at administration actions, I see a Middle Eastern catastrophe in the midst of which an Iranian situation is being ratcheted up. Then there's China, once upon a time the enemy of choice for the neocons and Rumsfeld, and now here we are this summer having the largest naval maneuvers since Vietnam, four carrier task forces, off the Chinese coast. Then—as with Cheney's recent speech—there's the attempted rollback of what's left of the USSR, which has been ongoing. On the side, you've got the Pentagon pushing little Latin American bases all the way down to Paraguay. So many fronts, so much overstretch, and no backing down that I can see. What do you make of this?

Bacevich: My own sense is that this administration has largely exhausted its stock of intellectual resources; that, for the most part, they're preoccupied with trying to manage Iraq. Beyond that, I'm hard-pressed to see a coherent strategy in the Middle East or elsewhere. In that sense, Iraq *is* like Vietnam. It just sucks up all the oxygen. Having said that, before being eclipsed by 9/11 and its aftermath, China was indeed the enemy-designate of the hawks, and a cadre of them is still active in Washington. I would guess that large naval exercises reflect their handiwork. Still, I don't think there's been a resolution within the political elite of exactly how we ought to view China and what the U.S. relationship with China will be.

Why the hell we're extending bases into Latin America is beyond me. Rumsfeld just announced that he has appointed an admiral as the head of U.S. Southern Command. Now this has almost always been an Army billet, once or twice a Marine billet, never a Navy one. I got an email today from someone who suggested that this was another example of Rumsfeld's "boldness." My response was: Well, if he was bold, he'd simply shut down the Southern Command. Wouldn't it be a wonderful way to communicate that U.S.-Latin American relations had matured to the point where they no longer revolved around security concerns? Wouldn't it be interesting for Washington to signal that there is one region of the world that does not require U.S. military supervision; that we really don't need to have some four-star general parading around from country to country in the manner of some proconsul supervising his quarter of the American Empire?

Now, I have friends who think that [Venezuelan President

Hugo] Chavez poses a threat to the United States. I find that notion utterly preposterous, but it does reflect this inclination to see any relationship having any discord or dissonance as requiring a security—i.e., military—response. I find it all crazy and contrary to our own interests.

TD: One thing that's ratcheted up in recent years is the way the Pentagon's taken over so many aspects of policy, turning much of diplomacy into military-to-military relations.

Bacevich: If you look at long-term trends, going back to the early Cold War, the Defense Department has accrued ever more influence and authority at the expense of the State Department. But there's another piece to this—within the Defense Department itself, as the generals and the senior civilians have vied with one another for clout. When Rumsfeld and [Paul] Wolfowitz came into office they were determined to shift the balance of civil/military authority within the Pentagon. They were intent on trimming the sails of the generals. You could see this in all kinds of ways, some symbolic. Regional commanders used to be called CINCs, the acronym for commander-in-chief. Rumsfeld said: Wait a minute, there's only one commander-in-chief and that's my boss, so you generals who work for me, you're not commanders-in-chief any more. Now the guy who runs U.S. Southern Command is just a "combatant commander."

Also indicative of this effort to shift power back to the civilians is the role played by the Joint Chiefs of Staff, which has been nonexistent for all practical purposes. Accounts of the planning and conduct of the Afghanistan and Iraq Wars make clear that they had virtually no influence at all. They were barely, barely consulted. Ever since Colin Powell was chairman of the Joint Chiefs and became a quasi-independent power broker, presidents have chosen weak chairmen. Presidents want top officers to be accommodating rather than forceful personalities who might hold independent views. I'm sure General Myers of the Air Force is a wonderful man and a patriot, but he served four years as chairman after 9/11 and did so without leaving any discernible mark on policy. And that's not accidental. It reflects Rumsfeld's efforts to wrest authority back towards the office of the Secretary of Defense.

TD: Isn't this actually part of a larger pattern in which authority is wrested from everywhere and brought into this commander-in-chief presidency?

Bacevich: That's exactly right. I've just finished a review of *Cobra II,* this new book by Michael Gordon and Bernard Trainor. A major theme of the book is that people like Cheney, Rumsfeld, and Wolfowitz saw 9/11 as a great opportunity. Yes, it was a disaster. Yes, it was terrible. But by God, this was a disaster that could be turned to enormous advantage. Here lay the chance to remove constraints on the exercise of American military power, enabling the Bush administration to shore up, expand, and perpetuate U.S. global hegemony. Toward that end, senior officials concocted this notion of a Global War on Terror, really a cover story for an effort to pacify and transform the broader Middle East, a gargantuan project which is doomed to fail. Committing the United States to that project presumed a radical redistribution of power within Washington. The hawks had to cut off at the knees institutions or people uncomfortable with the unconstrained exercise of American power. And who was that? Well, that was the CIA. That was the State Department, especially the State Department of Secretary Colin Powell. That was the Congress —note this weird notion that the Congress is somehow limiting Presidential prerogatives—and the hawks also had to worry about the uniformed military, whom they considered "averse to risk" and incapable of understanding modern warfare in an information age.

TD: And you might throw in the courts. After all, the two men appointed to the Supreme Court are, above all else, believers in the unitary executive theory of the presidency.

Bacevich Yes, it fits. I would emphasize that it's not because Cheney, Rumsfeld, and Wolfowitz are diabolical creatures intent on doing evil. They genuinely believe it's in the interests of the United States, and the world, that unconstrained American power should determine the shape of the international order. I think they vastly overstate our capabilities. For all of their supposed worldliness and sophistication, I don't think they understand the world. I am persuaded that their efforts will only lead to greater mischief while undermining our democracy. Yet I don't question that, at some gut level, they think they are acting on your behalf and mine. They are all the more dangerous as a result.

PART 2:
DRIFTING DOWN THE PATH TO PERDITION

TD: I'd like to turn to the issue of oil wars, energy wars. That seems to be what holds all this incoherent stuff together—minds focused on a world of energy flows. Recently, I reread [President Jimmy] Carter's 1979 energy speech. Isn't it ironic that he got laughed out of the room for his sweater and for urging a future of alternative fuels on us, while we latched onto his Rapid Deployment Force for the Persian Gulf? As you argue in your book, *The New Militarism*, this essentially starts us on what you call "World War IV."

Bacevich: I remember the Carter speech. I was a relatively young man at the time. In general, I have voted for Republicans, although not this Republican in 2004. But I did vote for Carter because I was utterly disenchanted with [President Richard] Nixon and [his National Security Advisor Henry] Kissinger. [President Gerald] Ford seemed weak, incompetent. And I remember being dismayed by the Carter speech because it seemed so out of sync with the American spirit. It wasn't optimistic; it did not promise that we would have more tomorrow than we have today, that the future would be bigger and better. Carter essentially said: If we are serious about freedom, we must really think about what freedom means—and it ought to mean something more than acquisition and conspicuous consumption. And if we're going to preserve our freedom, we have to start living within our means.

It did not set well with me at the time. Only when I was writing my militarism book did I take another look at the speech and then it knocked me over. I said to myself: This guy got it. I don't know how, but he really got it in two respects. First, he grasped the essence of our national predicament, of being seduced by a false and even demeaning definition of freedom. Second, he understood that cheap oil was the drug that was leading us willy-nilly down this path. The two were directly and intimately linked: a growing dependence on seemingly cheap foreign oil and our inability to recognize what we might call the ongoing cultural crisis of our time.

Carter gives the so-called malaise speech, I think, in July '79. The Russians invade Afghanistan in December '79. Then comes Carter's State of the Union Address in January 1980 in which he, in a sense, recants, abandoning the argument of July and saying, by God, the Persian Gulf is of vital interest to the United States and we'll use any means necessary in order to prevent somebody

else from controlling it. To put some teeth in this threat he creates the Rapid Deployment Joint Task Force, which sets in
motion the militarization of U.S. policy that has continued ever
since. So, July 1979 to January 1980, that's the pivotal moment
that played such an important role in bringing us to where we are
today. But of course we didn't understand that then—certainly I
didn't. In July 1979, Carter issued a prescient warning. We didn't
want to listen. So we blew it.

Fast forward to 2006, and President Bush is telling us, thank
you very much, that we're addicted to oil. I heard [House Minority
Leader] Nancy Pelosi on the radio over the weekend saying that the
Democrats now have a plan to make us energy independent by
2020. She's lying through her teeth. There's no way anybody can
make us energy independent by then. We needed to start back
in 1979, if not before. Even to achieve independence from Persian
Gulf oil will be an enormously costly, painful process that none of
the politicians in either party are willing to undertake. Gas is now
roughly three dollars a gallon. I heard some guy on a talk show the
other day say: "Whaddya think we should do? I think we should all
park our cars on the Interstate and stop traffic until the government
does something." What does he actually want the government to
do, I wondered? Conquer another country?

We Americans are in deep denial, unwilling to accept that
we're going to have to change the way we live for our own good.
Empire does not offer the recipe for preserving our freedom.
Learning to live within our means just might. Jimmy Carter was
the one guy, back in July of '79, who really had the guts to say
that. Unfortunately, he didn't have the guts to stick with it.

TD: I always wonder what would have happened if we had
dumped a bunch of money into R&D for alternative fuels
back then.

Bacevich: The funding for the Iraq War is now in the hundreds of billions of dollars. [Economist] Joseph Stiglitz projects that total costs could go to $2 trillion. What would a trillion dollars have done for research into alternative fuels? I don't know, but something . . . something! What do you get for a trillion dollars in Iraq? Nothin'. It's just nuts!

TD: I was amused, by the way, that you were born in Normal, Illinois . . .

Bacevich: . . . because the Normal School of the State of Illinois, the teacher's college, was there.

TD: I was also thinking about stereotypes of military men. You know, rigidity of mind and the like. What strikes me in your writings is that you seem more open to rethinking your worldview than almost any scholar around. So I was curious about the evolution of your thought.

Bacevich: Two key moments for me were the end of the Cold War and the Iraq War. The simple story would be that, for the first twenty-some years of my adult life, which coincided with the latter stages of the Cold War, I was a serving officer. I was a cold warrior in uniform. I therefore accepted the orthodox narrative of the Cold War and of the postwar era more generally. I was not oblivious to policy errors we had made and some of the sins we had committed, but as long as I was in uniform I was willing to accept that these were peripheral to the larger narrative. I did retain this notion that the Cold War was an emergency, a very long, serious one in which we as a nation had been called upon to depart from the norm. This was not the way things were supposed to be, particularly in regard to a globally deployed military establishment.

TD: Let me back you up for a moment to Vietnam. You fought there . . .

Bacevich: 1970–71.

TD: . . . and how did you come out of Vietnam?

Bacevich: For a variety of personal reasons, my wife and I decided to stay in the Army after my obligation was up . . . [He hesitates.] For those who are not familiar with military service, it may be difficult to appreciate the extent to which that life is all embracing. It's like being a monk. It's a calling. Soldiers work real hard. And much of that work is peculiarly satisfying. For most of my time in the service, women were few in number and on the margins. So it was a very masculine environment. This might seem retro, but men living among men and doing manly things [he laughs], there is a peculiar savor to that. At any rate, I bought into the institutional view of Vietnam—that *we* had been screwed. The politicians had screwed us; the media had screwed us; the American people had screwed us. They had let us down, and so my commitment was to an institution that, after Vietnam, was engaged in a comprehensive effort to reconstitute and restore itself—and its standing in American society.

In that context, the questions I was willing to ask about Vietnam or about U.S. foreign policy more generally were fairly narrow. Since getting out of the Army, since trying to make sense of the Cold War and U.S. foreign policy from a different perspective, I've come to see the Vietnam War differently as well. I can accept to some degree the argument that the meaning of Vietnam is to be found in the-military-gets-hung-out-to-dry, but that's not sufficient. And I've come to see the war as just utterly unnecessary, misguided, and mistaken. A monumental miscalculation that never should have happened, but that did happen due to some deep-seated defects in the way we see ourselves and see the world.

In any case, the Cold War essentially ends in 1989 when the [Berlin] Wall goes down; in '91, the Soviet Union collapses. I get out of the Army in 1992 and I'm waiting with bated breath to see what impact the end of the Cold War is going to have on U.S. policy, particularly military policy. The answer is, essentially, none. We come out even more firmly committed to the notion of U.S. military global supremacy. Not because there was an enemy—in 1992, '93, '94, there's no enemy—but because we've come to see military supremacy and global hegemony as good in and of themselves.

The end of the Cold War sees us using military power more frequently, while our ambitions, our sense of what we're supposed to do in the world, become more grandiose. There's all this bloated talk about "the end of history," and the "right side of history," and the "indispensable nation," politicians and pundits pretending to know the destiny of humankind. So I began to question my understanding of what had determined U.S. behavior during the Cold War. The orthodox narrative said that the U.S. behaved as it did because of *them*, because of external threats. I came to believe that explanation was not entirely wrong but limited. You get closer to the truth by recognizing that what makes us behave the way we behave comes from inside. I came to buy into the views of historians like Charles Beard and William Appleton Williams who emphasize that foreign policy is an outgrowth of domestic policy, in particular of the structure of the American political economy.

So I became a critic of U.S. foreign policy in the 1990s, a pretty outspoken one.

TD: You wrote a book then with the word "empire" in the title . . .

Bacevich: Yes, because I became convinced that what we saw in the '90s from both Democrats and Republicans was an effort to expand an informal American empire. Fast forward to 9/11 and its aftermath, and the Bush doctrine of preventive war as implemented in Iraq, and the full dimensions of our imperial ambitions become evident for all to see.

I have to say, I certainly supported the Afghanistan War. I emphatically believed that we had no choice but to take down the Taliban regime in order to demonstrate clearly the consequences of any nation tolerating, housing, supporting terrorists who attack us. But the Iraq War just struck me as so unnecessary, unjustifiable, and reckless that . . . I don't know how to articulate its impact except that it put me unalterably in the camp of those who had come to see American power as the problem, not the solution. And it brought me close to despair that the response of the internal opposition and of the American people generally proved to be so tepid, so ineffective. It led me to conclude that we are in deep, deep trouble.

An important manifestation of that trouble is this short-sighted infatuation with military power that goes beyond even what I wrote about in my most recent book. Again, it revolves around this question of energy and oil. There's such an unwillingness to confront the dilemmas we face as a people that I find deeply troubling. I know we're a democracy. We have elections. But it's become a procedural democracy. Our politics are not really meaningful. In a meaningful politics, you and I could argue about important differences, and out of that argument might come not resolution or reconciliation, but at least an awareness of the consequences of going your way as opposed to mine. We don't even have that argument. That's what's so dismaying.

TD: You've used the word "crusade" and spoken of this

administration as "intoxicated with the mission of salvation."
I was wondering what kind of "ism" you think we've been
living with in these years?

Bacevich: That's a great question, and it's not enough to say that
it's democratic capitalism. Certainly, our "ism" incorporates a
religious dimension—in the sense of believing that God created
this nation for a purpose that has to do with universal values.

We have not as a people come to terms with our relationship
to military power and to the wars we've engaged in and the ways
we've engaged in them. Now, James Carroll in his new book,
House of War, is very much preoccupied with strategic bombing
in World War II and since, and especially with our use of, and
attitude toward, nuclear weapons. His preoccupation is under-
standable because those are the things we can't digest and we
can't cough up. You know, at the end of the day, we, the missionary nation, the crusader state, certain of our righteousness,
remain the only people to have used nuclear weapons in anger—
indeed, to have used them as a weapon of terror.

TD: Air power, even though hardly covered in our media in Iraq,
has been the American way of war since World War II, hasn't it?

Bacevich: Certainly that "ism" that defines us has a large technological component, doesn't it? I mean, we are the people of technology. We see the future as a technological one and can't
imagine a problem that doesn't have technological solutions . . .

TD: . . . except when it comes to oil.

Bacevich: Quite true. In many respects, the technological artifact
that defines the last century is the airplane. With the airplane
came a distinctive style of warfare. The Italians dropped the first

bomb in North Africa; the Japanese killed their share of civilians from the air as did the Germans, but we and our British cousins outdid them all. I've been thinking more and more that our record of strategic bombing is not simply an issue of historical interest.

We are not who we believe we are and, in some sense, others perceive us more accurately than we do ourselves. The President has described a version of history—as did Clinton, by the way— beginning with World War II in which the United States is the liberator, Americans are the bringers of freedom. There is truth to that narrative, but it's not the whole truth; and, quite frankly, it's not the truth that matters a lick, let's say, to the Islamic world today. Muslims don't give a darn that we brought Hitler or the Third Reich to its knees. What they're aware of is all kinds of other behavior, particularly in their neck of the woods, that had nothing to do with spreading democracy and freedom, that had everything to do with power, with trying to establish relations that maximized the benefit to the United States and American society. We don't have to let our hearts bleed about that. That's the way politics works, but let's not delude ourselves either. When President George W. Bush says, "America stands for freedom and liberty, and we're coming to liberate you," it's absurd to expect people in that part of the world to take us seriously. That's not what they've seen and known and experienced in dealing with the United States.

TD: And, of course, within the councils of this administration, they threw out anyone who knew anything about the record of U.S. policy in the Islamic world.

Bacevich: Because those experts would have challenged the ideologically soaked version of history that this administration has attempted to carry over into the twenty-first century. Only if we begin to see ourselves more clearly, will we be able to understand how others see us. We need to revise the narrative of the American Century and recognize that it has been about a host of other things that are far more problematic than liberation. There can be no understanding the true nature of the American Century without acknowledging the reality of Hiroshima, Nagasaki, Dresden, Hanoi, and Haiphong.

TD: Do you, by the way, think that the reality-based community is catching up with the Bush administration?

Bacevich: It's catching up, but is it in a way that has political consequences? If we just toss Bush out and bring in . . . Who? Senator Clinton or John McCain? Will things be different? Somehow, I don't think so. Of course, there is something to be said for competence even in implementing a bad policy. Right now, we have incompetents implementing a bad policy, but the essence of the problem is the policy—not just the Iraq War but this paradigm of a Global War on Terror, this notion of unconstraining American power. That's what we have to rethink.

TD: Your thoughts on three military matters: what might be called the religionizing of the military; the Bush administration's setting up of a Northern Command in 2002 for the so-called homeland, which I find disturbing; and finally, what do you make of the now-normalized practice of presenting the costs of war-fighting as a non-Defense Department budget supplementary item?

Bacevich: I think the last thing in your list is outlandish and irresponsible. It's as if we're keeping two sets of books. But again, the administration abetted by the Congress plays these games and nobody seems to care. Still, it doesn't change the facts—that we're spending more on defense than the rest of the world put together. That has no precedent. And are we becoming safer and more secure and more prosperous? If we're not yet secure, does that mean we should be spending twice again as much? I have friends who think we should, or who at least believe that the defense budget is inadequate. I myself think that the flinging of money at the Defense Department ought to prompt Americans to reconsider the notion that the solution to our problems is to be found in the realm of military power.

I think the evangelizing issue reflects at least three things. Number one, the elite disengagement from the military after Vietnam. The Episcopalians don't sign up anymore, or the Presbyterians. Number two, the heightened political engagement of Christian evangelicals who, by the 1960s, had embarked on a crusade to save America from itself. Evangelicals have long seen the U.S. military as allies in that cause. American society may be going to hell in a hand basket with its promiscuity, its pornography, its divorce rates, its abortion, its women's rights, all these things evangelicals lament, but the military's a bastion of traditional virtue. Now, they misperceive soldiers in that regard, but I think that's one reason military service has a special appeal for evangelical Christians.

Third comes the politicization of the military. When I first became an officer, the tradition of being apolitical was still deeply rooted. As one consequence of Vietnam, that went away. The officer corps came to see its interests as lying with the political right. Evangelical Christianity is just part of a larger mix.

TD: So, you have an all-embracing world that has become more politicized, that's moved south, and that has few new streams of blood heading into it, unlike in the era of the draft or of the World War. What are the results of the military becoming less and less like American society?

Bacevich: I think it's bad news. The only good news—this is pure speculation as there's no evidence for it—might be that since the Iraq War is the handiwork of a conservative, evangelical, Republican President, perhaps members of the officer corps will begin to rethink where their loyalties should lie and will come to the realization that hitching their flag to the Republican Party is not necessarily good for their institutional interests. The officer corps loved [President Ronald] Reagan. He saved the military. And here we have, according to some people, the most Reaganite president since Reagan who seems to be doing his darnedest to destroy the military. That might have some impact.

TD: About a year ago you said, "The only way I can envision a meaningful political change along the lines that I would like to see would be in reaction to an awful disaster." Would you like to comment?

Bacevich: A disaster like that could go either way. One hates to speculate on this, but were there another 9/11, the likely result could be that Americans would rise up in their righteous anger and say, let's go kill them all. But it's at least possible to hope that such a disaster might offer an opportunity for people who are advancing alternative views to be heard.

One of the strange things about the Iraq War and other post-9/11 policies is that, except for gas being at three dollars a gallon, who the hell cares? Part of the cunning genius of the Bush administration has been the way it's insulated Americans from the effects of their policies. You know, 9/11 happens and they seize upon it to declare their Global War on Terror. The President says from the outset that this is a long war, that it may take decades, that it's comparable to the world wars. On the other hand, he chooses not to mobilize the nation. There are no changes in our domestic priorities; no significant expansion of the armed forces.

Well, why was that? In their confidence about how great our military power was, they calculated that what we had would suffice. That was a major miscalculation. But I think they also calculated that by telling Americans, as President Bush famously did, to go down to Disney World and enjoy this great country of ours, they would be able to buy themselves political protection. Even though opinion polls show that public support for the President has dropped tremendously, in a sense events have proven them right. They have not been held accountable for their egregious mistakes because average citizens like you and me don't really feel the pain in any direct way.

Now, if the President had said: We're going to cut back on our domestic programs; we're going to raise taxes because this is an important war and, by God, we need to pay for it; we need a bigger Army and so we're going to impose a draft. Then I think Americans might have been more attentive to what's been happening over the past four years. But alas, they've not been. Instead we've drifted down the path toward perdition.

12. A Guided Tour of Class in America

Barbara Ehrenreich

June 4, 2006

You turn into a middle-class, suburban housing project on the periphery of Charlottesville, Virginia, and at a row of attached homes you pull up in front of the one with the yellow "for sale" sign on the tiny patch of grass. Ushered inside, you take in an interior of paint cans, a mop and pail, and cleaning liquids. On the small porch that overlooks a communal backyard, workmen are painting the weathered wood railings a nice clean white. Later, when they're gone, we step out for a minute, on a balmy late spring afternoon, and she says, "You know what I need out here? Flowers!" And it's true, the nearest neighbor's small porch is a riot of red, orange, and purple blooms, while hanging from her railing are three plant holders with only dirt and the scraps of dead vegetation in them.

Not surprising, really. Barbara Ehrenreich, our foremost journalist of—and dissector of—class is regularly not here. Practically a household name since she entered the low-wage working class disguised as herself, in her already classic account, *Nickel and Dimed*, she reported back on just how difficult it is for so many hard-working Americans to get by. Then a few years later she repeated the process with the middle class, only to find herself not in the workforce but among the desperately unemployed who had fallen out of an ever meaner corporate world. Her most recent book, *Bait and Switch, The (Futile) Pursuit of the American Dream*, was the result. Now, she spends much time traveling the country talking to audiences about her—and their—experiences. She has become a blogger, is involved in launching a new group to help organize the middle-class unemployed, and in her spare time has even finished a new book.

Now, after four years in Virginia (at least some of the time), she's about to head north. She gestures at the bookshelves. "There are a lot fewer books this week than last. I'm giving them to the Virginia Organizing Project." And it's true, the place is clearly being stripped down for sale. But you have the feeling, looking around, that it was a no-frills life to begin with, as Ehrenreich herself, in her short hair, jeans, T-shirt, and sneakers, presents a distinctly no-frills look. (Suddenly, imagining her with an image makeover advisor in *Bait and Switch* trying to give herself that perfect corporate look of employability seems amusing.)

Her mind is wide-ranging and daring indeed. Some years back, in a book entitled *Blood Rites*, she even managed to turn traditional ideas about the origins of war on their head. She is a thoroughly no-nonsense national resource.

She's looking forward to a trip to the local gym, followed by a visit with her two grandchildren (the daughters of her daughter, Rosa Brooks, a law professor and columnist for the *Los Angeles Times*). We sit down at a paper-and-book cluttered dining-room table, which shows no evidence of having held a meal in quite some time, and—eye on the clock, no fooling around—begin.

Tomdispatch: You were at a graduation ceremony recently where the students were bouncing beach balls in the stands. The college president leaned over and whispered, "This is the problem with having the commencement in the afternoon. Some of these people have been partying for hours." In response, you wrote, "There are reasons, whether the graduates know them or not, to want to greet one's entrance into the work world with an excess of Bud." Could you start by explaining why an excess of Bud might be an appropriate response to leaving college today?

Barbara Ehrenreich: Well, a lot of graduates are simply not going to find jobs appropriate to their credentials. They're going to be waitstaff. They're going to be call-center operators. Their twenties could be spent like that. I recently got Jared Bernstein of the Economic Policy Institute to do some research on this. It's still tentative, but he found that 17 percent of people in jobs that do not require college degrees have them. Those are very often people in their twenties who can't get professional-type employment, or people in their fifties who have been through one too many lay-offs and are no longer employable because they're, quote, too old. So I was thinking of that, and then I was thinking that for a lot of those who do get jobs, you know, the fun is over. They're going to be sitting in cubicles and they won't be able to bounce balls around when they're in boring meetings with their bosses.

TD: The real earnings of college graduates fell by 5 percent between 2000 and 2004, so they also have that to look forward to.

Ehrenreich: There still is a real big earnings gap between college and non-college graduates, but it's begun to shrink. Jared tells me that the reason it was growing so fast in the nineties was not that college graduates were doing so well, but that low-wage people, blue-collar people, were doing so poorly. Their wages were being held down—and that remains true.

TD: In 1989, you published a book about the middle class, or the professional-managerial class as you call them, entitled *Fear of Falling*. The book was way ahead of its time. If you were titling a work on the subject today you might just call it *Falling*.

Ehrenreich: What I was thinking about then was the fear of inter-generational falling, the fear a lot of upper-middle-class people have that their children will not get into the same class, because you can't just bequeath your class status to them. They can't inherit. They have to go through this whole education thing. Now, it could be *Free Fall*, though it isn't quite that bad . . . yet.

TD: In *Bait and Switch*, the book where, as an investigative reporter, you sought a corporate job and found yourself in the world of the middle-class unemployed or anxiously employed, you wrote, "On many fronts, the American middle class is under attack as never before." What happened to the middle class between then and now?

Ehrenreich: In *Fear of Falling*, I was concerned with the distance between the professional managerial class and the traditional working class. I thought I saw a new class developing. The strict Marxist idea is: You've got the bourgeoisie. Everybody else is a wage earner and they're not that different, whether they're account-ants or laborers. And I was saying, no, there's a real difference here. The white-collar worker who sits at a desk is telling other people what to do in one way or another. Such workers are in positions of authority when compared to blue- and pink-collar people.

Back then, I was emphasizing the differences. Today, in *Bait and Switch*, what I'm emphasizing is the lack of difference, that the security the professional-managerial class thought it had is gone. The safest part of that class, when I was writing in the eighties, seemed to be the professionals and managers with corporate positions. Then something happened in the nineties. Companies began to look at even those people as expenses to be eliminated rather than assets to be nurtured. What I was seeing in the late eighties was this pretty tight middle class where, really, the only problem was to get your kids into it, too.

TD: Your fear was for your children. Now it's for you.

Ehrenreich: And of course, your children, too.

TD: In *Bait and Switch*, you describe life in the corporate world as a "perpetual winnowing process."

Ehrenreich: One way that shows itself now is in the requirement in so many jobs for an annual—or even an every six-month—evaluation. You're constantly on your toes, constantly being reviewed, and potentially always up for elimination.

TD: And how do you account for the change in corporate culture?

Ehrenreich: I'm not sure. This is partly a mystery to me, but the pioneers were people like [Sunbeam's] Al "Chainsaw" Dunlap and Jack Welsh at GE, who took pride in eliminating as many people as possible, white- as well as blue–collar, and were richly rewarded by seeing their stock prices rise and their CEO pay go up. Leanness became the currency, what you wanted to achieve. I think part of that—but I don't know enough yet to say this with confidence—had to do with the fact that top executives were increasingly being rewarded with stock options, so that the distance between management and ownership was no longer there. A CEO knew that if he could raise quarterly profits via cuts he would get handsomely rewarded. The easiest way to raise profits is to cut expenses and the biggest expense is labor. Of course, the better way to increase profits would be to sell a better product, or more of them, or at a higher price.

TD: You're famous now for having been in two worlds as an investigative journalist, the low-wage world of the working class in *Nickel and Dimed* and the middle-class unemployed one in *Bait and Switch*. You've also, it seems to me, been one of the relatively few members of the professional managerial class to gnaw at the issue of class regularly. I suspect on this issue you really feel your politics. What was it that got you to class analysis and what kept you there when so many others were heading in the other direction?

Ehrenreich: I'm sure it has something to do with my background. When I was born, my father was a copper miner in Butte, Montana. It was a hard-core blue-collar situation. But ours was an amazing story of upward mobility. My father managed to get through college . . . well, the Butte School of Mines . . . while he was a miner. He was, by his own account, a genius. [She laughs.] Eventually, he got out of the mines and ended up as a corporate executive. He started out doing research as a metallurgist and then got turned into an executive. So my childhood was sort of an unguided tour of American classes.

TD: For people I've known, leaping classes tended to be a complicated, painful experience.

Ehrenreich: Well, my dad was always a heavy drinker, but he was a falling-down drunk by the time he finished his career—or it was finished for him. He wanted all that. He wanted success. He wanted to make more money—not that we were ever wealthy, but we certainly got toward the upper end of the middle class. But he also had this social nostalgia for the mines and would often talk about men he had worked with, things that had happened. It was clear to me that that was a real world of much stronger ties among people.

TD: And that he had lost something?

Ehrenreich: Oh, yes! One thing that stuck with me and helped me when I was doing *Nickel and Dimed:* I had told him in the seventies about young leftists going to work in factories to organize the working class. He thought that was hilarious, but then he said something very interesting: "Do you know what they probably don't understand? If you want to do something like that, the first thing is you have to do your job right. The first thing is—do the work." As a miner he had known communists organizing in the mines, but wasn't always impressed with them because some of them weren't good miners.

TD: Is there less mobility, and less study of it, than there was in your father's day?

Ehrenreich: There is less. We don't compare well to Europe anymore on that score.

TD: You now have a blog. You travel the country extensively and, because of your books, you hear from blue-collar and white-collar people in various kinds of trouble. What sorts of stories do you hear these days? What don't we know?

Ehrenreich: Both chronic, long-term poverty and downward mobility from the middle class are in the same category of things that America likes not to think about. Periodically, we'll have some little focus on poverty, like post-Katrina, but then it goes away again. After the dot.com crash, there was a brief moment of thinking about downwardly mobile software people; then we forgot about them. But it's there all the time, these crises in people's lives.

When it comes to the media, anything about economic pain is what gets left out. People sometimes say to me, why do you always focus on the downside? Because morally that seems to be my obligation—to look at pain. Not to celebrate every instance of successful entrepreneurship, but always to think of who's hurting. That just seems like a basic moral requirement for everybody. But that's what's missing too often in the media—the pain.

Stories of pain. The forum on my Web site is full of them. People will just post them:

> *I have a master's degree in mechanical engineering. I give up. I've been searching for three years.*
>
> *I'm living with my parents now. I had to give up my apartment, my home.*
>
> *I'm working in a call center now.*

That's the kind of thing I hear, over and over. And then people are losing pensions, losing health insurance. That's happening across the board—to people in middle-class occupations, too.

TD: You recently commented, "Thanks to Reagan, Clinton, and Bush, we now have a government with vastly expanded military and surveillance functions and sadly atrophied helping functions. Imagine, for an awkward zoological analogy, a lioness with grossly enlarged claws and teeth but no mammary glands."

Ehrenreich: This was something I first wrote about in 1997 in an essay in the *Nation*, which they entitled "Confessions of a Recovering Statist." I talked about the shift of government, at the end of the Clinton years, away from the helping functions and toward the military, penitentiaries, law enforcement. At what point, I asked, do progressives have to say: "I don't want to expand the helping functions of this government because look what it's doing"? A nice example is public housing— okay, public housing's a good thing, but when you start doing drug tests on people to get in or stay in such housing, then it's become an extension of the law enforcement function of government.

I still raise that question. Today, we have this even larger federal government, more and more of it being war-related, surveillance-related. I mean it's gone beyond our wildest Clinton administration dreams. I think progressives can't just be seen as pro-big government when big government has gotten so nasty.

TD: And also when civil society has been stripped of so many of its "civil" capacities, including, as with Katrina, the capacity to rebuild.

Ehrenreich: Katrina's a perfect example of how militarized the government has gotten even when it's supposedly trying to help people. The initial response of the government was a military one. When they finally got people down there, it was armed guards to protect the fancy stores and keep people in that convention center—at gunpoint! I mean, this is unbelievable.

TD: And what about the fobbing off of the civil parts of government onto religious and charitable groups, often politicized?

Ehrenreich: It's partly that the evangelical churches have reached for these things, and then there's the faith-based approach coming from the Bush administration where the dream was: Let's turn all social welfare functions over to churches. A lot of the mega-churches now function as giant social welfare bureaucracies. I wouldn't have found this out if I hadn't been researching *Bait and Switch* and gone into some of them, because that's where you go when you want to connect with people to find a job. That's also where you find after-school care, child care, support groups for battered women, support groups for people with different illnesses. As government helping functions dwindle, the role of the churches grows. What's sinister is that so many of these churches also support political candidates who are anti-choice, anti-gay, and—not coincidentally—opposed to any kind of expansion of secular social services.

TD: Let's turn to the hot-button issue of immigration. For *Nickel and Dimed*, you went to places where there was still a low-wage white working class—Minnesota, Maine . . .

Ehrenreich: Not Key West, which was packed with immigrant workers. But I did choose my places carefully, because real ethnic sorting does go on. For example, my son, Ben Ehrenreich, who is also a freelance journalist, decided to get a job in a meat-packing plant in LA. When he showed up, sixty guys were there and he was the only Anglo. Though he speaks perfect Spanish, he was rejected because they just think: What's he doing here? Employers get it in their minds that a certain kind of work is done by a certain kind of person and we're not going to hire someone different. When I realized that was going on in Key West, I said: Next stop, Maine, where almost everyone is white and I wouldn't run into racial sorting. I couldn't have done *Nickel and Dimed* so easily in LA or New York because they would have thought: Blue-eyed, white, middle-aged woman; if she wants this job, she must have a serious drug problem. [She laughs.]

TD: The issue of class and immigration threatens to split what's left of the Bush administration constituency, but not just them. How do you read the class politics of immigration?

Ehrenreich: My son went to a Minutemen gathering in the southwest and the fascinating thing was that a lot of the leaders talked a very big anti-corporate line: The corporations are crushing us, we're the real Americans, and so forth. In their minds, the immigrants are part of the thing that's crushing them and it's so much easier to pick up a gun and go to the border than to confront your employer.

Then, commentators keep saying that Americans won't take the jobs immigrants take. It's not that native-born Americans won't do heavy work and hard work and sweaty work. The problem is that these jobs pay so little. What makes it possible for immigrant workers to live on such low wages is their willingness —at least temporarily—to put up with just impossible situations, with many people packed into a room. After all, what does immigration do, in corporate terms? It provides a group of people you can really, really exploit. As long as they're illegal, you can do anything you want to them. Like not pay them. Not at all. If you were going to take on the immigration issue seriously, you'd have to look at what NAFTA did to the economy and agriculture for working-class Mexicans. Much of the immigration stuff is standard scapegoating. I mean, we're not going to begin to get at the problem until we take a serious look at the economies of the countries that are exporting people. Illegal immigrants are not coming here for the climate. We need to ask: How would we help

Mexico, for example, become a place with stable employment and agriculture. Not with NAFTA, for sure.

TD: Isn't the other side of the immigration issue the outsourcing of jobs?

Ehrenreich: It's very hard to have a serious discussion of outsourcing when we have no safety net for people whose jobs are outsourced. It's calamitous to lose your job, and that experience does pit you against the software writer in Bangalore. The longer term issue is: How do we get together across those national boundaries, so that the software writer in Atlanta is talking to the one in Bangalore and saying, we're in this together.

TD: What about the lack of protest in our world, especially the middle-class world you visited in *Bait and Switch*? You've started a new organization to begin to deal with this, right?

Ehrenreich: You know, after I wrote *Nickel and Dimed*, so many middle-class people would say to me: Oh, what's wrong with these people? Why do they take it? Well, they didn't just take it! Even if they expressed defiance in ways that were not too productive, like laughing at the boss behind his back or regularly breaking little rules. With the white-collar people, though, it just seemed so internalized. I couldn't get over it, how beaten down people were, how they had internalized obedience. The fear of standing out in any way that might be noticed seemed to grip them.

Our new organization, United Professionals, had its launch meeting in Atlanta at the end of April. Its constituency is unemployed, underemployed, and anxiously employed white-collar people. Now, it's not a union. Obviously, you can't have a union for people with such vastly different employers and professions. But it will provide advocacy for universal health insurance, extended unemployment benefits, and the like. And some services. We're looking at ways of offering cheap health insurance and mostly what I call networking, not in the instrumental corporate fashion, but a coming together, people sharing their stories, trying to figure out for themselves what's going on, what they need to do.

TD: A little á la early feminism then.

Ehrenreich: I see so many parallels, because there's a huge stigma attached to unemployment. People who have been laid off are very ashamed and depressed. There's a need to come together and overcome that shame. In those early meetings in the feminist movement of the seventies, people were ashamed to talk about having been raped. They were ashamed to talk about having been molested as a child. To be able to say that has happened to other people proved transforming. So let's bring it out, let's see what the problem is here.

TD: Isn't this the problem without a name again?

Ehrenreich: Exactly. So I see the need for something at the same level of emotional involvement as in the early women's movement.

TD: What other solutions to white-collar distress do you imagine?

Ehrenreich: Obviously you want some employment rights like the French just fought to preserve—saying you can't be fired at will, that a procedure must be gone through. When I was in England recently talking about *Bait and Switch*, my publisher told me: "You know, people aren't quite understanding what you're saying, how you could be laid off or fired without any procedure." They didn't understand the concept of employment at will. So I had to explain that in America you have no rights: no right to your job, no right to a hearing. You could be fired for a funny expression on your face.

Some of the people involved with United Professionals are looking into the concept of fighting collectively for what are called transition rights. Let's say everybody gets laid off. This happened at a mortgage company in Fort Wayne, Indiana. Lay-offs of hundreds of white- and pink-collar people. They're all told individually, "Here's your little severance package; now, never say another word or we might take it away." They're trying to take this on as a group and respond, "No, you can't deal with us like that; we all want a severance package we can live with or at least that will get us through a few months."

TD: In that half-century-plus from the 1950s to the present, do you feel there's been a transformation of middle-class culture?

Ehrenreich: It's more sealed off for sure. If you're in the upper middle class you never have to interact with other classes, except with your servants or a cab driver or a manicurist.

TD: Until you get fired by your corporation, of course.

Ehrenreich: Yes, that's the surprise, but until then your children won't go to the public schools; you won't be using the public parks on weekends. You don't ride public transportation if you're in that class. They're really walled off.

TD: Back in 1989 you wrote of a "culture in which the middle class both stars and writes the script." What did you mean and is it still true?

Ehrenreich: There's been a lot of polarization within the professional-managerial class since the 1980s. There is now a huge gap, for example, between a journalist and the managing editor of the paper. The difference between the university provost and the associate professor of sociology could be a hundred thousand dollars a year. They're less and less in the same world. So I would modify that statement. The scriptwriters have gotten higher up.

TD: What would an anatomy of your professional-managerial class of 1989 look like now?

Ehrenreich: The main thing is there's just more leakage at the bottom, people falling out of it. In 1989, college education had expanded a lot, but not as much as today. Now, so many jobs insist on a college education. I have no idea why. I think they're just training people to sit quietly for long periods of time. Obedience training I guess is the phrase . . .

TD: . . . for dogs.

Ehrenreich: Yeah! I don't see where a typical BA even represents any serious skills. Obviously I'm for education, but there's a major element of rip-off here.

TD: What happened, by the way, to the famed 1950s man in the grey flannel suit? I was amused that, for your working class book, you could go to work more or less dressed as you are now, wearing a T-shirt and jeans.

Ehrenreich: I think you would need khaki pants.

TD: Right. But when you tried to make your way into the

corporate world, there was this constant stylistic retooling. No more single uniform.

Ehrenreich: The explanation for that—which sociologist Robert Jackall offered and my image makeover guy confirmed—is that by being precisely right in your appearance you signal that you'll conform in any other way they might want. You're sending a signal about your degree of compliance.

TD: Certainly the man in the grey flannel suit didn't expect to get a $300 million thank-you note when he retired. Here's a figure you had in one of your blog entries: "The top 10 percent of households saw their net worth rise [between 2001 and 2004] by 6.1 percent to an average of $3.11 million." I was wondering how you looked at the vast payoffs to CEOs, a tiny endowed elite, who will, in fact, be able to endow their children.

Ehrenreich: It's just plunder. You have your pay determined by a board of your buddies, often just other CEOs. They can take what they want. What was it in the paper today? Home Depot. [She grabs a newspaper off the table and begins rifling through it.] "The stock fell but the chief's pay kept rising." That's news? [She laughs.] Or it was Verizon? Stock tumbled and the CEO got a raise. They'll push down wages as far as they can, and if there's no union to stop them, they'll just keep going, and they'll push up their own pay. There's no limit to what they'll take!

TD: You've talked about the invisibility of the poor, the low-wage working class, and these middle-class people falling out of the corporate world, but in a weird way aren't the rich invisible, too?

Ehrenreich: Well, not that invisible, because they're always in the media spectacle, though they aren't studied enough. I think that the poor know much more about the rich than vice versa. You can get some sense of their lives from the entertainment media and, if you clean their houses or you wait on them in stores, you sort of see them. Whereas the other way around doesn't seem to function.

TD: What I was thinking, though, was: Who writes books today with titles like *Who Rules America?*

Ehrenreich: My fantasy after *Bait and Switch* was to go under-cover among the rich. I spent a long time talking to [*Harper's* magazine editor] Lewis Lapham about it, but we came to the dismal conclusion that I wouldn't pass. It's not only things like fingernails, but that a woman of my age should have had a lot of surgery. I would be a dead giveaway. Not to mention "How do you get access?" Too bad—I thought that would be so much fun to do.

TD: Looking toward the midterm and presidential elections, what are your thoughts?

Ehrenreich: I don't spend a lot of time thinking about electoral politics, though I'm kind of interested in John Edwards, because since '04 he's devoted himself to talking about poverty and he's showed up at picket lines and the like.

TD: In terms of the issues that matter to you, can you explain the difference between Democrats and Republicans to me?

Ehrenreich: [Laughs.] What kind of question is that, Tom!

TD: I've been writing a lot—based on that infamous presidential

Mission Accomplished banner of 2003—about what the Bush administration hasn't accomplished abroad. There, I believe, they're already standing in the rubble of their own project. But have they accomplished more of their mission more successfully at home?

Ehrenreich: No, because they haven't completely dismantled the welfare state. I mean, welfare itself is pretty much just a pathetic wage-supplementation program now, but they couldn't get rid of social security and they actually expanded Medicare. There's a trip wire people have not let them go over yet. I remember hearing Stuart Butler, a Thatcher guy who arrived from England at the end of the Reagan years, say that he felt this was a country where he could really see his goal, the destruction of the welfare state in all forms, being achieved. Well, they haven't done it.

However, one of the places where they've been most successful, as Peter Gosselin, an economics writer for the *LA Times*, has pointed out incisively, is in shifting risk to individuals. It's happening with the disintegration of the whole concept of insurance. Insurers don't want to insure the coasts anymore; they certainly don't want to give anybody health insurance who might ever get sick. That's one of the things they've done pretty well at. In the ownership society, you take care of yourself; don't bother us, it's your problem.

TD: When you look to the future, do you see some path other than this incredible one we're on that seems possible?

Ehrenreich: Oh, yes! I'm sort of a libertarian socialist type. There are a lot of things that just should not be in the market. Health care, that should be taken care of. I think there's a place for markets, but there's always going to be tension between markets and our mutual responsibility.

TD: If the polarization in the middle class you describe continues apace, do you imagine a moment when those dropping out of the old middle class and the corporate world may make common with . . .

Ehrenreich: That's my whole theme as I've trooped around the country talking about *Bait and Switch* to somewhat more middle-class audiences than I normally get with *Nickel and Dimed*. There's a lot in our society that makes people with college degrees and white-collar jobs think they're special and superior. But next time you're seeing that person pushing the broom, remember, you may be one year, maybe even six months, away from that yourself. You're not special, not in the eyes of the owners and the CEOs. So we've got to get together; we've got to bridge that divide, get over that snobbishness.

TD: Let's turn briefly to war. We're in a war period and you've offered a thoroughly ingenious explanation for the origins of . . . well, you call them humanity's blood rites in a book of the same name. You've suggested that they came not from our prehistory as aggressive hunters of prey, not even out of aggression, but out of fear and from an even earlier period, when we were the prey of other creatures. Of course, in a non-war situation in your two recent books you've been dealing with the prey. But I was wondering if you have any comments on our modern blood rites?

Ehrenreich: First, you said something interesting about looking at the prey in my books on economic themes. Well, yeah! And the way in prehistory that humans or hominids rose from prey to predators was through collective action. I mean, that is the great human trick. Weapon-making, too. We're smart at that. But there's a human ability that doesn't get enough attention—that ability to mobilize concertedly as a group. I think that's ultimately what tipped the balance in our favor. Other primates can jump around together to ward off a predator, but humans can do it so much more effectively. We're good at collective action. Similarly, to get out of these internal prey situations in our own economy, you've got to band together. That's not just a lesson from the last 200 years of labor history, but one of the deepest lessons from thousands of years of human experience.

Now, what do I think of wars at present? Well, the current war and the first Gulf War were, to a certain extent, rally events. That's a term sociologists started using fairly recently to describe something that leaders initiate for the purpose of manipulating mass emotions—in their favor, of course. [Former British prime minister] Margaret Thatcher was sinking in the polls when she did the Falklands War, just as the first George Bush was before Gulf War I, when he soared to something like 90 percent approval.

TD: And, by the way, the younger Bush before 9/11.

Ehrenreich: That's right. It was just sort of handed to him on 9/11. Of course, it was his choice to invade a random country in response. But that rally effect has not lasted and I don't think they can pull it off again. I don't think people are going to start waving American flags for the bombing of Tehran. The scarier thing would be another terrorist attack, which might mobilize some crazed, nonrational response. What do we hit next? Norway? Because these people are not understanding that terrorism doesn't pose a normal military challenge. What the U.S. is doing in Iraq is as silly as the British marching around in little files in the forests of North America in red uniforms and getting picked off by Americans hiding behind trees. There's just no clue as to what to do. Historically, if you don't make the transition to the next threat, if you're still fighting, basically, the Second World War, which is as far as they've advanced, you're not going to make it.

TD: Last thing—maybe a term that's disappeared might be worth reconsidering: class war.

Ehrenreich: I already use it when I'm talking to groups. I say, yes, there's a class war. It's totally one-sided and it's time for the rest of us to mobilize against the aggressors.

13. Reading the Imperial Press
Back to Front

Tom Engelhardt

JUNE 20, 2006

Nick Turse stands at the door, a frizz of curly black hair, a fringe of beard, in a dark T-shirt and green cargo pants. Slung over his shoulder is a green backpack (a water bottle sticking out of a side pouch) so stuffed that he might well have been on a week's maneuvers. When I mention its size, he says, "Genuine military surplus," smiles, and lets it drop to the floor with a thunk. Immediately, he begins rummaging inside it and soon pulls out a tiny box sporting drawings of futuristic robot warriors and covered with Japanese characters (but also with a tiny Made in China in English). "Knowing your tastes," he says, handing it to me. He found it at a toy store in Tokyo on his way back from Vietnam.

Young as he is, he's been in the government archives for years and is one of our foremost experts on American war crimes in Vietnam. In fact, the combination of historic crimes and toys first brought us together at a diner a block from my apartment, perhaps three years ago. I had written a book, in part on Vietnam, in part on how an American "victory culture" had once expressed itself in the world of children's play. He read it and was looking for a little advice on his work. Soon after, he began sending out to friends his own homespun version of Tomdispatch and put me on his e-list.

Overwhelmed by such send-outs, I ignored his for a while, but he had such an eye for the place where toys, entertainment, and the military-industrial complex merged that I finally found myself paying attention, and one day called him, asking if he could write a Tomgram on the subject. The rest, as they say, is Tomdispatch history. Now, in a busy life that includes writing two books and working a couple of jobs, he spends his spare time as the site's associate editor and research director—I may not have much money to offer but titles are plentiful—and has become one of its more popular writers.

As we walk into the dining room, reviewing our past history, he says wryly, "You found me in the cabbage patch." For a brief moment, at the dining room table, we're both absorbed in preparations. Cellophane wrappers come off tapes that are clicked into tape recorders. Then we seat ourselves and, for the first time since I began these interviews, I swivel my two machines so they face me.

Outside, on this late spring Sunday, the sky has darkened and rain is beginning to fall. Nick says into his tape—he's the pro here, having interviewed many vets from the Vietnam era—"May 21, 2006, Turse Interview with Tom Engelhardt." And when I give him a quizzical look, he adds, "I don't know how many tapes I've gone through and then thought: Who was I interviewing? Who is this guy?" Who is this guy turns out to be the theme of the afternoon.

Nick Turse: Was there some eureka moment when you created Tomdispatch?

Tom Engelhardt: It was more an endless moment—those couple of months after 9/11 when, for a guy who was supposedly politically sophisticated, my reactions were naïve as hell. I had this feeling that the horror of the event might somehow open us up to the world. It was dismaying to discover that, with the Bush administration's help, we shut the world out instead. What we engaged in were endless, repetitive rites that elevated us to the roles of greatest survivor, greatest dominator, and greatest victim, all the roles in the global drama except that of greatest evil one.

I'm also a lifetime newspaper junkie. I just couldn't bear the narrowness and conformity of the coverage when I knew that this had been a shocking event, but that there was also a history to 9/11. It only seemed to come out of the blue. I was a book editor by profession. I had published Chalmers Johnson's prophetic *Blowback* two years earlier. I became intensely frustrated with the limited voices we were hearing.

At the same time, watching the Bush administration operate, I became increasingly appalled. [There's a thunderclap outside.] Maybe it's dramatic license to have thunder booming in the background now.

Look, I had been at the edges of the mainstream publishing world for almost thirty years and I'd done useful work. I had nothing to be embarrassed about. I also had two reasonably grown-up kids and, looking at the world in perhaps early November 2001, I had an overwhelming feeling—maybe this was the eureka moment, though it crept up on me—that I couldn't simply go on as is. We're egocentric beings. We tend to move out from the self. Children are next, then spouse, friends, relatives, your city, your nation, the world. I couldn't bear to turn this world over to my children in this shape. I had no illusions about what I could do. I wasn't imagining Tomdispatch. I just felt I had to make a gesture.

Turse: What was your initial vision then?

Engelhardt: I had none. This is very much me. I was fifty-seven, an aging technophobe. Computers scared me. I had barely gotten e-mail.

Thinking about this interview today, a passage came to mind from a book I published years ago called *To the Ends of the Earth*. A British expedition to Greenland in 1818 had a first meeting with a small group of the most northerly people on the planet . . .

Turse: . . .these are Inuit?

Engelhardt: Yes, four Inuit. The Brits have an interpreter. "What great creatures are these?" the Inuit ask about the British sailing ships. They're houses made of wood, the interpreter replies. "No," they insist, "they are live. We have seen them move their wings." Later, one of the tribesmen is brought closer. Overcome with fear and astonishment, he cries out to the boat: "Who are you? What are you? Where do you come from? Is it from the sun or the moon?"

Now, I was that tribesman and, for me, the world of the Internet was that wondrous, fearsome boat. That November, I don't think I yet realized that you could read a newspaper online. But a friend e-mailed me a piece from an Afghani living in California—our Afghan War had just begun—who wondered what it was like to bomb rubble because, after all those years of civil war, that's all Afghanistan was. The image stunned me exactly because you couldn't find anything like it in our press. And so I made up a little list, maybe twelve friends and relatives, and sent it off with a note saying, "You've got to read this," and that started me wandering the Internet looking for other voices we weren't hearing.

"Voices from elsewhere, even when the elsewhere is here" was what I used to say about the kind of book publishing I did. I found Arundhati Roy. I started reading the British *Guardian*, various papers around the world, piling up pieces and sending them out with little comments that got longer and longer. Just an unnamed e-list. Then people from the ether started writing in: "Hey, could you put me on your list?" Some of them were journalists. I didn't even know how they found me. By then, I was doing it obsessively. I couldn't stop. Maybe a year later, I had this list of four or five hundred e-beings. At that moment, toward the end of 2002, the wonderful fellow who runs the Nation Institute, Ham Fish, first suggested sponsoring it as a Web site. It had never crossed my mind.

Even the name Tomdispatch began as a joke. Friends of a friend started saying about my e-mails, "We got another Tomgram today." It struck me as funny and I do think, no matter how grim things may be, you have to remain somewhat amused with the world.

Turse: So from a clipping service to a broader e-list and then a Web site.

Engelhardt: Next, I started asking friends to write original stuff for me. The first Tomgram—on Bush administration–induced smallpox hysteria—was by your former graduate-school advisor, David Rosner. The Web site barely existed then. Almost no one saw it, which was sad since the piece was very good. Remember, I had been editing and publishing for thirty years: Chalmers Johnson, Mike Klare, John Dower, Arlie and Adam Hochschild, Mike Davis, Jonathan and Orville Schell—and all of them you can read at Tomdispatch.

That's how it got close to where it is now, by complete happenstance, because I was too old to know better and just stumbled into this world where, along with the obvious disadvantages, my age has some advantages.

Turse: Tell me about them.

Engelhardt: I bring some old-fashioned things to the online world. However pressed for time, I still believe in the well-made, well-edited essay. And length doesn't scare me. Everyone online is supposed to have the attention span of a gnat, but counterintuitively I'll run pieces of up to ten thousand words. Sometimes the world just can't be grasped short. So length defines—and limits—my site. It signals that Tomdispatch is the product of obsessional activity, which means you probably have to be an addict to read it. On the other hand, I'm too old to fully appreciate people yakking at each other in something like real time. You won't find that at my site.

Because I started off writing for friends, my tone was informal, personal. I kept that when I went public. Though I don't write a lot about myself, I suspect people feel I'm speaking to them, as I hope I am.

Turse: What about that tagline at the site, "a regular antidote to the mainstream media" and, by the way, tell me about the poison?

Engelhardt: To start with that poison, as you put it, Tomdispatch is a 24/7 operation for which I don't have 24/7; but every day I try to read the *New York Times*, my hometown paper, cover to cover. Sometimes the *Wall Street Journal. The Washington Post*, the *Los Angeles Times*, and several others online if I have the time. Then I check Juan Cole, a great, thoughtful collecting site for Iraq and the Middle East and start visiting what I call "riot sites" like Antiwar.com or the War in Context that have a million headlines chosen by some interesting eye.

I've always claimed that, when you read articles in the imperial press, the best way—and I'm only half-kidding—is back to

front. Your basic front-page stories, as on the TV news, usually
don't differ that much from paper to paper. It's when you get
toward the ends of pieces that they really get interesting. Maybe
because reporters and editors sense that nobody's paying attention but the news junkies, so things get much looser. You find tidbits the reporter's slipped in that just fall outside the frame of the
expectable. That's what I go looking for. Sometimes it's like
glimpsing coming attractions.

Here are a couple of tidbits I picked up deep in the *New
York Times* recently.

There was an interesting front-page piece by Sabrina Tav-
ernise, "As Death Stalks Iraq: Middle Class Exodus Begins."
After the jump, pretty deep inside, there's this line: "In all, 312
trash workers have been killed in Baghdad in the past six
months." There it is—basic, good reporting that no one's going
to notice or pick up on. And yet it probably tells you just about
everything you need to know about life in Baghdad today. Forget
the security forces, forget top officials. Three hundred and twelve
garbage men slaughtered. Holy Toledo!

So that kind of reporting, hidden but in plain sight, can start
me on an Iraq piece. I mean, here's the thing about the American
press: If you have the time, it's all there somewhere. But who,
other than a news nut like me, has the time to look for it?

Okay, here's another. This one, which greatly amused me,
was tucked away on page twelve of the *Times*. First, though, I
have to say something about article placement. Every spring, I
become an editor to a group of young journalists at the Graduate
School of Journalism in Berkeley. And where do they read their
news? Remember, these are professional news junkies. They read
it online! Most of them do not read a daily paper daily. "Why
should I read the *L.A. Times* in print," one of them told me,
"when they've posted their major stories the night before?"

But if you don't read the paper paper, you don't see how it's arranged and you miss all the little stories, some of which may be very big, buried deep inside the fold. In a sense, my students don't understand the organization of a newspaper.

Take a little Jim Rutenberg piece, only ten paragraphs, headlined, "With the President as the Guest, the Hostess Sends Regrets," about how Republican House seats were starting to come into play. It was a story that would hit the front pages only days later. Here was the paragraph I loved, quoting a column elsewhere I had missed. "The situation has been different for others who have clearly snubbed the president, like the Republican candidate for governor in Illinois, Judy Baar Topinka. One of her aides told the syndicated columnist George Will last month that she wanted the president's help to raise money only 'late at night' and 'in an undisclosed location.'"

Read that and you already know a lot about American politics at this second. I was one of the few places, I'm proud to say, insisting very early on that there was no bottom to Bush's approval ratings. Read deep into the paper and into articles, and you know enough to write pieces that look predictive but aren't. Of course, this is also to acknowledge that most of the political Internet is parasitically based on reporting done in the mainstream media. Without money, what other possibility could there be?

Turse: So it's all there just buried in the back pages?

Engelhardt: It's the genius of the American press that you can always say something's been covered, even when nobody sees it.

Turse: So are they hiding it from us or don't the editors notice those last paragraphs—or care?

Engelhardt: None of the above, I suspect. My basic line is, if you put three CPAs—and my father-in-law was a CPA, so no disrespect intended—and three journalists on stage and ask them to talk about their professions, the CPAs would be the introspective ones. Journalists often don't seem to have a clue about how their world actually works.

That's probably one reason why it works as well it does. In states with propaganda machines, everyone knows how things work. If you were in the old Soviet media, you knew you could write what the state or Party told you to write. You knew you were a paid hack. The American media doesn't work that way. It's like a conspiracy of which nobody involved knows they're a part. It's genius itself.

Turse: Do you think you see the world differently than mainstream journalists or do you just say what they won't?

Engelhardt: I tell my students: Look for wherever you're askew our world, wherever there's just that little crack of space between you and society. Everyone has that somewhere. Otherwise when you go out to report, you'll just bring back what we all know anyway.

When I look back on the young Tom Engelhardt, I couldn't have been more American normal. I was deeply involved in what in a book I wrote I later came to call "victory culture," the parades, the military, the on-screen glory. I was an all-American boy in a way that maybe only a second- or third-generation American could be. You know, a Jewish kid who was completely hooked on American history, a nut in high school on the Civil War and World War II. On my own, I memorized the inspiring speeches of generals.

Yet when I look back—and I came from a liberal New York family (nothing radical there)—I would say that from an early age, for reasons that still puzzle me, I was deeply anti-imperial. Of course, that's in the American grain too. It still seems a defining aspect of me, and now of Tomdispatch. I am just against everything that goes with empires, of which, I think, we're one.

Back then, bored white kid, only child, living in the middle of New York City, probably feeling a little out of it even before teen awkwardness set in, I felt askew. And I hated how that felt at the time, but it's proved valuable since. When I read a paper, my eyes just seem drawn to things that not everybody notices.

Turse: Give me an example.

Engelhardt: Okay, here's a piece in the *Times* by John Burns, a fine reporter, on the new Iraqi government just now being installed inside Baghdad's fortified Green Zone, a unity government in which, as of today, the prime minister still can't name the three key ministers for security—this, in a country where the whole issue is security, or the lack of it. Anyway, Burns's piece is labeled "news analysis," and headlined, "For Some, a Last, Best Hope for U.S. Efforts in Iraq."

Now my brain works by association. I think best when I swim: metronomic motion, straight crawl. Like those Magic 8-Ball toys of my childhood, I just wait for the thoughts to rise onto the screen of my brain and surprise me. I love imagery. We're such a metaphoric species. My eye is always drawn to the metaphors we use without much thought.

I've been following the Iraq news intimately for at least four years now and the American imagery has told such a story: There were the first upbeat images after the invasion when we were teaching the Iraqi child—as the likes of Rumsfeld and Bush put it—how to take the "training wheels" off that bike of democracy. So fabulously patronizing. Then, as things got worse, you got your "turning points." (The President's the only one left mentioning those these days.) And with them went the "milestones" of progress, after each of which there would be a worse set of disasters until they kind of faded away and you got images instead of the invasion having opened a Pandora's Box in Iraq.

Then, maybe six months ago, Americans officials made it to the metaphoric "precipice" and soon after looked into the "abyss" of civil war before "taking a step back." You saw such imagery quoted in the press all the time, usually from the mouths of the anonymous officials who swarm through such stories.

Now, Burns, today, has the newest Bush administration image. I first noticed it when Condi Rice went to Baghdad at the end of April to twist arms and get the prime minister we wanted. Officials in her party were quoted as saying that this was "a last chance," which was, of course, absurd. I mean, this situation has been devolving for four years.

A month of sectarian catastrophe later, Burns's piece quotes yet more anonymous American "military and civilian officials" who feel they are "witnessing what might be the last chance to save the American enterprise in Iraq from a descent into chaos and civil war." If you keep reading, you find that we're now at a "critical juncture," kind of a turning point without the optimism; then, that the Americans "played a muscular role in vetting and negotiating over the new cabinet." Now that's a wonderful phrase, like we're at the gym.

Turse: It's the strong arm.

Engelhardt: Yes, but so much more polite. Then you discover that our ambassador, Zalmay Khalilzad, "acted as a tireless midwife in the birthing of the new government." Now, if this were, say, the Russians and some Central Asian autocracy, it would be strong-arming the locals and creating a puppet government. And then, part way in, those "milestones" arrive. The piece is a compendium of images from the Bush experience in Iraq—with some new gems thrown in. This is just the automatic writing of the press in a hurry. But for me, it would be a jumping-off place for a piece.

Reading newspapers, I'm often aware of what an imperial planet we're on. Things only work in one direction. Sometimes, just for the hell of it, I imagine flipping the directional signs.

For instance, a recent front-page *New York Times* piece about the CIA went essentially like this: Good news! Despite all its well-known problems, the Agency has bolstered its corps of spies, ramped up its on-the-ground capabilities, and we're finally on the verge of breaking operatives into closed societies like, say, Iran. I'm thinking: Whoa, it doesn't even faze us to proclaim to all and sundry that we have the right to mobilize vast numbers of covert operatives and put them in any other society of our choosing, for any kind of mayhem we might desire. We broadcast that fact on the front pages of our major papers.

So flip this story. Blazing headlines, the *Tehran Times*. The Iranians announce that, despite years of problems, their intelligence agencies have just bolstered their spy corps significantly and proudly expect to be capable soon of seeding the closed society of Washington with covert teams of operatives. We would be outraged. We'd be bombing them tomorrow! The fact is we're allowed to talk and write in a way permitted to no other people on Earth. It's imperial freedom of speech.

Or imagine January 2008. A new American administration is coming into power and the "news analysis" in an Iraqi paper praises the "muscularity" of Iraq's minister to Washington and the way he "midwived" the birth of the new government. Of course, it's not even imaginable. There is no such world.

Turse: If you wrote something like that, it would be labeled satire.

Engelhardt: I say to my students: Writing, like everything else in the universe, is essentially an energy transfer but a very weird one. The energy of writing is something you hook a reader with. It can drive readers through a piece. Even if you're writing about terrible things, there should be pleasure to the writing itself. And humor, parody, satire, they're powerful tools. When things strike me as absurdly funny, I don't hesitate, though our world is now so extreme that satire can easily be mistaken for the real thing, as confused or outraged letters from readers often remind me.

Turse: The site has become home to diverse voices. What makes a Tomdispatch writer? Is there a defining trait you're looking for?

Engelhardt: I can only explain this with an image. When I was young, we kids would go hunting for clams with our toes. The question naturally was, How do you know what one feels like? Of course, nobody can tell you. You just feel around until, amid the empty shells, stones, and live crabs sooner or later you hit a clam. Then you know.

Ditto Tomdispatch writers. Ditto how I operate in life. Many Tomdispatch writers I already knew. I had edited their books. Tomdispatch is a nonsubmission site, because I'm the only one answering the mail and I'm usually working another job or two. I just can't deal.

The real adventure of my site, by the way, is all those e-letters pouring in. This wows me. I check the site e-mail and there's a convoy commander from Iraq telling me about his experiences, or an anti-imperial conservative from some southern state, or residents of small towns all over America.

In the nineteenth century, people fled small towns for the big city. Now, when they feel isolated, they flee onto the Internet looking for company. So I get letters regularly from people who sign off with the name of a town in Kansas or Montana or Texas, and in parentheses maybe, "pop. 250." Sometimes, they'll add something like: "From Red State Hell." Wonderful letters from people I would never in a million years meet: Iraqi exiles, Germans who want to tell me about our President, an American expat in Athens who let me know that a Greek college student had recommended the site to him. Imagine that!

I try to reply to everything, at least a few words. But every now and then I get an e-letter where I just go: Wow, I have to do something with this! So here's an example of how a Tomdispatch writer got started. Elizabeth de la Vega had just retired as a federal prosecutor when she wrote in. She had a few kind words about the site, but mainly she wanted to offer some comments on a piece I had posted on the Plame case. Well, I doubt I had gotten a letter from a federal prosecutor before, and her Plame comments were riveting.

When I have the urge to use something written privately to me, I respond quite diffidently. I don't want to pressure anyone into making private comments public. But I did ask her about writing hers up. She replied that she'd never written anything other than a prosecutor's brief before, but that she'd try—and she was a natural. She's been writing for the site ever since.

Stumbling across someone like her, it's part of what makes life fun for me.

Turse: Any idea who the typical Tomdispatch reader is?

Engelhardt: Based on those letters, including periodic waves of hate mail from Bush people—though they've been quiet of late— I suspect the readership is a lot broader than the alternate press version of Tomdispatch would have been back in the sixties, my other moment of activism. Of course, those years weren't what we now believe them to be either. All through that period, for instance, I was involved with dissident GIs, even though the history books tell us we didn't have anything to do with each other.

But the wonderful thing about the Internet is that you can't know who your audience is. Not really. I mean, we know Tomdispatch has about 17,500 subscribers, who get free e-mail alerts notifying them that a piece has been posted. Those pieces then get picked up and reposted by all sorts of sites. Some give me figures; some don't even have them.

Then there are the little blogs that pick up the pieces and just bounce them around, and then there are the personal pass-ons and e-lists like Tomdispatch was before it had a name. I get letters all the time saying, I pass your stuff on to fifty or one hundred friends, relatives, workmates. I figure anything I post is read by at least 75,000 to 100,000 people and that's probably conservative.

People write in corrections, appreciated because both of us are lousy proofreaders; they also write strong critiques and sometimes very angry letters. They order me to write shorter, to stop being such a know-it-all. People regularly tell me things I simply *must* do. You've *got* to cover the real story about hidden American casualties in Iraq! They don't realize that we're the only ones here. You and I joke sometimes: Yes, I'm sending my crack Tomdispatch team to Germany immediately to check it out!

Generally, though, I just look at the world as best I can, put my fingers on the keyboard, and bam! The amazing thing is that most of my life I've been such a slow writer. Give me a four thousand-word assignment and I could still be in knots a month later.

Now, four thousand words can come out in twenty-four hours. If I were religious, I would say I was possessed and the next question would be: Whose voice am I channeling? In fact, I know it's mine in some grim moment weirdly made for me. If I ever had two seconds to go back to writing fiction—because doing my novel, *The Last Days of Publishing*, was one of the quiet joys of my life—I might write about possession.

Turse: How do you define what you do at Tomdispatch? Are you a news editor, a journalist, a commentator, or an Internet activist?

Engelhardt: Except in a couple of very limited circumstances, I don't pretend to be a journalist at all. Every now and then, I go to some event—I covered the demonstrations in front of the 2004 Republican Convention and then the Republican delegates on the convention floor—and essentially ask people why they're there. In our media, we almost never hear people speak in more than little snippets. That's the nature of journalism, really.

So we seldom hear their real voices or how they actually think, and they almost invariably turn out to be more eloquent and complicated than we expect. In those moments, I do think of myself as some kind of citizen journalist.

I'm always fascinated by how comfortably we humans hold complex and contradictory views without being too bothered. I don't find it odd, for instance, that the neocons or Bush administration people thought they were manipulating us and also believed in many of the things they were being so Machiavellian about. Yet most people prefer either/or. Either they were manipulating us or they were true believers.

Here's what marks me as not a journalist: I can go to the event, but I can't go back the next day. I don't have the psychic energy. I find approaching strangers too hard.

As for the site, someone else should tell me what it is and what I am.

Turse: All right, but I'm going to try to pin you down on some definitions anyhow. You came of age in the heyday of the New Left and the turbulence of the sixties. Politically and ideologically, how did you define yourself then, and how about today?

Engelhardt: In the sixties I was still such an American kid. I grew up dreaming of doing exactly two things. I wanted to go into government service, the State Department, and become a diplomat. I didn't know they basically didn't favor Jews. And then there was a journalist, a friend of my parents named Robert Shaplen, who wrote about Vietnam for the *New Yorker*. He had that reportorial tough-guy, weathered look to him, but he was sweet as hell to me when I was a kid. I admired him greatly and dreamed about being him.

Journalism or diplomacy, either way I would serve my country. That feeling held deep into the sixties, even though Vietnam began making me really angry. As Iraq drives some people today, Vietnam drove me—right into a kind of unexpected opposition, starting in maybe '65. In '64, I was still half-defending the war, or at least the so-called peace candidate, Lyndon Johnson, against Barry Goldwater. I was shocked when, after the election, Johnson turned out to be such a warmonger.

By '67, I had really moved. In '68, I turned in my draft card, began doing draft counseling. But—and this is the complexity of human beings—in the midst of it all, I also wanted out of graduate school and applied to the USIA [United States Information Agency]. A propaganda outfit. I told them I wouldn't go to Saigon. A hopeless thought, actually. I could read French and was studying Chinese. It was like having a bull's-eye on my forehead, but I was dreaming of someplace like Brazil where I would present my country in a better light.

And then they accepted me! But the vetting took so long that, by the time they made the offer, I couldn't imagine doing it. Still, as late as 1968, I wasn't quite either/or yet. The rest of the sixties, by which we usually really mean the early seventies, I defined myself as on the left. Later, through another series of happenstances, I settled into normal life as a book editor and . . .

Turse: [He laughs] . . . joined the establishment.

Engelhardt: I became established in any case.

Turse: And now?

Engelhardt: We're in such a weird time and the Internet is such a strange beast. Leftists, rightists . . . I deal, for instance, with some great anti-imperial libertarians who fear what's happening to our civil liberties and are upset about our imperial course, and on that we agree.

In fact, as I age and watch the Bush administration wreak havoc on the planet, I've come to think of myself as more conservative, in the literal sense of conserving what's human and valuable; in the sense of seeing things in the world I came out of worth conserving that are being frittered away . . . no, thrown to the winds by these alien people who run this eerie thing they call our "homeland." But, of course, the word "conservative" has already been appropriated by people I can't abide.

In a funny way, I probably define myself less and less, and yet, put my fingers on a keyboard, and I know what I think. And if you read Tomdispatch, you'll know too.

Turse: So is Tomdispatch providing a service to the country?

Engelhardt: When I interviewed Ann Wright, one of three State Department diplomats who resigned in protest as the invasion of Iraq rushed toward us—a brave act—I asked her what she thought her military and State Department careers and her antiwar activism had in common. "Service to America," she said. And here was the thing, I had written the word "service" next to the question beforehand. So I replied, "Hey, I knew you were going to say that," and I showed her. I've come to feel particular sympathy for many of the people you write about, Nick, in your "Fallen Legion" series, people in government or the military who thought they were serving their country and find themselves serving officials they can't bear, who have betrayed them and the country. In that sense, Tomdispatch has come to feel like my version of service to country.

Of all the things that people write me when they're angry, the one that most gets my goat—and also makes me laugh—is, Go back to . . .

Twenty years ago, it would have been Russia, but now, depending on the moment, they'll put in China or maybe France. Part of me thinks: a plane ticket and a croissant or some Peking Duck. Sounds like a good couple of weeks. But my deeper feeling is, hey, you jerk, this is my damn country and I'm not going anywhere!

Turse: Switching gears, what started you doing these Tomdispatch interviews?

Engelhardt: Well, the site just continues to develop, probably because I'm a bit of a restless personality. In the years when I was mainly a book editor, I published a certain amount of oral history. My boss then edited the miraculous Studs Terkel and he used to call me in on Studs's manuscripts, like the second team, just to do a final read-through. More recently, I've edited a couple of Studs's books. I also, for example, edited Chris Appy's incredible oral history of the Vietnam War from all sides, with an appropriate title for this interview: *Patriots*. So I have an appreciation for the glories of the interview.

Last summer, I realized I had access to Howard Zinn and
Boston Globe columnist James Carroll, and I just thought, well,
they probably won't write for me, and interviews, that's something I've never done. I'll take a shot at almost anything on the
page. I thought, why not try? So I picked up the two cheapest
tape recorders I could find, which are now in front of us, and it's
turned into a new forum for people I admire.

Turse: What would you like readers to do with what they learn at
Tomdispatch?

Engelhardt: We're barraged by information, so many images, so
much noise, so many fragments. Even the cultural wallpaper's
screaming, I like to say. In addition, a striking thing about the
media in the first few years after the 9/11 attacks was its demobilized state. Here we had a thoroughly mobilized administration,
looking at the globe in the largest geopolitical terms, connecting
the dots—sometimes terribly—in a planetary way.

Officials like Cheney clearly think of the world in terms of
energy flows. They think in terms of interlinked military bases
and global military power. They've been thinking big, thinking
strategically, connecting disparate countries. They look at Russia
and, as old Cold Warriors, they think: Rollback. So they're
considering Estonia, Ukraine, and Uzbekistan in the same
frame. You read the press in this period, and you can find a
piece about Estonia, another about Ukraine, and yet another
about Uzbekistan, but not together. You can read a piece about
Uzbekistan, about Afghanistan, about Iran, about Israel, about
Iraq, about Turkey. But from mainstream American coverage
generally, you would have no idea that those countries were
near to, or related to each other, or that our leaders were thinking
about them in the same breath and via sweeping geographic
labels such as "the arc of instability."

The press, in those first few years, was striking in not connecting the dots, even when reporting well on specific subjects. What I think Tomdispatch does best is to connect those dots. My hope is that, when you read a dispatch, it will provide a connect-the-dots framework so that the next little bits that wash over you, you'll be able to slot them into something larger, and say, oh, that makes a kind of sense.

You don't have to accept my way of framing things, but maybe, at its best, Tomdispatch gets you thinking about how to fit these pieces together.

Turse: And what if, as readers start to see things in this larger framework, they're outraged and come to you for some guidance . . .

Engelhardt: Sometimes they do.

Turse: . . . and want to do something. What advice would you give them?

Engelhardt: I'm going to disappoint you on this one, Nick, because the advice I give is terribly limited. I have no hesitation about putting the world together in immodest ways, right or wrong; but I'm modest indeed about telling people what they should do in the world.

I don't see any reason why, because I'm capable of connecting those dots, I should become an oracle. Usually what I write back is very simple. I always suspect that people already know what they should do. There's always something to do in one's world, after all. But who am I to tell them what it is? So I don't.

Oddly enough, if I had anything to tell them on the subject, it would be this: I'm proud as anything of the pieces I've posted at Tomdispatch, especially since many of the authors could be writing for far bigger places. But I'm proudest of all that I didn't do a very American thing, which is to post for a while, get discouraged, and go home.

That was the story of the prewar antiwar movement. I predicted before the invasion of Iraq that the huge antiwar movement would only get bigger. Boy was I wrong. I've been wrong about many things in my life, but one of the bleak miracles of this period is that, to take an example, just about everything that's happened in Iraq looked obvious to me from the beginning. If you were to go back and read the things I wrote just before or after the invasion, it's clear that I sensed more or less what was going to happen. Only on the antiwar movement was I wrong. When they didn't stop the war, so many of them got discouraged, packed their bags, and went home.

Fortunately, I learn from the authors who write for me. Rebecca Solnit, for instance, has taught me a great deal about how history works, about the fact that simple cause-and-effect—we tried, we failed—isn't going to cut the mustard. As she points out, you mobilize a huge movement, then you can't figure out for years, if ever, what it's actually done, and yet it's invariably done something strange, affected someone somewhere. History, she says, isn't like a game of checkers, it's like the weather. History scuttles sideways like a crab. This gives me hope. This keeps me going. We just never know.

So here I am, almost sixty-two, doing this almost five years now nonstop, and I've never taken the tent down, never left the campgrounds, never left the battlefield. And I'm quite proud of that.

Turse: I was just about to ask you what the most heartening thing about Tomdispatch was for you.

Engelhardt: Just the feeling that I've hung in there and, if someone asks, that's really the advice I do give. I don't know what you should do, but do it and don't stop when it doesn't quite work out, when you don't get the results you want.

Turse: So what's your vision for Tomdispatch? You've gone from clipping service to mailing list to Web site. Now you've got a book of interviews coming. Where would you like to see it in five years?

Engelhardt: A five-year plan, Nick? You know me better than that. I'm usually worried about the last five minutes and the next five. The rest I leave to the gods. Maybe I'll wake up tomorrow morning and that voice in me will have abated, and maybe that'll be that. Proud as I am about having lasted this long, there's nothing wrong with Tomdispatch not going on forever.

I don't believe in thinking too carefully about future plans. Not as a lone individual in this world. Spend too much time considering what you want to do and you probably won't do it, because it'll look hopeless. So whatever it is, maybe it's best just to close your eyes and try.

Acknowledgments

Like much that exists in the world of the political Web, Tomdispatch is a minimalist, basement operation, and yet a whole community of sorts lurks just behind the onscreen logo. Let me start by thanking Ham Fish and Taya Kitman for The Nation Institute's long-term, enthusiastic support without which Tomdispatch would simply not exist online. Nick Turse has been an online lifeline and daily phone companion for the past two years. He's the fastest human search engine on the planet, and he's made my Tomdispatch life one regularly worth living. Then there were the interviewees in this book, all of whom showed patience indeed while a rookie interviewer tested his modest skills on them. I can't thank them enough, nor all the writers, thinkers, journalists, and historians who were willing to put fingers to keyboard for Tomdispatch, at first for nothing and then for a pittance, to make the website as surprising and informative as I hope it is. In addition, there are the readers of Tomdispatch, a voluble bunch who never hesitate to offer criticism, but also to share bits of their lives and thoughts, and to offer regular encouragement. They are my secret adventure.

Thanks go to Ruth Baldwin and Carl Bromley of Nation Books for taking a gamble and suggesting that my interviews should be collected into this volume. They did me a great favor; whether they did the same for themselves remains to be seen.

Finally, deep thanks to my dear wife, Nancy, for everything—including tolerating the speeded-up, swept-away life that Tomdispatch makes mine.

About the Author

TOM ENGELHARDT created and runs the Tomdispatch Web site (www.tomdispatch.com), a project of The Nation Institute of which he is a Fellow. He is also consulting editor for Metropolitan Books and the co-founder of its American Empire Project series. He is the author of *The End of Victory Culture*, a history of American triumphalism in the Cold War, and of a novel, *The Last Days of Publishing*. Each spring he is a Teaching Fellow at the Graduate School of Journalism at the University of California, Berkeley.

About Tomdispatch.com

Tomdispatch.com began in November 2001 as Tom Engelhardt's unnamed e-list of commentary and collected articles from the world press. In December 2002, it gained its name, became a project of The Nation Institute, and went online as "a regular antidote to the mainstream media." It now posts Tom Engelhardt's regular commentaries and the original work of authors ranging from Rebecca Solnit and Mike Davis to Chalmers Johnson, Michael Klare, and Elizabeth de la Vega. Nick Turse (who also writes for the site) is its part-time associate editor and research director. Tomdispatch is intended to introduce readers to voices and perspectives from elsewhere (even when the elsewhere is here). Its mission is to connect some of the global dots regularly left unconnected by the mainstream media and to offer a clearer sense of how this imperial globe of ours actually works. The series of Tomdispatch interviews collected in this book began in September 2005 as a periodic (and still ongoing) feature of the site.